Controlling the Weather

Edited by
Howard J. Taubenfeld

Controlling the Weather

A Study of Law and Regulatory Procedures

The Dunellen Company, Inc., New York

© 1970 by the Dunellen Publishing Company, Inc.
145 East 52nd Street
New York, New York 10022

International Standard Book Number 0-8424-0017-6.

Library of Congress Catalogue Card Number 76-132981.

Printed in the United States of America.

Research supported by
Southern Methodist University,
Institute of Aerospace Law, and by the
Atmospheric Sciences Section,
National Science Foundation,
under NSF Grant
GA-10202

Contents

Preface

In the relatively few years since the beginning of scientific interest in weather-modification efforts, the subject has become one of lively concern not only to scientists and commercial modifiers but to legislators and others interested in the legal, political, economic, and social consequences as well. While dispute continues within the scientific community as to the precise effects of various modification efforts, reports of the Special Commission on Weather Modification of the National Science Foundation (NSF) and of the Panel on Weather and Climate Modification of the Committee on Atmospheric Sciences of the National Academy of Sciences (NAS), both issued in 1966, concluded that a limited capacity to modify certain weather conditions, under certain circumstances, already demonstrably existed.

At the present time, efforts to modify the weather are actively being conducted in a dozen countries in addition to the United States, underscoring the likelihood of advances in the state of the art. Experiments and operations have been concerned primarily with precipitation augmentation, hail suppression, lightning suppression, and fog clearance. The beginnings of efforts to understand and perhaps influence severe storms—hurricanes and the like—have also been made.

At the same time, in the United States there have already been more than a dozen suits based on modification activities which have reached the courts. Over half the states have enacted some form of legislation relevant to this field. Several bills have been introduced in Congress. Several federal departments and agencies are engaged in research, operations, and/or funding activities in this and related fields.

This activity began when, just after the end of World War II, Langmuir, Schaefer, and Vonnegut succeeded in the experimental modification of clouds through "seeding" with dry ice and, shortly thereafter, with silver iodide crystals. In the two and a half decades since, the study of weather and of its modification has proceeded along several lines. On the one hand, the development of computers, of satellites to survey large areas of the world, and of other devices has led to a greater understanding of the atmosphere and of the interrelated phenomena which produce "weather." This is an ongoing story. At the same time, several government agencies, many scientists, and numerous commercial modifiers have been conducting laboratory and field experiments and field operations which tend to indicate that man already can, by intent, modify to some degree and in some locales certain weather phenomena. Moreover, unintended modification of climate by discharge of pollutants, change in type of land use, and many other factors are increasingly being recognized as meriting study and, to some degree at least, regulation.

As early as 1957, the Advisory Committee on Weather Control to the U.S. Congress reported that on the basis of statistical evaluations, cloud seeding of storms in the winter and spring months in the mountainous areas of the western United States "produced an average increase in precipitation of 10 to 15 percent from seeded storms with a satisfactory degree of probability that the increase was not the result of natural variations in the amount of precipitation." The Committee also found that seeding from the ground with silver iodide generators was a valid cloud-seeding technique.

For nearly a decade thereafter, these conclusions were tested and checked with varying degrees of skepticism. To attempt to make fair evaluations, two major study groups were created in the 1960's. In November 1963 the Committee on Atmospheric Sciences of the NAS appointed a Panel on Weather and Climate Modification to "undertake a deliberate and thoughtful review of the present status and activities in this field, and of its potential and limitations for the future." On June 16, 1964 the NSF announced the appointment of the Special Commission on Weather Modification to review the state of knowledge on weather and climate modification, to make recommendations concerning future policies and programs, including that of the NSF, and to analyze modification potentials for nonmilitary purposes. The reports of both the Special Commission[1] and of the NAS group[2] were completed in 1965. Both groups worked essentially with the same data.

As to the scientific prospects, the Special Commission found, in summary, as follows:

1. Several cubic miles of super-cooled cloud droplets can be transformed into ice crystals by seeding with dry ice or silver iodide. Super-cooled fog on the ground can be dissipated. No practical approach to the dissipation of warm fog is at hand.

2. While the evidence is still somewhat ambiguous, there is support for the view that precipitation from some types of clouds can be increased by the order of ten percent by seeding. If the results are confirmed by further studies they would have great significance. The question of corresponding decreases of precipitation outside the target area is unresolved.

3. Results from attempts to suppress hail in the United States are as yet inconclusive but more promising results in other countries are leading to the establishment in this country of a program that should provide a more definitive answer.

4. Experiments in lightning suppression are beginning to show some promise.

5. Modification of hurricanes has reached the stage of preliminary field experimentation but the results, so far, are inconclusive.

6. Changing the course of intensity of extratropical cyclones and altering climate over large areas remain as problems for the future. No serious attempt has yet been made to control tornadoes.

7. Inadvertent changes in climate as a consequence of human activity (e.g., urbanization, air pollution, increase of atmospheric carbon dioxide by burning fossil [fuels] are amenable to analysis and deserve early attention.

With respect to the scientific prospects for the future, the Commission finds that attractive opportunities exist. Advanced experimental techniques and application of sophisticated concepts in statistical design promise to reduce the present uncertainty in the interpretation of field experiments. The scientific exploration of weather and climate modification is passing from the speculative phase. Within reach are mathematical and laboratory modeling techniques that permit the simulation of atmospheric processes. By these means it should become possible to assess in advance the probable consequences of deliberate intervention.

---

1. *Weather and Climate Modification.* Report of the Special Commission on Weather Modification, NSF (Washington, D.C.: NSF 66-3, 1966).

2. NAS-NRC, *Weather and Climate Modification Problems and Prospects,* Vols. I and II (Washington, D.C.: NAS-NRC 1350, 1966).

Weather modification programs are in progress in many parts of the world. Over the last few years the conclusions cited above generally have been supported, but not in all instances. For example, the possibility that cloud seeding might decrease precipitation in some situations appears more likely today than was the case in 1966. There is growing attention being given to the effects of cloud seeding on the weather far downwind of the so-called "target area." Progress has been made on the use of physical and mathematical models to predict and evaluate the effects of cloud-seeding activity. Much of the scientific community now appears more ready to accept the notion of intentional weather modification. Obviously far more research as well as experiments and operations will be necessary before the limits of man's ability to modify intentionally and to deal with unintentional modification can be determined with great accuracy. Numerous studies and reports now exist, including those already mentioned, which detail the scientific problems and prospects and which identify the social, economic, legal, and regulatory problems as well.

For various reasons it seems likely that the potentially profitable subject of weather modification is ripe for more intensive development. The likelihood of increased activity of a research or operational nature made it seem very important to study the requirements of an appropriate regime for controlling weather-modification activities so that society would be assured they are conducted to advance the public interest to the highest degree.

In an effort to build on past studies and to make creative suggestions as to how the promising field of weather modification might be regulated by society to advance the public interest, the Institute of Aerospace Law at Southern Methodist University Law School, with support from the NSF, organized a Task Group on the Legal Problems of Weather Modification Activities in 1968.

Professor Howard J. Taubenfeld, Director of the Institute, was designated Director and Principal Investigator of the Task Group. Other full members who prepared studies, included herein, and who participated in the drafting of the Task Group's Report are Professor Ray Jay Davis, Law School, University of Arizona; Professor Ralph Johnson, Law School, University of Washington; Professor Sho Sato, Law School, University of California at Berkeley; and Dr. Rita F. Taubenfeld, Institute of Aerospace Law, Southern Methodist University. Each of the major participants was assigned a particular part of the overall study. Dr. Rita Taubenfeld was asked to investigate the questions of social norms, the public interest, and their relation to modification activities; Professor Johnson looked into federal organization for the control of weather modification; Professor Davis analyzed regulation practices, present and potential, at the state level; and Professor Sato studied the involvement of local government entities in weather modification. Dr. Louis J. Battan, Associate Director, Institute of Atmospheric Physics, University of Arizona, provided scientific guidance, prepared the supporting paper on the present "state of the art," and commented on the Report. Professor Arthur Murphy, Law School, Columbia University and Edward Morris, Esq., of the California Bar, participated in the Task Group's work in varying degrees but did not participate in the preparation of the Report. Dr. David G. Barry, now Vice Provost, Evergreen State College, Washington, assisted at one meeting of the Task Group. Peter H. Wyckoff, Program Director for Weather Modification of the NSF, provided invaluable assistance throughout the work of the Task Group.

Each member of the Task Group was selected on the basis of prior work concerning weather modification activity or especially relevant expertise. The work of the Task Group was conducted during 1968-1970 through a series of group meetings, individual interviews, study and analysis, and the interchange (oral and written) of ideas as well as drafts, memoranda, and critiques. For the Task Group's meeting in January 1969 invitations were extended to interested federal agencies, to all states' Attorneys-General, and to all known practicing modifiers. Interviews were also conducted at various times with senators, congressmen, federal and state officials, and others interested in modification.

What follows then is first the Report with recommendations of this Task Group on the Legal Aspects of Weather Modification Activities. This focuses on suggesting an appropriate type of regime for the regulation of weather modification in the public interest. Following are the study papers prepared by members of the Task Group covering the picture of where we now stand scientifically, the problems of defining the public interest in this field, and surveys of some of the alternative existing patterns of regulation of modification activities at the federal, state, and local levels. This provides the political, legal, and institutional background upon which the future regime is likely to be built.

The members of the Task Group wish at this time to recognize the invaluable assistance they have received during the course of their work. Special thanks are due to Margaret Seifert, SMU, for secretarial assistance; to Joseph Russell, Esq., and Dr. S. Bhatt, SMU, for service as research assistants; to Dean Arthur M. Sammis, Hastings College of the Law and to Bronson, Bronson and McKinnon, San Francisco, for making conference facilities available; and again to Peter H. Wyckoff and others at the NSF for their continuing and generous assistance. Specifically too, this research was supported by Southern Methodist University and by the Atmospheric Sciences Section, National Science Foundation, under NSF Grant GA-10202.

One special point must be made clear. At the close of their work on this project, the members of the Task Group reviewed the Report which follows. Although there was general agreement on the Report, it should not be assumed that every participant necessarily subscribes to every recommendation included therein; indeed, in two places specific demurrers are noted.

Dallas, Texas	Howard J. Taubenfeld
March 1, 1970	Director and Principal
	Investigator

Controlling the Weather

1   Report of the Task Group on the Legal Implications of Weather Modification

In the roughly 25 years since Langmuir and his associates conducted the first scientifically conceived efforts to modify local weather, considerable strides have been made in the meteorological sciences. A capacity to modify the weather intentionally, in certain ways and in certain places, seems now to be generally accepted. Some 29 states have legislated with respect to weather modification activities; federal funding for research and some operations, while modest compared with that spent in other scientific areas, is at a significant level; several bills concerning weather modification have been introduced in Congress. Yet it is fair to say that despite these developments, much basic knowledge remains to be acquired; modification techniques need to be developed and demonstrated; and an overall political-legal regime is yet to be established to facilitate the socially regulated pursuit of socially useful experiments and modification activities and the safe, orderly development of knowledge and technology. It is to be hoped that such a regime could help minimize losses and help assure appropriate, socially desired recompense for those who may be especially burdened by developments which are otherwise deemed desirable by their community.

At least in recent decades, the astoundingly rapid development of science and technology has been accomplished by a growing awareness of the need to use political organization and legal mechanisms to aid, shape, guide, and even direct social developments—not merely to prevent harm once it is perceived but also to prevent the infliction of unnecessary harm. In such areas of concern as the uses of atomic

3

energy, outer space technology, and pollution, to name but a few, here have been increasing efforts at the international, national, and even local levels toward preventive law—that is, the investigation of needs and problems in advance of catastrophe and the development of techniques both to prevent a problem from becoming a crisis and to meet problems before human loss and suffering occur. The impetus behind this Report and its supporting studies is the realization that intentional weather modification may be an area of development requiring just such efforts.

At present the most optimistic reports concerning developed technology indicate that, so far, man has made at most a conscious impact on certain local weather conditions.[1] We still lack much of the fundamental knowledge needed to begin to understand how major weather patterns might be controlled or altered and are not even certain of all the effects created by present interventions into the atmosphere. Further scientific investigation is desirable on a wide scale, but local problems associated with modest local weather-modification activities are with us even now.

The Present Legal Regime in the United States

The Task Group has been able to proceed on the basis of a number of solid and penetrating recent studies of the present law concerning weather modification in the United States.[2] It has not sought to redo these compilations and analyses. Rather, as already noted, it has taken as its task the suggestion of alternate routes to the social control of modification which decision makers might pursue once goals and opportunities are clarified. Nevertheless, a very brief review of the already developed present "regime" seems appropriate here before proceeding to suggestions for future action.

To date, the federal government has been the major contributor of funds for weather modification research and, through several agencies, has also conducted substantial laboratory and field-research operations itself.[3] It conducts such international negotiations as are necessary to permit experimentation (for example, for hurricane seeding), which might affect the interests of other nations. Within the government, modification programs have been coordinated through intergovernmental-agency cooperation.[4] While several different bills have been introduced in the Senate and in the House, which would involve greater federal control, coordination, and regulation or would create a modification study group or potential control agency or at least create the role of federal "lead agency" in the field, no such legislation has made any significant progress through Congress to date.[5] The only federal exercise of a regulatory nature is the authority given to the NSF to require reports of weather-modification activities, exercised from 1966 to August 31, 1968.[6]

No reports to date substantiate "damage" sustained by persons or property due to federal activities as such. Of course, as the frequency of conflicting expert testimony in the reported U.S. law suits suggests, it has been difficult to prove a causal connection between alleged injuries and weather-modification activities. This is due in part to the migratory nature of weather elements. The courses of storms and rain clouds are erratic, and their effects vary considerably. No two storms are exactly alike. Moreover, the sciences of weather forecasting and cloud physics are not yet developed enough to either describe satisfactorily the precipitation mechanism or to predict precisely what would have happened naturally without modification efforts. It is extremely difficult for a plaintiff to show, for example, what damages resulted from modification activities specifically and what would have been the normal results of the weather forces had they not been subjected to modification efforts.

Moreover, even if our knowledge were more certain, where the federal government (or, indeed, any government) is the moving force, there are well-known special difficulties under present laws, rules, and procedures in obtaining appropriate recompense for injured parties. There may indeed often be no legal redress available to persons injured thereby under the present law. A citizen damaged as the result of federal activities can often sue for damages under the Federal Tort Claims Act, but this is not true if the damage is caused by the exercise of one of the government's so-called discretionary functions.[7] Courts have to date generally held weather forecasting to be a discretionary function. They may well also consider modification of the weather by the federal government to be a discretionary function. Nevertheless, substantive inroads have been made by the courts into this exception in recent years, and public policy might best be served by allowing damaged parties to recover provable losses from governments.

Moreover, in fields where risks are high, the federal government has on occasion fostered activity and development by relieving its contractors of liability for tort claims against them. The Atomic Energy Commission (AEC), can relieve a licensee from liability arising from nuclear incidents by assuming that liability itself. The Veterans Administration and the Public Health Service can indemnify contractors where particularly hazardous conditions are involved as can the Department of Defense; yet note that NASA was expressly refused this authority. If government agencies which support weather modification were authorized to indemnify their contractors, this might encourage the development of the technology. The bothersome questions remain: Should the government in effect subsidize weather activities in this way? If so, which ones? Should the subsidy be for research and some forms of commercial operations as well? What standards of liability and of proof of loss should be set? What should government policy be with respect to conflicts in interest in the type of weather regarded as desirable by different affected parties?

In some respects, the problems presented in cases involving airport construction close to private residences may prove analogous to some of the weather modification cases. Courts have long held that airplanes can fly over land without getting the permission of every property owner. However, in certain cases airports have approach and takeoff patterns which bring aircraft very close to homes. The U.S. Supreme Court has held that the invasion of the superadjacent airspace by aircraft, though within the federal airway, may so affect the use of land as to constitute a taking.[8] In state cases, operating under even broader constitutional language, taking and damaging have given rise to compensable claims.[9] It is permissible for a government body to "take" or "damage" property rights, but appropriate payment must be made to the property owner affected. The responsibility of a government for losses caused by its weather-modification activities should also be considered in light of the loss-distribution scheme presently compelled by the federal and state constitutions. Thus it would be permissible for governmental bodies or their agents to modify the weather on a continuous basis, but only if they compensate landowners whose property is thus taken or permanently injured by such modification.

States have already shown a surprising amount of interest in weather-modification activities.[10] Already more than half have enacted statutes dealing with at least some aspects of weather modification. These statutes can be divided into two broad classes: those which aim at active control of weather modification, including the collection and evaluation of scientific information, and those which aim primarily at the collection and evaluation of information with a minimal licensing requirement. In the first, larger group restrictive laws require a license or registration for an operator and for operations. In most, a license can be obtained only after a statement is filed showing the qualifications of the operator, his financial responsibility, and the nature of the proposed work. Few of the states, however, list specific competence requirements. The methods of assuring financial responsibility differ widely. Except in a few instances, these demands also tend to be modest. Boards or commissions evaluate these factors, with a number of states having special weather control boards, presumably with special expertise in the field. Often public notice is required before activities can be undertaken. Most states charge fees for licensing, registration, and the like. After the conduct of the weather-modification activity, most require reports.

Several states assert sovereign rights to the atmospheric moisture within their borders. A few states limit weather activities which may affect other states. Maryland bars all weather-modification activities, and Pennsylvania and West Virginia have adopted laws which restrict or eliminate weather-modification activities. Since much weather research needs the atmosphere as a laboratory, such statutes may interfere with research and experimentation in the regions in question. It has eliminated commercial operations as well.

On the issue of liability, the laws of several states exempt the states and their instrumentalities from liability for modification operations. In no state is a private person exempt from such a liability.[11] A bond or liability insurance or proof of financial responsibility is a common prerequisite for private operations, as noted above. Texas' statute seeks to promote modification efforts by expressly stating that modification activities are not inherently ultrahazardous, although the rule was adopted with no legislative discussion of the potential impact of this section.

Thus far, at least, there do not appear to have been any multistate activities concerning weather modification. As noted, the laws of a few states already have provisions dealing with interstate accommodation; however there are no reported regional or interstate operations by the states, and no interstate compacts in this field exist. Indeed, while some state universities normally funded by the federal government are leaders in modification research, the states themselves have neither sponsored nor invested much in research or operations.

At the local level, there has been considerable interest in modification in some areas of the country. Some cities (for example, New York and Dallas) have funded efforts to increase precipitation in times of drought. The Los Angeles Flood Control District has sponsored a substantial number of operations. Weather-modification districts, exist or have been proposed in some states (the Dakotas, Texas, etc.), especially for hail suppression where the land use is relatively homogenous. Airport operators have also been involved in local fog-dispersal efforts. At least one local government prohibited modification.[12] We will return to this point in the next sections.

The Overall Pattern to Date

Research

At the present stage of the development of the art of weather modification, perhaps the single greatest need is for a massive attack on the question of understanding geophysical, atmospheric, and related phenomena.[13] Indeed, it may well be that the identification of the socially "best" resolution of all the questions posed hereafter for action by decision makers is impossible or fraught with unnecessary risks until the necessary scientific knowledge is obtained.

At the present time, weather-modification research, laboratory and field, is largely funded by the federal government. Total federal spending in the National Atmospheric Sciences Program is on the order of $248 million for the fiscal year 1968, $212 million for fiscal 1969, and $202 million for fiscal 1970.[14] This includes the Department of Defense. While the drop is largely explained in the ending of funding for planetary programs, it is not a very large sum in a total federal budget of over $200 billion, and, it must be noted, in this country the federal government funds the overwhelming bulk of research in this field.[15] Moreover, the figures themselves are slightly misleading in that much of these funds has been spent on aeronomy (studies of the very high atmosphere) and on planetary atmospheres, both of which are only distantly related to weather modification and are unlikely to have a material effect on advancing modification knowledge.

Also included within these figures is the total sum allocated to weather-modification research itself. Here, total funding was about $12 million for fiscal 1968 (including about $2 million from the Department of Defense), $11.3 million for fiscal 1969, and $11.8 million for fiscal 1970. Once again, it appears that, nationwide, the federal government directly or indirectly supports most of the research in this field. It is of course only fair to note that much of the remaining work in the atmospheric sciences develops knowledge which is directly in point for the modifier; yet the totals allocated to research in modifica-

8

tion have been quite modest despite the suggestions of major study groups which have examined the prospects and possibilities.[16]

The Task Group recognizes, of course, that weather modification is normally not a goal in itself; it is essentially another way of accomplishing other ends. At this time, modification research in the federal government involves some seven operating agencies, departments, and administrations. The Bureau of Reclamation of the Department of the Interior funds over a third of all activities and is largely concerned with precipitation modification and increased water resources. The NSF funds all kinds of studies at about $3 million annually and the Environmental Science Service Division (ESSA) of the Department of Commerce, funding about $1.5 million annually, studies most aspects of modification including general basic research. The Forest Service is studying lightning suppression. The Department of Defense funds studies through all arms of the services (Army, Navy, and Air Force); the Department of Agriculture and the National Aeronautics and Space Agency (NASA) have funded modest efforts; and the Department of Transportation through the FAA has shown some interest in fog clearance. Each mission-oriented agency has been predominantly interested in operations relevant to its own special missions. Despite the suggestions in various bills introduced in Congress, there is no designated lead agency for modification. Federal activities are coordinated to a degree by the Interdepartmental Committee for Atmospheric Sciences (ICAS), a committee of the Federal Council for Science and Technology. ICAS thus has as its own missions: "(1) to survey and evaluate the national research effort in the atmospheric sciences, (2) to examine the role and activities of federal agencies therein, and (3) to make recommendations for appropriate allocation of responsibilities among the federal agencies."[17] For research and operations then at the federal level, there are a number of essentially mission-oriented agency and department programs. There is coordination through ICAS, but there is no genuinely centralized program much less a "czar" for design of an overall program which might attempt to stress fundamental understanding of weather and modification phenomena and for allocation of roles and funds among agencies.

Operations

At this time, modification operations are conducted by universities, government agencies, and private operators. There is no federal legislation controlling research or operations, though reporting by all opera-

9

tors was required in 1966-1968 by the NSF and may again be required under proposed legislation, making ESSA the recipient of the reports. The states have funded little research or operations, but over half have legislated with respect to weather modification. Local units of government have to date authorized and paid for some modification activities and in one instance attempted regulation.

This embryonic legal regime has only partly been filled by court decisions. Only a dozen or so cases have been decided and they do not answer many of the most interesting legal questions one could raise, not to mention the questions of appropriate mechanisms of control, supervision and fair sharing of the benefits and costs to which this study is rather more specifically dedicated.[18] The cases nevertheless point up several key problems.

In all but two of the cases, the modifiers have succeeded in avoiding liability for their operations, and in all but one of these the decision was based on failure to prove that the damage was attributable to the cloud seeding and the negligence of the modifier.[19] The other involved attempts by drought-stricken New York City to increase precipitation in its reservoir area. The court held that attempts to modify could be made even over the objections of a potentially damaged party where it was necessary to balance the conflict of a remote possibility of inconvenience to a resort and its guests against giving the ten million inhabitants of New York City and surrounding areas an adequate supply of pure and wholesome water. The Court would not "prevent a possible private injury at the expense of a positive public advantage" and thus invoked principles of equity and public policy.[20]

These few cases do raise some of the important issues for legal policymaking in re weather modification. They suggest, for example, that in the short run it may be easier to enjoin modification activities than to collect damages for the results, given the difficulty of proving a cause-effect relationship and the likelihood of varying scientific opinion on the subject of the effectiveness of modification in any particular instance. To date, scientific opinion suggests that proper seeding can lead to an increase in precipitation. The special panel of the NA of S in 1966 stated: "There is increasing but still somewhat ambiguous statistical evidence that precipitation from some types of cloud and storm systems can be modestly increased or redistributed by seeding techniques." The Panel apparently regarded 10 to 20 percent precipitation increases as modest ones.

Hail suppression has also been reported as successful in some tests in the Soviet Union and in this country. Cold fog clearance is operational. Yet to date and for some time to come it is in the nature of the activity that proof as to the specific outcome of any *single* act of weather modification is unlikely, though an average effect over time and repeated trials may be estimated. This might well lead courts and other decision makers to favor injunctive or preventive action when the specific effect of a certain weather modification act on a certain day cannot be demonstrated.

In short, the problem of obtaining damages due to the difficulty in demonstrating a cause-effect relation added to the difficulty of proving "negligence" (if such a showing were required) and the unpredictability of court processes are likely to lead to a stress on prevention of weather-modification activities by threatened parties or on some system of providing compensatory payment (perhaps through an insurance scheme) without requiring a showing of a "wrongful" act. Whether or not there is a property right in weather, it is clear that property owners normally have a capital investment in their weather, and any imposed damages to the value of their property is really similar to a "taking." Weather modification is likely to produce such events. These are unlikely to be politically popular. Those who favor a relatively free development of weather modification will have to consider if it is not ultimately in their interest to favor an absolute standard of liability or at least to provide for securely arranging full compensation for losses imposed without a showing of negligence.[21] Even so, the fact that it is very difficult to demonstrate specific damages from weather modification presents a problem to the design of any compensation system which is keyed not to compensating all individuals for the effects of bad weather, whatever the cause, but which attempts to restrict compensation to those whose bad weather is wholly or partly the result of what may well be considered generally socially desirable weather-modification activities. Given present knowledge, the problem of devising reasonable but not overrestrictive standards of proof of causation and of damage appears difficult but important to try to resolve. It should be an important focus of research.

More generally then, the cases raise the implicit question of which weather-modification activities should be encouraged, permitted, or enjoined. As the New York City case suggests, it is likely that modification may promise great net social benefits, even if some losses are imposed. Thus not all potentially damaging weather-modification activities should be prevented; but modifying would imply an imposed redistribution of weather or welfare as well as some sort of utilitarian calculus. Insofar as it can intervene with nature, society is likely to wish to favor the attempt to seek the greatest good for the greatest number from its weather, even if this injures the status quo rights or property values of some minority. As noted above, this need not rule out the granting of compensation to the damaged parties. Such indeed may be their constitutional right.

Future Courses

This Task Group has engaged in its work with the common assumption that the technology needed to proceed with effective weather modification of several types on a local and even a regional scale is available or is likely to be developed in the near future. Since the potential utility of such techniques seems clear in many cases and since there also appear to be related risks, such as the possibilities of local and even widespread loss, the Task Group has examined the present state of legal arrangements and institutions dealing with intentional modification activities. We seek herein to suggest patterns which will permit society to protect carefully prepared and carried out legitimate experimentation and operations while assuring that any person truly injured by developments felt to be useful for society as a whole is duly compensated.[22] We have proceeded also with the understanding that despite great advances in the last two decades, we are still far from a full understanding of weather in its natural state, far from developing the mechanisms by which man can successfully alter weather patterns and phenomena, and far from the ability to state precisely all of the exact effects of each modification activity.

With this in mind, we move to the key question: What legal-administrative system for control of modification activities is likely to yield the fairest results from the social point of view? Thus far, the states which have acted on the matter seem to have concluded that a relatively loose licensing system plus access to the courts is likely to suffice to protect the modifiers, their clients, and those likely to be damaged by their activities. Since we do not know the scientific facts as yet, we cannot judge whether this system creates miscarriages of justice, but the industry is still very immature and modest in scale. It will be interesting to follow the activities of the licensing boards and of the courts over the years. Even present state standards of professional competence and responsibility of weather modifiers need upgrading. As weather modification activities become more prevalent, the need for further legislative policy directives to the courts and licensing boards will prove more pressing, especially concerning the desirable approaches to deciding conflicting claims to the same weather and to problems of liability and compensation.

When this happens it seems likely that whatever the pattern of social control of modification, a modern democratic society will be under pressure to protect victims of weather modification by assuring compensation to anyone who can prove a measurable loss due to the activities, whether the act is that of a government, private party, an experimenter, or operator. In any case if total losses are not less than the gains of modification, it can be presumed to be socially inefficient to modify on normal definitions of efficiency. Fact finding on these issues will remain a challenge to the agency charged with determining compensation.

The whole thrust of experience to date suggests the need for controlled experimentation aimed at understanding weather and weather mechanisms if the promise of weather modification is to be achieved with minimal social frictions. When successful, such studies should finally help establish the direct effects of specific acts of modification more clearly, or they should clarify the limits within which such knowledge seems feasible.

In the regulation of weather modification, community and private interests should, as always, be calculated and compared. Insofar as weather is transient and is not bounded by political borders and since experimentation over broad areas with interstate impact is or may become necessary, the utility of at least uniform minimum standards with respect to professional licenses, operational permits, and standards of liability seems beyond question. Reporting, both before the activity in order to allow potentially damaged parties to assert their rights and to prevent interference and contamination and afterwards to permit the collection and evaluation of scientific data, is crucial to progress. How can all of this best be managed?

The Report of this Task Group takes as its starting point existent studies of the present state of the art and of the institutional and legal arrangements evolved thus far. Certain other comments and points of reference must be made before proceeding into our suggestions for the future.

First, whether or not any programs of intentional weather-modification activities should be undertaken at all and, if so, by whom, at what levels, and with what safeguards are basic questions for decision makers, public and private. One of the papers forming the core of this study makes suggestions as to the appropriate criteria for deciding on the size of the federal weather-modification effort, and most of the other papers comment to some extent on related issues.[23] In principle, however, we do not attempt here to estimate the total benefits and total costs of intentional weather-modification activities—a difficult calculation under any circumstances, and we do not feel we need to answer the question as to the social utility of weather modification ab initio. Rather, we assume, on the basis of experience, that modification technology already exists and that interest in research and operations is sufficiently great so that there are and will be programs of intentional modification. This implies that an adequate institutional and legal framework for their regulation is essential so that such activities will conform to the public interests. The implications of achieving adequate regulation should in turn throw some light on some of the implied costs of safely developing new technology in this potentially hazardous field and aid society to make its rational calculus.

Second, while not seeking to usurp the role of the democratic decision maker in this federal society of representative governments and majority rule, we can point out that society as usual cannot avoid choosing an allocation system and a distribution policy in re weather modification. In an ideal world of rational choosers this would involve a choice of an optimal amount of intentional weather-modification research, experimental and commercial, to be regulated consistently with the achievement of a general maximum of welfare. We have suggested that, in this highly charged matter of modifying the national environment, society will, for various reasons, probably not only want compensation to be possible but to be paid as a means of assuring that only socially useful projects are undertaken while losses from intervention with the status quo of nature are minimized. Choices of the regime under which this or any other distribution policy might be managed, once it is agreed upon, are a principal focus of interest of this Task Group. The choice of optimal distribution policy again is a separate question from that of the choice of optimal institutions of regulation.

Third, this Task Group has concentrated its attention on what we call intentional rather than inadvertent weather-modification activities. While the problems are intertwined, this Report does not attempt to consider the problems caused by inadvertent modification—that is, modification arising from human activities which may in fact affect the weather on a greater or lesser scale but are designed expressly for some other purpose. Thus we exclude in general the serious current and future problems of pollution of all types, of urbanization, etc., all of which have had and may increasingly have a direct effect on the atmosphere and hence on the weather.[24] Some have argued that in fact a total regime is necessary—one which would deal with the environment and the atmosphere as a unit, including all activities which affect the weather as well as all other aspects of the human environment.[25] While this approach may seem reasonable in the long run and such a program might in time prove politically feasible and acceptable on a national basis, it would introduce many complex, politically difficult distributive issues into the discussion. Therefore the question of a regime for intentional modification activities seem both pressing enough and sufficiently severable at the present research stage to warrant investigation by serious students now.[26]

Fourth, as the papers attached to this Report indicate, it is wise to keep in mind that the concept "intentional weather-modification activities" as used here is a broad one and takes in a number of programs which vary widely in their scope, cost, significance, and likely impact on the public. We include basic research into atmospheric phenomena (laboratory, theoretical, etc.), efforts to augment and inhibit precipitation, efforts to suppress hail and lightning, efforts to clear fog of all descriptions, efforts to understand and control major storms, and efforts to control weather patterns on a regional, national, or even international scope. Different activities may require different treatment within an overall regime.

Recommendations

Research

Under the federally subsidized decentralized, competitive-research programs, which have been in effect for 20 years, some significant progress has been made in developing an understanding of the theoretical aspects of the atmosphere and weather-modification mechanisms, but the progress has been inadequate. Except in the clearing of supercooled fogs, only modest progress has been made in the development of operational programs.[27]

If the relevant decision makers decide to increase substantially the funding for weather-modification research in order to discover fundamental knowledge, to understand better man's total environment, and to form a more rational basis for the overall guidance and control of intentional weather-modification activities, how should it be handled?

First, it seems clear to this Task Group that the vast bulk of funds for research will continue to come from the federal government. While state and local governments have funded operations to some degree and research to a very modest degree and while universities and corporations (for example, General Electric) have funded relevant research on their own, it seems clear that wide-scale basic research, especially in matters of general national interest, has been and quite appropriately will continue to be financed primarily by the federal government.

Whatever the level of expenditures, research into the atmosphere or, more narrowly, into weather modification could in theory be undertaken largely by a new major institute or agency which would virtually blanket the field. It could be concentrated in one or a few existing entities. As expanded, it could depend on variations of the present mix in which some federal agencies undertake or support research in fields akin to their operational interests while others support universities, consortia of universities, and other research groups in basic and field research of all types, with coordination achieved through superimposed government action. Such a program could be assisted perhaps by developing a monitoring role for one of the already interested agencies. Alternatively, some special new entity at the federal level could be established to plan, direct, coordinate, and monitor a national program in weather-modification research in addition to or in cooperation with the mission-oriented programs.

It is recognized that fragmentation of control over programs may lead to wasteful duplication and even to interference between projects. Moreover, while achieving modest success in coordination to date, intragovernmental consultation in this field, organized through ICAS, has had its difficulties with various agencies over the years. Its success appears to have depended on the strength of the chairman and on the willingness of the members to cooperate. It has yet to be proven where truly large sums of money for allocation among member agencies might be involved.

At one end of the continuum of possibilities for the future direction of federal weather-modification programs is the creation of a monolithic research agency which might diminish problems of coordination, unnecessary duplication of effort, and the like. Yet such a politically difficult move seems neither inherently necessary in the weather-modification field or compatible with the usual pluralistic U.S. policy approach to matters of scientific research, which has always stressed competitive research programs. It implies the risk of any monopoly,

16

including among others the risk of a certain sterility and a lack of adequate variety, coverage, and vitality to the effort. While more moderate alternatives combining the present mission-oriented agency approach a special national program for weather improvement—perhaps the new Council on Environmental Quality should be studied—the Task Group suggests, in general, that the basic lines of the overall federal research effort continue in roughly the present pluralistic form.[28] However, expenditures probably need to rise sharply, especially expenditures on the pursuit of basic knowledge as in the field of cloud physics as pursued at present through NSF and by other federal agencies. The NSF, with its mission to further the pursuit of basic knowledge throughout the country, is at present the major supporter of university and other basic research programs in this field. This effort needs vigorous expansion. At a minimum, the principal objectives should be to obtain a clearer picture of the atmosphere and on the precise effects of each type of intentional modification effort as well as other relevant factors so that those charged with regulating and controlling related human activities can effectively aim for the maximum gain to society as a whole and the least uncompensated loss to individual members thereof.

As prospects of larger funding emerge, it may prove necessary to control conflict between the federal agencies. This can probably be facilitated by vigorous action within the Office of the President. Of great concern to us are the important functions of advising the President and his advisers on the relevant national goals and priorities with respect to modification and the direction of research and the appropriate allocation of funding between agencies. This could be handled by the recommendations of a vigorous ICAS or by any new group set up by the President or his Science and Environment Advisers. As always in the end the President, with the help of his budget advisers, will have to make the final executive decisions and see that his various advisers and his Administration defend them in Congress.

Without such a major research effort focused on obtaining relevant new knowledge, it will remain difficult to regulate weather-modification operations for the general welfare. The Task Group, therefore, feels that if the mounting of a major research effort does not prove possible or promise success within a reasonably limited time under the existing, decentralized, pluralistic federal mechanisms (augmented perhaps by a new national weather-modification policy group in the Office of the President), it would favor another examination of the alternative means of organizing, focusing, and coordinating weather-modification research, including the possibility of selecting a lead agency or establishing a major new centralized research entity on the federal level.[29]

Operations

To date, intentional weather-modification activities both at the research and the applied levels have been conducted directly by federal agencies, by universities on their own and with government support, by state and local government entities, essentially through use of contractors, and by private persons, including corporations on their own pursuant to commercial contract and pursuant to contracts and grants from government agencies at various levels. Basic weather-modification techniques are simple, easily understood, and easy to use, at least at an unsophisticated "backyard-generator" level.

Whatever the pattern of an overall weather-modification regime eventually adopted by the appropriate U.S. decision makers, attention will have to be given to the questions of who will be permitted to operate in this field and what his responsibilities will be. At present, for example, an individual clearly able to demonstrate harm caused him by a modification activity might find that his ability to receive compensation might depend in large part on the legal liability of the operator. This Task Group does not, however, recommend the limitation of the right to conduct activities to a particular class of operator. There seems ample room for operators of all present types. The real issues, to which we turn next, are those of assuring that *all* operators are competent; that operations are responsibly planned to minimize risk and maximize scientific and commercial gain; and that all specific losses are compensated.

Reporting, Monitoring, Licensing, and Liability

At present, as we have noted, intentional weather modification is being carried on in many parts of the country by or under the auspices of many types of entities. While there has been little effective federal legislation to date, half the states, a few local governments, and a dozen courts have already created an embryonic legal regime. Weather, broadly speaking, is inherently in many respects more than a local phenomenon and inevitably moves without respect to any governmental borders. A failure to act at the national level or state level is, as usual, itself an action and a decision.

In considering the shape of a more affirmatively created regime, the

18

Task Group has attempted to keep several sometimes divergent factors in mind. These include the following:

1. the above-noted present lack of sufficient knowledge as to the precise scientific basis for weather modification, for the precise description and prediction of atmospheric phenomena, and for the precise description of the effects of a particular modification activity;

2. the level and nature of the funding of present weather modification research and operations;

3. the variety of interested parties, researchers, modifiers, and those potentially adversely affected;

4. the history of coordination, operations, and attempts at legislation at the federal level; the history of state legislation and of lawsuits; and the demonstrated intensity of feeling generated at times by weather-modification activities;

5. the need for democratic control over technology which has within it the seeds of potentially vast changes in the overall human environment;

6. the fact that "intentional weather modification" is a term used to cover a broad range of technological possibilities ranging from those which appear to have quite a local impact at most, such as fog clearance at airports (though these too may be at or near state or national borders); to those of a potentially substantial, broad impact, including precipitation augmentation or inhibition and hail and lightning suppression; and then to those of regional, national, and even worldwide significance; attempts to deal with major storms, such as hurricanes, and even to affect weather patterns broadly enough to be called "weather control";

7. the preference in this nation for reliance on the most efficient, effective local unit of political decision and action available to meet a need (though often with guidance and/or financial assistance from higher levels of authority which also may involve minimum standards of safety, for equity and to avoid local biases). In general also it seems wise to avoid the proliferation of unnecessary new institutions.

8. the usual desire to permit a role for private enterprise to as great a degree as promises to be safe and effective, given society's aims.

The Task Group is also well aware of the fact that inadvertent modification through pollution, industrialization, etc., plays a far greater role in affecting weather today than does man's direct efforts to intervene intentionally. It may be that, in time, as some have suggested, intentional modification and efforts to control inadvertent modifica-

19

tion should be placed in one major federal agency whose task would be to monitor and, as possible, "control" the atmosphere as a totality. At present, the President's new Council on Environmental Quality is concerned with both aspects. As noted, this Task Group feels, however, that the problems are at present severable conceptually, and that intentional modification has reached the stage where there is a need for action in the creation of an overall regime for the regulation of intentional-modification operations whatever the other problems involved caused by industrialization as such, by pollution, by population pressure, and the like.

With these points in mind, the Task Group offers the following suggestions on the regulation of weather-modification operations:

1. Reporting and Monitoring. Even without other controls, it is essential, in order to avoid interference and conflicts between projects and to aid in obtaining the information for evaluating field research and operations' results, that there be a centralized, obligatory procedure for reporting the nature (and results) of all intentional-modification activities. Many states now require reporting, but this decentralized, partial system appears to us to be quite inadequate, even if the state requirements were generalized and made uniform and even if information from state agencies were easier to obtain and more regularly used. Activities are likely also to take place across state borders. We propose that, as with the authority formerly possessed by the NSF, *all* intentional-modification activities be reported promptly to a federal entity to be charged with receiving and promptly disseminating this information. No researcher or operator would be exempt except, presumably, the Department of Defense on a showing by the Secretary of Defense to the President of the need for such exemption to preserve national security. Such reports should also be made simultaneously available to such states or state agencies as may so require.

Moreover, we propose that the chosen federal entities to be described below compile and disseminate information on prospective modifications and on the stated results of modification efforts and, *in addition,* that it be charged affirmatively with the responsibility of organizing the monitoring of the country (and appropriate adjacent areas) both in the field, if possible, and through surveying reports and studies by others to determine whether or not modification activities were all being reported, and also to identify other important emerging factors in or inputs into the atmosphere which would affect modification research and operations. Such monitoring could be carried out through the facilities of other agencies.

20

2. Licensing. In the field of weather modification, licensing contains two different elements. As with some other activities, it seems appropriate, as the states which have legislated on this question have done, to consider separately the licensing of individuals and the licensing (granting of permits) for a weather-modification operation.

We propose that operators be licensed by the federal government. In the American federal system, certain kinds of activities of a national import—aviation, for example, patent attorneys, and others—have been subjected to a system of federal licenses for those seeking to perform the operation. For a variety of reasons, often including historical accident, others including practice in medicine, law, etc., operating motor vehicles and the like have been left for state licensing of personnel. The advantages of securing standardization of operators' educational requirements and technical capacity seem apparent. Where purely technical standards are involved there seems to be no conceptual reason for preferring local political control at the cost of uniformity. In any case since weather respects no state boundary and since operators are likely to conduct activities in many states and to affect the citizens of many states by their activities, it seems reasonable to suggest that federal standards for an operator's license be set and that a federal entity issue the license once an individual shows his competence. It seems likely that there would be little or no objection from the states whose licensing requirements were superseded; there would probably continue to be support from operators for a federal license. As with aviation, this would be a first step in assuring the competence of all the operators who may, in fact, as the technology progresses, cause serious risks to many if their operations are not wisely conducted.

Again, as with aviation, there might be some who would be exempt from a license requirement, just as military aviators are not licensed by the civilian authorities. Presumably no license would be required of laboratory experimenters; licensing would be required only of those whose work is in or directed toward affecting the atmosphere itself. There might also be exemptions for one conducting a sudden emergency operation and the like, but in general the exemptions should be as limited as possible.

In contrast to the utility of federal licensing of operators, the question of licensing operations needs consideration at different levels of government. As we have noted, intentional-modification activities range from some that in all likelihood will have results limited to quite small geographical areas to others that will inevitably affect large areas. It is our assumption that, weather being an inherently national issue,

21

Congress would preempt all regulation and, indeed, even bar all intentional-modification activities in the national interest if it was convinced that this was essential (as a few states have done, at least on a temporary basis). Having the constitutional power to act does not mean, however, that Congress inevitably will preempt the field, or that it should. In many areas too, where federal minimum standards are set, local authorities are given substantial leeway in setting their own regulations to meet local needs.[30]

Thus, once standards were ascertained for determining the likely effects of a given kind of modification activity, a license for that activity might be issued by the appropriate entity, either federal or state, on a showing of compliance with all standards.[31] Such licenses could be issued for each operation, as defined, or for a series of similar operations (for example, fog clearance at a particular airport for a particular length of time, such as a year). Thus where it could be determined scientifically that a certain activity had only highly local effects and no state boundaries were involved, licensing would be effected at the state level, avoiding the need to invoke federal machinery.[32] Where an activity affected more than one state or nation it would be licensed federally.[33] We deal hereafter with substantive standards for licensing.

All such licensing should normally require, inter alia, local and/or general advance notification, a hearing if appropriate objections were made by appropriately interested parties, provision for emergency exemption from normal procedures, and obligations to report and to assure compensation of injured parties. Government field operations at all levels should also be subject to the duties to notify, report, and compensate, and there is no inherent reason why some form of licensing or some substitute therefore should not apply to them.[34]

All operations which might have an international effect would be licensed by the federal government. In this, but in all other cases as well, it is clear that an operation could be barred if the public interest, as defined by the relevant decision-making authority, would thus be best served.[35]

3. Liability. To date, the question of compensation for those damaged by a weather-modification activity has been left essentially to the courts, and thus far complainants have in all but one case failed to convince a court of a causal connection between the activities complained of and an alleged damage.[36] This means that the question of standard of care, of the general insistence on negligence as a basis of

fault, has not been litigated. The laws of several states now require a showing of (generally modest) financial responsibility on the part of would-be modifiers. One state, Texas, declares by law that weather modification is not an ultrahazardous ("liability without fault") activity. There are conflicting reports as to the availability of substantial amounts of liability insurance for modifiers. Suggestions have been made that most coverage is now provided by foreign insurers. The adequacy of present and prospective insurance facilities deserves careful, further study in view of our recommendations as to liability.

The problem of compensation is complicated by the fact that government agencies conduct operations. While the doctrine of sovereign immunity is on the decline with respect to state activities, the federal government, though liable for ordinary torts committed within the territorial United States, is liable only if negligence is proven and if the activity is "nondiscretionary."

While it is always argued that the creation of a standard of nonfault liability tends to hamper the development of an industry or technology, there seems no immutable reason to favor the development of the industry and technology at the expense of those who lose therefrom. While it would be legally very inconvenient for the future of modification efforts to suggest that each man has a property right to his normal weather, the fact is that the capitalized value of his real property often does depend in part on its normal weather. Therefore an uncompensated imposition of worsened weather which would affect the capitalized value of such property is very much like an uncompensated taking, which, profitable or not, would normally not be permitted to a private party without consent and would require compensation if undertaken by a government. Thus, a legal regime which allows private parties to modify so long as they provide adequate compensation may be viewed as generous to the modifiers who engage in an activity which can be expected to frequently cause damage as well as gain. Recall too the important point that unless compensation for such damage is possible, the results of modification would be economically inefficient from the social point of view on the most common standards of these concepts. If modification districts for supervising or carrying out operations were normally designed so that the modifiers recieved all the gains of modification, or if they were compensated for the costs to them of benefits they did not receive, and if the system of securing insurance fairly reflected the risks, requiring assurance that all costs imposed by modification will be compensated could be viewed as one desirably decentralized, automatic mechanism for assuring that only economically feasible and efficient modifications would take place.[37]

It is the Task Group's overall view therefore that the concept of absolute liability is appropriate for weather-modification activities. At the present stage of lack of knowledge of the precise effects of each modification effort, of lack of knowledge and experience on which to base a reasonable standard of care, and of the possibility of widespread loss, it is reasonable to require any modifier causing demonstrable damage to make good the losses, without respect to whether or not his activities could be classed as negligent. Ability to respond in the event of a major weather incident should be obligatory. The need to prove causation will remain a problem. Presumably new knowledge of the mechanisms of modification might make it possible to leave the resolution of this issue in litigated cases to state and federal courts.

We have already noted that the availability of liability insurance for modifiers deserves careful study. With the standard of absolute liability adopted, the government may feel that insurance against liability should be subsidized from the start, if it is desired to favor initiative in modification efforts and not to allow the initial status quo of property rights to block otherwise potentially efficient modifications. In any case, as modification activities increase and as causation becomes more credible and more easily proved, available insurance coverage by today's standards might well become inadequate or an impediment to the growth of modification. At such a time a program for "weather incidents" similar to that adopted for "nuclear incidents" should probably be adopted. This involves the establishment of an insurance requirement for each incident with federal "insurance" available for amounts over a stated minimum and up to a stated maximum ($500 million in the nuclear energy field).[38]

The Task Group proposes that all modifiers be subjected to this liability rule, including federal, state, and local government agencies.[39]

4. Operations. Subject to the recommendations already made, it appears to the Task Group that the present mix of those authorizing operations—federal agencies, private individuals and companies, some state or local agencies—is appropriate for the future as well. In many instances weather-modification districts, which might well extend beyond state borders on the model of river agencies, the Port of New York Authority, and the like may be the most appropriate agency for conducting or contracting for operations if they can be designed to be effective, flexible, and solvent.

24

At the federal level, the half dozen or more agencies with interests in modification would continue to conduct operations in accordance with their missions with the Congressionally supported allocations of funds. The Task Group proposes that none of the existing agencies be asked, in addition to its research and operational roles, to be responsible for the other activities to be carried on in our proposed program at the federal level: supervising, reporting, monitoring, or licensing federal-level operations. We deem it appropriate to separate regulation from research and operations so that no one will be forced to be both regulator and regulatee, a basic notion in the democratic process.[40] These new regulatory functions can be carried out best by a new entity, the Weather Modification Regulatory Board.

The role and the norms to be applied by this new entity would be defined and regularly reviewed by Congress. The statement of purpose of the legislation establishing the Board would as usual specify Congress' general objectives, such as equity, efficiency, and the decision of conflicts of interest on the basis of the "general welfare." These would have to be further specified in the body of the legislation in which, inter alia, Congress can be expected to indicate its choice of the appropriate concept of equity to be applied. For example, it might choose to require that equity and efficiency both be pursued in a general private-enterprise framework by requiring that compensation be assured to all without necessity of proving fault before licenses for modification are granted. It might be expected to suggest that, in order to promote equity, efficiency, and political representativeness, modification districts should be designed wherever possible to include all affected parties, both gainers and losers. Then all affected parties would be called upon to contribute to the support of modification and would share appropriately in the decision making of the districts and in the benefits produced. It might be expected to specify that efficiency in pursuing the general welfare can be taken to mean that when conflicts among parties arise, the net national output should in general be maximized unless Congressional policy directives impose other additional norms or social objectives or specific standards, such as the requirement to favor poverty areas in case of conflict of interest or the like.[41] Probably some ban should be included in the legislation prohibiting operations designed to modify the large-scale circulation or to induce major regional or continental-scale weather modifications until these have been fully explored in computers and their implied results have been deemed socially desirable by the President and

Congress. Detailed regulations and technical standards for implementing the Congressional policy decisions would be set and implemented by the Board.

In view of frequently reported past difficulties in assuring that independent regulatory agencies pursue the public good as envisioned by the appropriate political decision makers rather than becoming captive to the industry regulated, efforts should be made to assure the responsiveness of the Weather Modification Regulatory Board to the overall values and policy preferences of the most important elected official with the whole nation as his constituency, the President as well as to Congress. This might be partly achieved by putting the Board in the Office of the President rather than creating it as an independent agency. Or it might be that the agency could be created independent but that Congress which would determine the number of members of the Board and how they were to be chosen could assure such responsiveness to the President by having members appointed for a relatively short term of office, perhaps for two years with one-half being replaced yearly. Some experiment in increasing the responsiveness of the regulatory agency to the changing general interest seems in order.

Presumably, appeal would be possible from the decisions or actions of the Weather Modification Regulatory Board to the federal court system, normally after all internal appeals procedures were exhausted. Special procedures can be devised for emergency operations.

Congressional interest and control over the federal program of weather modification will be reflected both in its control of the Weather Modification Regulatory Board's budget and of the allocations made to the mission-oriented agencies and in the funding of broad-scale research.

We are thinking then of an overall system in which the regulatory, allocative, and operational functions can be conceptually distinguished. In general the regulatory functions (registry, licensing, etc.) would be performed centrally at the appropriate state or federal-government level. General allocation between competing regions and major issues for statewide or multiregional areas would tend to be made at the statewide or national level by the decisions of the relevant weather-modification regulatory boards among competitive projects. These could be appealed from to the courts. General legislative guidance on the norms to be applied would exist, and legislative and executive pressure could likewise be expected to be brought to bear on the Modification Regulatory Board's policies if they seemed too inconsistent with pressure-group interests, with the mission interests of the Government mission-oriented agencies, or with the general interest. The results of such pressures would depend in part on the design of the relationships between the Board, the President, and Congress. This is a matter worthy of careful attention.

Purely local aspects of allocation and operations would be locally organized, at least at the first stages, and only in cases of conflict or disagreement with the policy of the modification district would local allocation issues be brought for contest before the central regulatory machinery or finally before the state and federal court systems. In general emphasis in this system would be placed on primary reliance on decentralized decision making in which central government action focuses upon regulation and upon programs aimed at creating weather-modification knowledge, providing certain desirable social services, and acquainting the relevant local entities with their opportunities, while allowing them to pursue their local self-interests in such a way that the results satisfy the local majorities and at the same time conform to the general interest.

It is this Task Group's view that this program will permit the nation to safely exploit weather-modification capabilities primarily on the basis of local and private initiative as rapidly and safely as the appropriate decision-makers deem wise. Such encouragement and regulation will assure that this capability develops in a manner consonant with "(a) equity, as defined by the legislature or the legislature and the President and the courts, interpreting the public will on these issues, (b) reasonable technical safety in modification activities, considering the costs and benefits of improving safety, (c) optimal efficiency in the use of weather resources of the nation, given the tastes of the society for output and for weather and the alternative output potentials of society, and (d) adequate consistency with attempts to achieve all other social objectives, such as economic stabilization, national security, etc."

Notes

1. See Battan, "A Brief Survey of the Scientific Aspects of Weather Modification," *infra*, this study, hereinafter cited as *Battan*.

2. E.g., Davis, *The Legal Implications of Atmospheric Water Resources Development and Management* (Final Report for the Bureau of Reclamation, Oct., 1968); Taubenfeld, ed., *Weather Modification and the Law* (1968); Taubenfeld, *Weather Modification: Law, Controls, Operations* (NSF 66-7, 1967).

3. See generally National Science Foundation, *Weather Modification, Annual Report, 1968,* (NSF 69-18, 1969); Interdepartmental Committee for Atmospheric Sciences (ICAS), *National Atmospheric Sciences Program, Fiscal Year 1970* (ICAS Report no. 13, Jan. 1969), hereinafter *ICAS 13;* Johnson, "Federal Organization for Control of Weather Modification," *infra* this study, hereinafter cited as *Johnson.*

4. *ICAS 13, passim; Johnson, passim.*

5. See *Johnson,* passim.

6. From and after September 1, 1968, reports were requested on a voluntary submission basis. Response was disappointing where no indirect pressure, as for example, through the modifier being one who conducted operations under a federal grant of contract, existed.
   At the time of preparation of this Report, legislation locating a report-receiving function in ESSA was under consideration.

7. A "discretionary function" is, broadly speaking, one which a government agency is not obligated to perform by a specific statute but which is performed as a public service.

8. Griggs v. County of Allegheny, Penn., 369 U.S. 84 (1962).

9. For discussion see Sato, "A Report on the Role of Local Governmental Units in Weather Modification: California Microcosm," *infra,* this study, hereinafter cited as *Sato.*

10. See Davis, "Strategies for State Regulation of Weather Modification," *infra,* this study, hereinafter cited as *Davis.*

11. Victoria, Canada *does* provide for such exemption for a licensed person.

12. Ayr Township, Ordinance, June 13, 1964. See Pennsylvania *ex rel* Township of Ayr v. Fulk, No. 53 (C.P. Fulton County, Pa., February 28, 1968).

13. For this, the work of all "atmosphere-oriented" researchers is vital, but so is that of, for example, oceanographers and others whose work, directly or indirectly, contributes to man's basic understanding of the physical mechanisms controlling the world in which he lives.

14. See *ICAS 13;* p. 25. Note that in the broader field of atmospheric sciences, in addition to the entities mentioned herein as funding weather-modification research, we find HEW and the FCC. The largest contribution to research, though, is through NASA with Defense second, including the Air Force which supplies over half the Defense budget; the NSF is third as a major entity; *ICAS 13,* pp. 23 ff.

15. Ibid., p. 3.

16. NSF, Special Commission on Weather Modification, *Weather and Climate Modification* (NSF 66-3, 1966); National Academy of Sciences (NAS), Committee on Atmospheric Sciences, Panel on Weather and Climate Modification, *Weather and Climate Modification—Problems and Prospects* (2 vols., 1965); Newell, *A Recommended National Program in Weather Modification* (ICAS Report No. 10A, Nov. 1966); Sewell, ed., *Human Dimensions of the Atmosphere* (NSF 68-18, 1968). Note too that, for all "social, economic, legal, and ecological studies" of the potentials of this conceivably radical capability, the sums funded were $400,000 in fiscal 1968 and 1970 and $350,000 for fiscal 1969.

17. *ICAS No. 13*, p. 3.

18. The questions are many and are noted in varying forms in the studies cited in footnote 2 above.

Just to survey some of the primarily legal questions these would include: Who "owns" the weather or particular "parts" of it? Is there already confusion due to conflicting rules? Is liability insurance available and on what terms? Who is liable for damage caused by modification activities? On what theory or theories? To whom? Who is exempt from liability? Does a landowner have a vested right in the weather in any sense? What courts should hear these cases? The rules of which state should apply? Are the clouds like wild animals, needing "capture" to permit special use? Are they like oil and gas in place under the land? Are they like water in the Western U.S. so that a first appropriator gets special rights or like water in the rest of the U.S. where one has a right to normal use free of "unreasonable" interference from "upstream" neighbors? Should ordinary rules requiring a showing of negligence be applied to modifiers? How do we establish standards of "reasonableness" in a new field? Should the standard be "absolute liability" once causation is shown? Many other social, political, ecological, economic, and scientific questions, etc. have also been raised. See also W.R. Derrick Sewell, ed., *Human Dimensions of the Atmosphere*, NSF 68-18, Feb. 1968.

19. The cases have been analyzed in several studies and are again reviewed briefly in Professor Davis's paper. They will therefore only be noted here. Of the two cases in which a modifier received an adverse decision, one, Southwest Weather Research, Inc. et al. v. Duncan, 319 S.W. 2d 94- (Tex. Civ. App. 1958) enjoined activity paid for by farmers who used the services of a commercial modifier in an effort to suppress hail, at the behest of adjoining ranchers, on a theory of some sort of ownership by the ranchers in the clouds over their land. The other, a criminal prosecution in Pennsylvania, found the modifier guilty of violating a Township ordinance which prohibited modification. See supra note 12.

20. Slutsky v. City of New York, 97 N.Y. Supp. 2d 238 (1950). The

court also stated, without further discussion or citation of legal authority, that the landowner had no vested rights in the clouds or the moisture therein. Even if the activities were not stopped, however, if the resort had been able to prove specific damages, the City would presumably be liable to pay for such injury or such taking for a public purpose.

21. One member of the Task Group has reservations concerning the advisability of establishing a system of compensation based upon strict liability principles. In his view it may well be justifiable to impose strict liability for some losses caused by some kinds of weather modification activities, but it is doubtful whether all types of provable losses caused by all varieties of weather modification activities should be compensable without regard to fault.

22. The supporting papers analyze, from the points of view of normative decision making in a democratic society and of local, state, and federal government arrangements the future possibilities in detail.

23. See Rita Taubenfeld, "Social Norms, the Public Interest, and the Regulation of Weather Modification," *infra,* this study, hereinafter cited as *R. Taubenfeld.*

24. See esp. *Johnson, passim.*

25. See, *e.g.,* Gordon J.F. McDonald, "Science and Politics of Rainmaking," *Bull. of the Atomic Scientists* (October 1968), pp. 8-14, esp. 13-14.

26. The federal Interdepartmental Committee for Atmospheric Sciences (ICAS) noted in its 13th Report (January 1969), for example, that (p. 4):

A detailed review is also underway of all the aspects of weather modification activities with a view to recommending the necessary reporting regulations, licensing standards, program coordination mechanisms, and federal legislation to insure an adequate national weather modification program. The inability of the weather modification program to push forward at its full potential reflects the uncertainty of the Congress in dealing with pending goals in this area and the acceleration of this program to its proper pace should be one of the major efforts of ICAS during the coming year.

27. See *Battan, passim.*

28. It may well be that the new Council on Environmental Quality in the Office of the President would be able to provide publicity, guidance, and leadership in support of such a basic research program

under the existing decentralized federal-research apparatus or alternatively, it might well be able to study and propose the adoption of a more centralized basic-research program perhaps in cooperation with the Science Adviser if this proved necessary because of a continued failure to achieve momentum under present decentralized arrangements.

29. One member of the panel feels past experience with the limitations of voluntary cooperation via ICAS suffices to suggest "that it will be necessary to designate an agency as having 'lead responsibility'."

30. As one example, the FAA has authority to set noise standards for certification of aircraft but, despite the desire of U.S. airlines, it has not taken the opportunity of setting them for airport operations (except perhaps at Kennedy Airport). The FAA has sought *not* to preempt the field despite the airlines' desire for uniformity under these conditions. It has urged that local authorities should set the standards to accord with airport and community needs. Cf. the discussion in American Airlines, Inc. v. Town of Hempstead, 272 F. Supp. 226, aff. 398 F. 2d 369, cert. den. 393 U.S. 1017. It may also be that the Agency fears that the setting of these standards might involve the federal government in numerous suits of the type now being brought for nuisance and for taking of property due to aircraft noise against airport owners and operators.

31. In pure logic the appropriateness of the level of the group decision-making entity chosen would be determined by the scope of the region to be directly affected by the activity in question and the preferences of the polity as to the preferred level of decision making. We have assumed that the polity will prefer control to lie with the most local level of government that can contain and effectively control the whole range of effects from any activity.

32. Perhaps fog clearance at the Denver Airport would prove to meet the test, for example. It should be remembered that the allocation of water resources insofar as intrastate problems are concerned has been determined primarily by the states. A federal allocative scheme for cloud resources might greatly affect the surface supply rationed by the states.

33. It is probably possible through interstate compacts (which need congressional approval) for interested states to work together in undertaking modification operations. Such arrangements are, however, awkward at best and might prove neither flexible enough nor politically manageable enough to permit the design of an adequate multistate-modification district. But regulation or licensing through such arrangements would seem infeasible.

34. Again, the Department of Defense might be willing to seek presidential approval for some of its operations at least for proceeding

31

without exposing its goals, methods, or results. Even then it might be possible to require the Department to specify the regions in which its modification activities were to take place so that effects on other programs could be taken into account by scientists. It might be possible to require them to minimize their interference with civilian programs in general.

35. In analogous procedures, the CAB can, for example, dismiss an application or a complaint against a procedure on the basis of the "public interest" even though the complaint is legally sufficient and even without a hearing. We do not propose to go this far.

36. In Pennsylvania and West Virginia, legislation now leaves this issue in part to weather boards. See *Davis, passim.*

37. If the modification districts did not internalize all benefits this distortion could be largely corrected if parties not within the modifying unit who receive benefits were taxed by the relevant political authority in favor of the district or in some other way required to contribute their share to the costs of modification.

38. See also S. 2875 (1966), discussed *infra* in *Johnson.*

39. Note that, in addition to this form of procedure, a government may also be held to pay adequate compensation where it takes someone's property for public use, even if this means only a diminution in that property's value occasioned directly by governmental activity on other property. This has been true, for example, in some airport noise cases.

Of course, if Congress approved, federal contractors could be indemnified against loss, but Congress thus far has generally been unwilling to permit such indemnification in other fields.

40. Occasionally, as with the AEC, it has been deemed appropriate to permit the same entity both to operate, to set standards, to license, etc. This has led to much criticism. Certainly the rather special factors connected with nuclear energy, its secrecy, and its military uses are not foreseeable for weather modification. Other entities too, the CAB, for example, which have been charged with multiple and conflicting authorities, have run into major difficulties. The CAB is both to regulate the airlines and to promote air transport (52 Stat. 973 (1938), now the Federal Aviation Act of 1958, 72 Stat. 737, 49 U.S.C. § § 1301-1542 (1964)). It has had great difficulty in determining what the overall U.S. public interest requires, especially in airline-bus (and other surface forms) competition. See for example, Transcontinental Bus System Inc. v. CAB, 383 F.2d 466 (5 Cir. 1967), cert. den. 390 U.S. 920 (1968).

41. The bases for many of these normative choices are analyzed hereafter in *R. Taubenfeld.*

2   The Scientific Aspects of Weather Modification

Louis J. Battan

In recent years there has been growing optimism that it should be possible to exert a significant influence on the weather. The degree of optimism depends to a certain extent, on the weather-modification expert whose opinion is sought. This uncertainty is one of the reasons for the complexities facing authorities confronted with legal questions. Anyone who examines the growing mass of scientific literature on weather modification quickly realizes that the uncertainties exist because of the paucity of precise information about the nature of clouds and precipitation and because of the small number of carefully designed and executed field experiments.

Clearly much needs to be learned about the science and engineering aspects of weather modification, but at the same time it should be recognized that a great deal has been learned over the last couple of decades. In this brief summary, the status of present-day knowledge will be outlined.

Fog Dissipation

There is overwhelming evidence that supercooled (that is, water clouds with temperatures below 32°F) fogs and cloud layers can be caused to dissipate by introducing ice crystals in the clouds. The most common procedures for doing this involves seeding them with pellets of dry ice or the smokes from burning certain reagents, such as silver iodide and lead iodide, or by releasing propage gas. The result of such an operation is a light shower of ice crystals and snowflakes which sometimes reach the ground.

Engineering techniques for clearing supercooled fogs over airports by a sufficient amount to allow airplanes to land and take off have been developed and are being used in the United States, USSR, France, and probably elsewhere as well. In the United States, dry ice was first employed on a practical basis for clearing airports in 1963 by United Airlines. Since then an increasing number of air carriers have taken advantage of this cloud-seeding technique to improve the efficiency of their operations.[1]

Clouds and fogs at temperatures above 32°F are called "warm clouds" or "warm fogs." According to W.B. Beckwith, they represent roughly 95 percent of the dense fogs in the United States and cost the airline industry nearly $75,000,000 annually through cancellations, diversions, and delays.[2] A generally accepted practical technique for their modification does not yet exist. During World War II, oil burners were used to heat runway areas and cause the fog to evaporate and cloud ceiling and visibility to improve sufficiently to allow airplane movements. This scheme, known as FIDO, is not regarded as practical under peacetime conditions. The same is generally true of other techniques involving only heat.

In recent years U.S. Air Force scientists have been experimenting with jet engines mounted so as to blow hot air over fog-covered runways. They have also proposed that under certain conditions, helicopter wakes may lead to the dissipation of warm fogs.[3] It still has not been shown that these techniques are practical.

Some 30 years ago, H.G. Houghton and W.H. Radford dispersed calcium chloride particles and fine sprays of solutions of this chemical into warm fogs on Cape Cod. Condensation took place on the salt particles, and they grew at the expense of the fog droplets which evaporated. As a result, visibilities improved. In recent years, there has been a revival of interest in such a technique or variations thereof. They involve seeding fogs with salts aimed at causing a transformation of the fog droplet-size spectrum.[4]

Flynn and Beckwith reported tests aimed at dissipating warm fog by seeding them with so-called polelectrolytes surfactants and vaporized salt brine.[5] The aim of the operations was to "cause water droplets in the fog to coalesce, reducing droplet count per unit volume and thereby increasing runway visibility." The exact nature of the chemical substance has not been revealed. The conclusions of the investigation were generally optimistic, but some scientists who witnessed the tests have not been convinced that it was demonstrated that warm fogs were effectively dissipated.

Although occasional hopeful results appear in print, it still is premature to claim that a practical scheme exists for effectively dissipating warm fogs and low-stratus clouds.

Precipitation

Most weather-modification activities in the United States have been concerned with attempts to increase precipitation. A special panel of the National Academy of Sciences stated that, "There is increasing but still somewhat ambiguous statistical evidence that precipitation from some types of cloud and storm systems can be modestly increased or redistributed by seeding techniques."[6] The Panel apparently regarded 10 to 20 percent precipitation increases as modest ones. In many practical applications such increases can be quite important.

In 1969 the Panel's conclusion still is valid as far as it goes, but it does not go far enough. The evidence on hand indicates that in certain types of weather systems ice-nuclei seeding might cause a reduction of precipitation.

Project Whitetop was a carefully designed and executed program involving the airborne ice-nuclei seeding of summer clouds in Missouri. It ran for a 5-year period, from 1960-1964, under the direction of R.R. Braham at the University of Chicago. Evaluation of rainfall data was first carried out by Decker and Schickedanz at the University of Missouri.[7] Over the primary target areas, on seeded days, the overall rainfall was significantly less than on not-seeded days.

Various experimental programs have concluded that ice-nuclei seeding have increased precipitation at the ground. One can cite the following programs as examples: (1) a project was conducted in Switzerland.[8] (2) one was conducted in Israel.[9] Rainfall differences of some 10 to 80 percent have been reported depending on the precise nature of the analyses.

In some seeding tests, the results have differed depending on the specific meteorological conditions involved. An excellent example is found in the long-period winter program in eastern Colorado. Mielke et al., have reported that the effectiveness of ice-nuclei seeding depends crucially on cloud-top temperatures as well as on wind speeds at middle layers in the atmosphere.[10] At cloud-top temperatures warmer than $-20°C$, there was substantially more snowfall on seeded days. When temperatures were $-27°C$ and lower, less snowfall fell on seeded days. At intermediate temperatures, differences between precipitation on seeded and not-seeded days was small. The observed differences appear to be consistent with the known physical processes of snow formation.

Other programs could be cited to illustrate the point that the results of ice-nuclei seeding tests have depended on meteorological conditions. For example, Simpson et al., used numerical models of convective clouds to select those clouds whose vertical extent and precipitation might be augmented by means of cloud seeding.[11]

The view that the effects of cloud seeding might range from an increase, to nothing, to a decrease appears to be subscribed to by an increasing number of authorities.

Only recently has this concept been getting serious attention. Although there are some encouraging exceptions, such as the one already mentioned, it usually is not possible to specify with confidence those storm systems likely to give precipitation increases. There is some evidence that in the case of individual cumuliform clouds, it sometimes is possible to identify those likely to be beneficially modified by cloud seeding.[12]

A question of major importance in connection with cloud-seeding programs concerns effects in regions outside the primary target area. A common query is, "What happens downwind? If you increase the rain on your farm, will you decrease it on mine which is downwind of yours?" The evidence is conflicting. On the basis of crude theoretical considerations of precipitation efficiency, it would be suspected that modest rainfall increases over a target area of say 100 to 1,000 sq. mi. would have no detectable effects downwind. On the other hand, analyses by research groups in various countries have led to diverging claims. In most instances, it has been reported that when rainfall over the target area was greater following seeding, the positive anomalies were also observed downwind to distances of perhaps 100 mi. or more.

A note of concern about this question has been raised by J. Neyman, et al., who analyzed rainfall data in and around the location of Project Whitetop.[13] They claim that as a result of the ice-nuclei seeding of summer cumulus, there was an "estimated average loss of rain" of "21 percent of what would have fallen without seeding" over a circular area 360 mi. in diameter. In subsequent articles, Neyman and his colleagues have made stronger statements indicating their belief that seeding caused very widespread decreases in rainfall. This view has been questioned by Battan, who has argued that the observed differences in the rainfall on seeded and not-seeded days may have resulted for reasons other than the cloud seeding.[14] He has suggested that an alternative hypothesis having greater meteorological plausibility should be examined before claiming widespread rainfall decreases.

At this stage, the crucial questions of possible effects outside the primary seeding area are not resolved. Clearly *if* seeding in one area can have effects over regions more than 100 mi. from that area, there are likely to be large numbers of disputes. It is essential that the question of so-called "downwind effects" be given a great deal of attention by atmospheric scientists.

In summary, it should be noted that present knowledge of the effects of ice-nuclei seeding on rainfall still is not so far advanced that any operation can be regarded as a purely engineering enterprise. On the other hand, there is a great need for increasing numbers of applied-research programs to resolve the uncertainties now existing and to supply the data needed for engineering designs of future programs. The Bureau of Reclamation has embarked on such a program in the upper Colorado River Basin.

Suppression of Hail Damage

In the Soviet Union the major share of funds invested in weather-modification work has been used in the development and application of techniques to reduce hail damage to crops.[15] At least four separate practical projects are in existence in the regions north and south of the Caucusus Mountains and in Moldavia. These projects "protect" more than 6,000,000 a. of farm land. Developing hailstorms are seeded with ice nuclei, lead iodide for the most part, but sometimes silver iodide. In general, the aim has been to encourage the growth of many small hailstones in place of relatively fewer large damaging ones. If this could be accomplished, hail damage would be reduced because the small hailstones would melt almost completely during their some 10,000 ft. of fall from the freezing level to the ground.

The Soviet techniques for ice-nuclei seeding call for the delivery of the reagent directly into the cloud at altitudes where the temperature is between -5 and $-10°C$ (an altitude of perhaps 18,000 ft.). This is accomplished either by means of 70-mm artillery or rockets. In the first instance a shell contains the seeding reagent which is dispersed when the shell explodes within the cloud. In the rocket technique, a pyrotechnic mixture is ignited when the missile is in the cloud.

Soviet scientists have claimed spectacular success in all their projects. They have quoted benefit-to-cost ratios ranging from 4 to 1 to as high as 17 to 1. Hail-suppression activities are now carried out as engineering projects. Unfortunately it has not been possible to make an independent analysis of their data, and no research group outside the USSR has yet made an independent test of the technique.

Furthermore, the degree of success claimed has raised skeptical eyebrows among meteorologists who recognize the great variability of weather events and the lack of understanding of natural mechanisms of hail production.

Hail-modification experiments in other parts of the world have yielded mixed results. In a carefully designed research program conducted over a seven-year period in Switzerland, it was found that silver-iodide seeding by means of ground-based generators did not reduce hailfalls. As a matter of fact, it appears that the seeding may have increased the occurrence of hail.[16]

It has been reported that silver-iodide seeding as well as rockets containing explosive charges reduced hail damage in Kenya.[17]

In Argentina it was concluded that in certain types of storms, silver iodide might increase hail while in other types of storms it might decrease it.

In the United States, hail-modification research programs, which have been modest in scope, have failed to supply convincing answers to the question of whether or not hail damage to crops can be reduced. Attempts have been made to equate effectiveness of seeding to the quantity of seeding reagent employed, but so far it has not been possible to make a convincing case.

In the United States, legal controversies have arisen as a result of cloud-seeding operations aimed at hail reduction. People opposed to the operations have claimed that the cloud seeding caused a reduction in the quantity of rainfall. If a hail-suppression activity is instituted during a period of drought, such as was experienced over Pennsylvania in the early sixties, an uninformed individual could be led to the erroneous conclusion that the seeding caused the drought. There is no evidence to support such an allegation.

In the case of the Swiss project (called Grossversuch III) which was designed to test if hail could be reduced, more rain occurred on seeded days.[18] In three of the four hail-suppression programs in the Soviet Union, it was claimed that the effects of seeding on rainfall were not examined. In Moldavia, it was concluded that the seeding did not reduce rainfall.

In summary, it can be said that the available information would not support the claim that ice-nuclei seeding for the purpose of hail suppression has caused a reduction in rainfall.

It is generally agreed that in the United States, research on hail and hail-modification needs to be substantially enlarged. For several years several government (particularly the NSF) and nongovernment agencies have been working on a plan for a so-called "national hail-research program." Until such a program comes into being, it appears that little progress will be made in understanding the nature of hailstorms and the development of effective schemes for modifying them.

Influencing Lightning

Because of the tremendous damage to forests as a result of lightning-caused fires, there has been considerable interest in the development of techniques for reducing the occurrence of cloud-to-ground lightning. Developing thunderstorms have been seeded with ice nuclei in attempts to modify the mechanisms for electrical charging and discharging within the storms. Results of carefully conducted field experiments started in 1960 by scientists of the U.S. Forest Service, and though they indicated that fire-producing lightning might have been decreased by ice-nuclei seeding, they still have not proved this hypothesis. More research on the effects of massive ice-nuclei seeding on the electrical properties of clouds is needed.

Other techniques have been proposed to modify the electrical structure of thunderstorms, but to date none have been shown to be effective.

Violent Storms

The scientific literature contains speculations about how tornadoes might be modified, but no tests have been conducted. As a matter of fact, very little serious attention has been given to this very important problem. One reason why they have not received adequate attention is that their small sizes and brief lifetimes make them difficult and expensive to investigate. Nevertheless, in view of the destructiveness of tornadoes and the number of injuries and deaths they cause, it is essential that they be given a higher priority by atmospheric scientists.

In terms of property damage, no atmospheric phenomena can compete with the hurricane. A single storm, Hurricane Betsy, which passed over Florida and then into Louisiana during the early part of September 1965, did 1.4 billion dollars worth of damage. Hurricane Camille in August 1969 ravaged Mississippi, doing damage in the hundreds of millions and causing more than 300 fatalities.

A hurricane is a tropical cyclone having winds exceeding 74 mph and sometimes approaching 200 mph. The storms affecting the eastern United States originate over the warm waters of the South Atlantic and move westward towards Florida. Most storms turn northward along a curved path and then northeastward over the colder waters of the north Atlantic where they weaken.

The storms produce giant waves which inundate low-lying land. The sea water combined with torrential rains may produce widespread flooding leading to extensive damage, fatalities, and injuries. The powerful winds around the hurricane center obviously contribute to the destruction. To compound the hazards, tornadoes frequently occur within the hurricane.

The first attempt to modify a hurricane was made by Irving Langmuir and his colleagues on October 13, 1947 when he seeded a hurricane with Dry Ice. The hurricane followed an unexpected course, and Langmuir concluded that the seeding may have been the cause. This view was not shared by most atmospheric scientists.

In 1961 hurricane Esther was seeded with silver iodide, and it was subsequently observed that there were changes in the "eyewall" clouds and a 10 percent decrease in the maximum wind speeds. Since 1962, Project Stormfury, a cooperative project of the U.S. Navy and the Environmental Science Services Administration has been concerned with learning about the properties of hurricanes and with testing the effects of cloud seeding on them.[19] In 1963 hurricane Beulah was seeded with heavy doses of silver iodide, but the observed changes were small. On August 18 and 20, 1969, hurricane Debbie was seeded with silver iodide, and according to a press release from the Office of the Secretary of Commerce dated December 4, 1969, maximum wind speeds decreased from 98 to 68 knots the first day and from 99 to 84 knots on the second seeded day.

Doubts have been raised, particularly by the theoretical work of Dr. Katsuyuki Ooyama at New York University, that tampering with the cloud "microphysics" can significantly alter hurricane intensity or path of travel. On the other hand, the possibility that ice nuclei can do so cannot be ruled out. Furthermore, Project Stormfury will supply valuable information about the properties of hurricanes. Continuous experimental and theoretical studies may lead to an effective technique for modifying hurricanes.

It should be recognized that hurricanes have some beneficial results. They produce large quantities of much-needed rain water to the southern and eastern United States. If the paths of all hurricanes could be deviated away from the mainland, the damage by strong winds, high waves, and heavy rain would certainly be reduced, but over a period of years there would be a distinct water shortage in the southern and eastern United States.

Of course, if the intensity of the tropical storms, that is, the wind velocities, could be greatly reduced, while the storms followed their normal tracks, the land areas would still get the much-needed rain without having to pay the price of damaged property and lost lives. Such a solution to the hurricane problem appears to be far in the future, judging from the very modest research programs now underway.

Large-scale Weather or Climate Modification

There is little doubt that, by changing the landscape and emitting gases and particles into the atmosphere, man is inadvertently changing the weather and climate in cities.[20] It has been speculated by a number of scientists that large-scale atmospheric pollution has inadvertently modified the climate of the Earth.[21] The implications of such a possibility are so enormous that they need much greater attention than they are getting today.

It has been suggested that some day it might be possible to intentionally alter the climate over large regions of the Earth. Various schemes for causing a slight warming of the polar regions of the world have been offered. If the northerly latitudes could be warmed even slightly, the general air circulation over the globe would be changed and so would the climate. Unfortunately, no one knows how they would change.

At present, no attempts are being made to actually warm up the Arctic. It appears that none of the proposed schemes for doing so is practical. The general view of atmospheric scientists is that before any attempt is made to purposefully modify very large-scale weather and climate, it is essential that the possible consequences be known. At the present time, work is in progress to develop improved laboratory and mathematical models of the global atmosphere.[22] Once they are available, it should be possible to introduce artificial sources of heat and calculate their effects on the climate, in other words on temperature, rainfall, winds, etc. Until such factors can be adequately predicted, it would be hazardous indeed to attempt to consider intentional modification of the global atmosphere. It appears that no such experiments are likely during the next decade.

Summary

In this statement on the status on weather modification, no attempt was made to give a comprehensive review of the existing and rapidly growing voluminous literature. The publications in the list entitled "For Additional Information" at the end of this report give much more detailed and extensive bibliographies. The purpose of this paper has been to briefly summarize, for the nonscientist, what the author regards as our present state of knowledge.

In general, the dissipation of supercooled fogs over airports has reached the engineering stage, but techniques for reliably and economically clearing warm fogs still have not been developed.

Cloud seeding can cause changes in the precipitation reaching the ground. Results have ranged from increases to decreases amounting to some tens of percents. In certain special cases, progress has been made in identifying those meteorological conditions where positive results can be expected.

The effects of cloud seeding on rainfall outside, particularly downwind, of the primary seeding area still are subjects of speculation with reports of increases predominating, but at least one claim of possible large decreases. This crucial problem needs to be resolved as quickly as possible.

Claims of spectacular success in hail-damage suppression by means of ice-nuclei seeding have continued to come from the USSR, while in other parts of the world results have been mixed. Expanded research and experimentation is being planned in the United States.

Programs of research aimed at the modification of violent storms—especially tornadoes and hurricanes—are very modest in scope. Unless research efforts are greatly enlarged, little progress is likely in the future.

The design, conduct, and evaluation of a weather-modification operation involves the application of new scientific concepts. Unless such an operation is under the direction of a person having professional scientific training and experience, it is likely to yield nothing of value. It is essential that standards be established to identify persons having the competence and credentials to carry out weather-modification programs.

Finally it needs to be emphasized, as was noted at the start of this essay, that one of the chief obstacles to more rapid progress in the field of weather and climate modification is the ignorance of details of the nature of atmospheric phenomena. It is not correct to say that in order to predict and control the weather we must fully understand it. On the other hand, the better we understand it, the more likely we will be to learn to predict and control it. Unfortunately there are too many aspects of cloud, precipitation, weather, and climatic systems of which we know very little. Some of them have been mentioned earlier. An examination of the survey prepared by MacDonald et al. reveals many others.[23]

In view of the fact that the weather and climate influence the lives of almost every living thing on the planet Earth, it is distressing that the research efforts in this field of study are so poorly supported. A catalogue of deaths, injuries, and financial losses by violent weather events is very visible evidence of the effects of the atmosphere. More subtle, but more widespread, are such effects as abnormally wet or dry spells which govern the food production on which man depends.

The total federal government support for weather-modification research has been 11.37, 11.32, and 11.77 million dollars during Fiscal years 1968, 1969, and 1970, respectively. In light of the crucial relation of this work to man and his existence and considering the scale of federal science and technology expenditures, these sums seem unbelievingly inadequate. It surely is in the national interest to expand programs of study aimed at learning the fundamental processes of the atmosphere and to adequately support field tests of appropriate weather-modification procedures. Unless these steps are taken, progress in the development of practical techniques for beneficially modifying the weather will be too long delayed.

Notes

1. W.B. Beckwith, "Supercooled Fog Dispersed for Airport Operations," *Bull. Amer. Meteor. Soc.,* 46 (1965). pp. 323-327.

2. Beckwith, "An Analysis of Airport Fog Dispersal Operations," *Proc. First National Conf. on Weather Modification* (Boston: Amer. Meteor. Soc., 1968), pp. 361-371.

3. V.G. Plamk and A.A. Spatola, "Cloud Modification by Helicopter Wakes," *J. Appl. Meteor.,* 8 (1969), pp. 566-578.

4. J.E. Jiusto, R.J. Pilie, and W.C. Kocmond, "Fog Modification with Giant Hygroscopic Nuclei," *J. Appl. Meteor.,* 7 (1968), pp. 860-869.

5. R.G. Flynn and W.B. Beckwith, *Airline Warm Fog Dispersal Test Program* (Washington: Air Transport Assoc., 1968), p. 104.

6. J.F. MacDonald et al., *Weather and Climate Modification—Problems and Prospects,* Vols. I and II, Publ. 1350 (Washington: National Academy Science — Nat. Res. Council), 28 pp. and 198 pp.

7. W.L. Decker and Schickendanz, "The Evaluation of Rainfall Records from a Five Year Cloud Seeding Experiment in Missouri," *Proc. of the Fifth Berkeley Symposium on Math. Statistics and Probability* (Berkeley: Univ. Calif. Press, 1968), pp. 55-64.

8. P. Schmid, "On 'Grossversuch III,' A Randomized Hail Supression Experiment in Switzerland," *Proc. of the Fifth Berkeley Symposium on Math. Statistics and Probability* (Berkeley: Univ. Calif. Press, 1967), pp. 141-160.

9. K.R. Gabriel, "The Israeli Artificial Rainfall Stimulation Experiment: Statistical Evaluation for the Period 1961-65," *Proc. of the Fifth Berkeley Symposium on Math. Statistics and Probability* (Berkeley: Univ. Calif. Press, 1967), pp. 91-113.

10. P.W. Mielke, L.O. Grant, and C.F. Chappell, "Elevation and Spatial Variation Effects of Wintertime Orographic Cloud Seeding," *J. Appl. Meteor.,* ix, no. 3 (June 1970), pp. 476-88.

11. J. Simpson, G.W. Brier, and R.H. Simpson, "Stormfury Cumulus Seeding Experiment 1965: Statistical Analysis and Main Results," *J. Atmos. Sci.,* 24 (1967), pp. 508-521.

12. W.L. Woodley, *Precipitation Results from a Pyrotechnic Cumulus Seeding Experiment,* Tech. Memo. ERLTM-AOML 2, E.S.S.A. (August 1969), 50 pp.

13. J. Neyman, E. Scott, and J.A. Smith, "Areal Spread of the Effect of Cloud Seeding at the Whitetop Experiment," *Science,* 163 (1969), pp. 1445-1448.

14. L.J. Battan, "Whitetop Experiment," *Science,* 165 (1969a), p. 618.

15. Battan, "Weather Modification in the USSR—1969," *Bull. Amer. Meteor. Soc.,* 50 (1969b).

16. Schmid, op. cit.

17. T.J. Henderson, "An Operational Hail Supression Program near Kericho, Kenya-Africa," *Proc. First National Conf. on Weather Modification* (Boston: Amer. Meteor. Soc., 1968), pp. 474-483.

18. Schmid, op. cit.

19. R.H. Simpson and J. Simpson, "Why Experiment on Tropical Hurricanes," *Trans. N.Y. Acad. Sciences,* Ser. II, 28 (1966), pp. 1045-1062.

20. R. Bryson and J.E. Kutzbach, *Air Pollution,* Resource Paper No. 2 (Washington: Assoc. Amer. Geographers, 1968), 42 pp.

21. MacDonald, op. cit.

22. Ibid.

23. Ibid.

3 Social Norms, the Public Interest, and the Regulation of Weather Modification

Rita F. Taubenfeld

Introduction

This paper is divided into three parts. Since this is a normative discussion, the first part is an attempt to synthesize and make a contribution to the general theory of the generation of relevant social norms by which social decisions can be evaluated in a democratic-type system. The later parts attempt to seek out and apply relevant norms for the evaluation of the U.S. Government's and private programs of weather-modification research and operations. In the second part a current question, Should a major federally subsidized program in basic weather-modification knowledge be undertaken, is examined as an example. The third part focuses on some alternative normative policy choices and institutional strategies for establishing regulatory machinery intended primarily to regulate weather-modification activities in this society.

A final summary comment on the generation of overall optimal social policy on weather modification is appended.

The Criteria of Social Welfare

We wish first to discuss the generation of social values and preferences and the choice of social norms in a model society with a federal type

Special thanks are due to all the members of the Task Group, especially to Sho Sato and Ralph Johnson, and to Dr. Ruth Morgan for helpful suggestions and comments.

47

constitutional system of representative government which relies on a complex constitutional strategy primarily employing majority-rule legislative processes, the results of which are initially interpreted and administered by a huge, complex, bureaucratic administration under the direction of an elected chief executive. These majority-rule decision processes are balanced and constrained by a judiciary which interprets a written and unwritten constitution. The Constitution was designed to rely on such constitutional strategies as the "separation of powers" between the three main branches of the central government, the executive and his administration, the legislative and the judiciary, a specified but moving "division of powers" between the central and state governments, "checks and balances" among all the institutions for decision making on the federal level, regular reapportionment, and regular elections with secret ballots (in which more than one important political party freely participates), all combining to achieve a set of idealized majority-rule processes which would minimize the likelihood of a permanent tyranny of either the majorities or the minorities being established. We further assume that the social institutions provide that individual economic choices among goods and services are to be expressed as far as possible in what is to be kept a "workably competitive" market system. The market and the social system together are to allocate roles among competing aspirants. The market mechanism is therefore to be regulated by the central institutions of government, and the outcome generated by the private market together with the social system is to be regularly corrected by the central political institutions for economic and social and political aims it fails to achieve automatically.

For this model constitutional society we assume that a scientific opportunity, the capacity to seek to modify the weather, seems to promise to yield to heavily socially-subsidized, concerted, scientific study. If society does not pursue this study, mission-oriented agencies of the government administration and parties in the private sector both of which are interested can be expected to continue to undertake some weather-modification activities without full scientific understanding of their mechanisms and the costs and benefits they generate—unless, of course, such activities are prohibited or regulated. Political questions posed for this paper include: Should such a society undertake this costly scientific study? To what extent? And whether or not it does so, what institutional provisions should it make for the social regulation of such weather-modification activities?

When we ask such broad gauge normative questions we are ulti-mately asking about the hierarchy of values and goals of the society in question. Who should decide such normative questions? The obvious general answer is the relevant decision makers. In a rational choice framework they can be expected to decide in accordance with the expected benefits and costs of their alternative available options in such a way as to maximize their expected satisfactions or welfare.

A first question then is who are the relevant decision makers in terms of whose values and preferences alternatives are to be evaluated? We have assumed representative choice institutions. We shall assume that the ideology of the society requires that the values and preferences of all members of the society are to count in the social evaluation and choice processes on the basis of one-man one-vote with a majority-rule decision rule.

An even more fundamental issue must be raised. How do we determine in a society the extent to which the members will decide on the matters in question?[1] In this paper we accept the political facts that the major focus of decision making and norm choosing is the ongoing national state.[2] When we seek to define the public interest, it is the public interest of the national state we seek.[3] But we assume an open political system. Therefore for each state some international interest exists, the state cares about what would happen to it, because other states exist in a very loosely integrated international system. To this extent the state can be expected to internalize aspects of consideration for the welfare of other members of the international system into its own value and preference systems. It must also be sensitive to the requisites of self-defense in such a system. Thus even if a state felt that all states would be better off not investing in weather modification in this decentralized international system, there are reasons to feel that it could not afford not to pursue such experimentation. This would be the case if, as is likely, it believed other states would not do likewise and if it believed there was some significant possibility that weather modification could become an important military weapon or even a total weapon.[4]

It is to be noted that we have easily slipped into the almost unavoidable convenience of discussing a state's values, preferences, costs, benefits, and comparing these with those of other states. Of course, a state is a composite; it does not have a mind or a true subjective with which to consider values and preferences in order to make rational choices. We have noted that in our model state actual policy choices are made by the relevant decision makers who turn out to be legitimately chosen representatives of the general public. They are made by means of the whole highly complex apparatus of political choices. In this model representative society, the general population will retain some loose control over the political choice apparatus primarily through the rather blunt mechanism of periodic elections in which more than one party freely participates, allowing it to replace the current set of representative decision makers and many of the administrators dependent on them by their challengers. Between such elections, decisions are made *inter alia* in the legislative branches of the government, usually after searching investigations attempt to throw light on the public interest. It can be expected that the self-interests of the actual representative decision makers are also important in the actual choice processes. Hard bargaining takes place between the decision makers including vote trading, which often ties various independent issues of different importance to different groups together into a package. Decisions are also made by the chief executive and his administration both because they initiate legislative action and because they implement legislative and executive policy decisions. If disputes arise in our model representative democracy as to the meaning or constitutionality of the choice which evolves, the judicial system may be called on to interpret or amend the outcome. It is becoming customary to point out that such a complex, modern political-choice system in a representative democracy is reminiscent of the separation of ownership and control of a large modern corporation.[5]

Control in the system lies primarily with the chosen decision makers in the legislative, executive, and judicial organs rather than, as in direct democracy, with the "owners", the members of the electorate. In general the citizens of the society neither decide nor effectuate social choice directly.[6] Since we have assumed in our model democracy that the values and preferences of the people should nonetheless provide the yardstick by which to evaluate governmental policy, we are left to face the important problems—long belabored and still unsolved—of political theory and of welfare economics of defining and objectifying the social-value system and the social-preference structure or something which may be called the "will of the community," the "Public Interest," or the "Social Welfare Function," etc.[7] In our case we mean to seek to find the (preferably internally consistent, well-integrated) system of social values and preferences which has been appropriately aggregated from all the component values and preferences of citizens by

50

which to judge the social outcome. We have already specified that this aggregation would be made on the direct democracy basis of one-man one-vote majority rule. We will call this the democratic social-preference structure and social-value system.[8]

Such a social value and preference hierarchy would be very useful, both in judging the outcome of the whole complex social-decision process in terms of the aims of the citizens of the society after the facts of choice and implementation. It would of course also be useful ex ante in aiding the process of rational social choice itself in guiding the policy choices of actual legislators, executives, administrators and the judiciary—in other words, of the actual social decision makers and implementators by the socially correct value system and set of preferences. Indeed the press of economists in quest of the social-welfare function was primarily motivated by the desire to be able to refer to a synoptic map of all social preferences so that it would be possible to perform economic maximization as pure technicians who simply guided society to the maximized achievement of social welfare as defined by the appropriate decision makers—in a democracy, all the members of society. If an agency of social decision making, Congress, the Department of Health, Education and Welfare, the Civil Aeronautics Board, or the Weather Modification Board could only be allowed to refer directly to such an objective, internally consistent, well-integrated social-preference structure, society could always be placed somewhere on its welfare frontier by fully instructed apolitical technicians. If they failed to so place society, this could be clearly evident to all who could consult the objectified social preferences. If society wished the social preferences to be binding on its decision makers, only choices between equally socially good but mutually exclusive alternatives would still be left for political choice by representative decision makers. (It would be most unreasonable biologically to assume a strong social ordering in nature so that no irreducible social ties would exist.) Presumably such choices would be made on the basis of constitutionally specified criteria for such pure political tie-breaking.

Unfortunately, however, it turns out that there is no simple way to objectify the democratic social value and social preference structures.[9] As noted the actual role of a representative legislator or an administrator includes, inter alia, attempting to estimate, on the basis of his various informational sources, the relevant social values and preferences as part of the process of making the optimum social choice. This is an important function of the democratic political-choice apparatus, essential to the process of optimal social choice in which—hopefully— social preferences are applied to social alternatives so that the best available alternative can be selected. Because these processes of estimation and selection are not subject to an objective check against a blueprint of the objectivized social preference structure, in actual practice the representative decision maker has room to misinterpret the social values and preferences of his constituents. He also has the opportunity and quite probably the need to allow considerations of his own self-interest to dominate his political choice activities, even though he may be the chosen representative of many other citizens whose subjective values and preferences can only enter the actual social process by means of being reflected in his decision-making activities.

After it became clear that the correct social-preference hierarchy was not going to be a readily available, clear-cut, objectified datum, some economists have taken the position that the technician in a democracy must regard the values and preferences revealed by the choices of the legislature as binding, even for advice and evaluation purposes.[10] Yet, as we have just suggested the choice of the legislature, when it is finally made, is not necessarily likely to reveal the relevant social values and preferences (of the citizenry as aggregated on a one-man one-vote majority-rule basis) of even a model democratic society. Of course it is probably less likely to do so in actual, highly imperfect, democratic political-choice processes.

It will probably pay us to briefly review five major sources of distortions between actual social choices and the choices implied by the democratic aggregation of social values and preferences in a representative democratic government.

The first set of difficulties stems from the problems implicit in aggregating the subjective preferences of those whose values and preferences are being represented by the representative, administrator, or voter. Many problems arise from the fact that the subjective of any one individual is only partly realized and imperfectly objectivized at best.

Problems arise both because people do not know what they want and do not really understand themselves very well, and because of difficulties in objectifying this sort of information, if it is known, in a world in which only a few alternatives are likely to be presented for choice. Thus most people, even the eminently self-aware, undoubtedly do not have in mind a stable, complete ordering of all social-alternative actions on a given issue, though preferences among the basic values may be more complete and stable. Indeed, one of the reasons for having representative decision makers is to relieve the represented parties of the burdens of decision-making on innumerable social issues. In fact when an issue becomes of current political importance, much public exploration and community dialogue must take place in order to illuminate the alternatives. These are necessary self-education processes for decision makers and constituents alike. Thus the social preferences on the issues in question only take shape dynamically over time and over this education process. (The public and the members of the legislature tend to learn about their own values and preferences on these issues and about the content of the actual restricted, few alternatives available for their evaluation in terms of their preferences simultaneously.) The static format which calls for all relevant alternatives (or sometimes all conceivable alternatives) to be evaluated prior to all choice processes clearly abstracts from these dynamic processes and from real world selectivity, self-ignorance, and resistance to and costs of rational calculation. It also abstracts from changes of taste, changes of opportunity, or changes of environment. Furthermore, even if an individual were self-aware and calculative and there were no problems of changing conditions, the ripeness of issues for selection can be expected to vary. At any one time some issues will be genuinely resolved in his mind, and some will be resolved only in the process of resolution. The notion of relatively complete static social preferences probably can be viewed as relevant only to the last stages of the decision process on any single issue—when the temporary final decision is about to be made. No stable-preference ordering for all issues and alternatives in all conceivable contexts can be expected to exist at any one time or to be available for discovery.

As to problems of discovering the social consensus given the limited opportunities for most people to objectify the data of subjective preferences in practice, more vocal individuals express their current subjective values and preferences and propose alternatives reflecting these preferences more frequently in the press, the pulpit, at the lecturn, and in the many social organizations and lobbies which attempt to persuade the delegated decision makers of their view of the social welfare. Opinion polls and letters to decision makers, many actions in the private sector, such as acts of philanthropy, and many actions in the courts, can offer samples of the values or preferences of the voters on many issues, but the process of deriving an overall, representative set of aggregated, socially subjective preferences must remain very partial and imperfect, a challenge to representative and chief executive alike. Presumably more diligent efforts at sampling public opinion as to values and preferences of the voters are possible, however. Despite the fact that, in some ultimate sense, the subjective in all its complexity is ineffable and unknowable by selective efforts to objectify it, there is no reason to suggest that good approximations of the summation of such subjective evaluations of values and preferences of the members of a society on one or a few issues at any one time is in principle impossible. At present it is very inadequately and haphazardly pursued by the decision makers.

In actual choice processes people can only make their subjective preferences known by choosing among the specified alternatives, given their opportunities, including the sequences in which alternatives are presented. These may very inadequately reflect their overall subjective valuations after they have finally developed and analyzed them. Thus at any one time actual choices may only poorly reflect the current state of the preferences of the winning coalition of decision makers among the alternatives posed and nothing more.

A second important source of divergence between actual social choices resulting from actual decision making and those implied by the democratic social-value system and social preferences arises from the fact that the subjective values and preferences of the members of a representative's clientele are likely to be divergent and mutually inconsistent, especially in purely distributive issues, such as, for example, which of two equally (socially) good designs or contract offers is to be chosen. Even if the subjective-preferences structure of the component individuals of the group were perfectly known and even if it were agreed that they should be aggregated by direct democracy majority-rule processes, how could they be expected to yield a single, internally consistent group-preference structure where many highly conflicting values and preferences exist and each man's opinion is to be represented equally in the social choice?[11] Arrow and subsequent writers have shown that under his assumptions in which intensity of component preferences are not evaluated, this was only possible if individual preferences were, if not identical, at least based on mutually consistent underlying values so that preferences would be "single-peaked" or conform to other similarly restrictive assumptions on the types of allowable preference structures or the number of alternatives among which the citizens could freely choose.[12] The fact is that if people in a democracy divide into groups which disagree bitterly and

54

irreducibly, there may be no consistent majority social-value or social-preference hierarchy. Yet underlying agreement is not necessarily to be expected, especially on distributive issues in which one man's gain is another man's loss. Thus on distributive issues no majority social preferences for the representative decision maker to discover may exist. This seems important for issues like those that would be implied if major modification of the weather-switching type ever became possible. People's preferences and interests might bitterly conflict on the choice of an ideal weather pattern for society. This also suggests the important point that not only is a basic consensus on values including especially distributive values probably essential to stable democratic choice systems, but also a basic consensus on distributive mechanisms including final social tie-breakers.[13] A stable democracy must be based on an explicit or implicit fundamental social bargain on distribution policy and mechanisms. We conclude that, if great basic differences of opinion among the constituents of a decision maker exist, he may well be unable to discover a clear-cut democratic public interest to guide his choice of behavior, since no stable majority preferences may exist. The social decision rules may specify that under such circumstances society will remain at the initial status quo condition. This cannot be taken to imply that the status quo reflects the public interest on the issue in any substantive sense, despite the fact that it is chosen. It reflects the social agreement to be bound by the results of the groups' legitimate decision processes. Again at any one time some issues may be resolved in the sense that a majority consensus has been hammered out on them; some may be unresolved and some may be in the process of resolution in which a majority consensus is being created. Again, over time the contents of these categories can be expected to change.

We have been supposing that a representative is supposed to reflect the social values and preferences in his choice behavior. The third source of divergence between actual choice and ideal choice, even in a model representative government which we will discuss here, revolves around the question as to whether a representative or a local administrator should feel obliged to follow the dictates of the social value and preference functions of his constituency or of the society as a whole where these may diverge or whether he should do what he thinks is best after considering everything—in other words, vote the way his own social preferences dictate.

Without exploring the a priori pros and cons we can note that in a typical representative legislature, elected representatives seeking reelection from a geographically bounded constituency are in fact under pressure to reflect the interests of their regions rather than society as a whole, except as the latter enters the calculations of their constituents. Those elected at large, central government administrators in general, and the chief executive in particular, are under pressure to seek to pursue the general welfare of the whole group even over strong, intensely pressed sectional interests.[14] These divergent incentives of the chief executive and the legislature can be regarded as fortunate if society wishes social-choice mechanisms to rely primarily on one-man, one-vote majority rule (which applies equal-intensity weights to each man's choice), and yet somehow society also wishes them to reflect varying intensities of interest of the component parts of the society.[15] In actual legislative processes such varying intensities of interest tend to be reflected on the basis of the varying achieved political power, drive, negotiating skill, and luck of the representative decision makers. For it can be assumed that in actual decision processes the legislature will forcefully express its special sensitivity to the intensity with which component subgroups weigh their preferences even after the chief executive and his administration have expressed their views of the more equally weighted social interest.[16] In any case it should be noted that our assumed direct democracy majority-rule aggregation processes we have proposed for the aggregation of social values and preferences do not provide the opportunity for vote-trading processes of negotiation, which is another major source of divergence of such a social preference scale from the results of actual legislation processes.

The fourth source of divergence between the results of actual choice processes and the outcome implied by the democratic social value and preference system in an idealized society is one on which political scientists have focused: the likelihood that conflict will exist between the groups' preferences, even if these were perfectly known and consistently aggregated and stable and well integrated, and the values, preferences, and self-interest of the representatives themselves, including their preferences for their own welfare, power, and reelection. Politically, the self-interested incentives of the actual decision makers are to assure major financial and political bases of power for themselves among their constituents. Other psychological sources of divergence between the preferences and judgments of a decision maker and his constituents exist. Both administrators and representatives, for example, may well have a different time preference from that implied by their reading of the aggregated preferences of their constituents or of the society as a whole.[17] The all too human tendency for them to want to show results in the relative short run during their terms in office could readily produce such a bias in favor of heavier investment in capital for future production as well as in favor of many government projects which the social preferences of the society might not rank highly, given all the alternatives and the costs. A representative and an administrator are at best self-fulfilling humans with imperious needs and aspirations of their own and not just aggregation machines.

To all this we must add a fifth consideration: the indivisibility of the choice of a representative. For a representative is not chosen for each issue but for a large group of often imperfectly foreseen issues which will arise during his period in office. There are normally only a few candidates offered. The opportunity to choose the best compromise normally can be expected to mean that people must vote for representatives with whom they do not agree on many issues. Once again this implies another important set of sources of divergence between actual social choices and the democratic social preference hierarchy.

In sum then even in an idealized majority-rule representative government with its complex constitutional guarantees there are good reasons for not expecting the acts of the legislature or the government as a whole to faithfully reveal a socially maximized achievement of some actual democratic social value and preference hierarchy at any given time.[18] Thus constant efforts in our idealized representative democracy with its complex constitution of choice to produce a consensus on social values and on a social preference structure and to correct the actual acts of choice of the actual complex choice institutions in terms of the democratic public interest remain necessary.

Thus we cannot look upon the data of past choices of the actually imperfect existent governments as the revealed preferences of the society in question even at the time of enactment. Past choices reflect past political bargains, past political power alignments, and luck—not necessarily the public interest. To survey them is to survey ex post, past political success rather than ex ante social preferences. Although the desire to rely on available objective data of actual acts of choice is understandable in addition to the already surveyed defects of such a strategy, in an actual imperfect democratic government it would clearly be strongly biased in favor of the past and the status quo effective division of political power in the society. As such it would be more suited to predictive than to normative analysis. Thus we can conclude that although the evidence of past choices is likely to be of some interest, especially on well-developed or largely decided social-policy issues, because it is the legitimate decision makers' choices after careful consideration of the alternatives given the decision processes, there is really no substitute for exploratory normative analysis of the democratic public interest. This should be undertaken by technical experts and by others who can attempt to weigh all the relevant evidence. In addition, of course, direct surveys of public opinion after it has matured on an issue can be fruitful in estimating the content of the democratic social preferences.

In general it seems likely that the chief executive elected by and responsible to the nation at large has the political incentives and the greatest resources at his command for obtaining information as to the content of the democratic social value structure and the social preference structure of society at any time and on any set of issues. As the chief decision maker for the polity he can be viewed as likely to be the temporary best source of information about the public interest. But he too is necessarily an imperfect embodiment of the social welfare, the public interest, or the will of the community, for problems 1, 2, 3, 4 and 5 exist for him, too. Thus pressure on him by the legislative and judicial branches of government and by subsidiary levels of government can all play a fruitful role in bringing information to him, especially as to the relative intensity of feeling of different groups and sections and also as to the aggregated "subjective" values and preferences of the community as a whole, which he only imperfectly knows and which he in fact of course must lead as well as reach.

Unfortunately, all this suggests that although greater efforts at surveying public tastes on a one-man one-vote basis in the last stages of the decision process on important issues seems indicated, we cannot expect to be able to answer our initial normative questions by simple reference to a generally agreed, neatly aggregated objectified social value structure and social preference hierarchy; nor could we, even in our model representative democracy. But at least we know that for an issue as inchoate as the appropriate policy towards weather modification we should look to find independent evidence of the content of democratic social preferences—independent of the actual choices, past or future. Indeed since we are not going to undertake a survey of the relevant values and preferences here, and it would no doubt be premature to do so in this preliminary paper, we can do no more than present one man's exploratory interpretations of the probable issues and the current evidence concerning the relevant parts of the still

58

emerging social value and preference hierarchies in our society insofar as weather modification activities are concerned. Our analysis suggests that such exploratory excursions are likely to be necessary in the early stages of opinion formation on contentious issues. Moreover our analysis has suggested that we look for clues as to the treatment of these and closely analogous type issues to all sections of opinion, to the chief executive, especially. For, given his incentives and his strategic position as far as information as to values, preferences, and alternatives are concerned, he appears to be the appropriate major innovator and evaluator of new social programs. We know to counterweight his choices by the opinions expressed in the whole governmental apparatus of decision making and most particularly in the legislature with its independent sources of search and information, its immediacy to the pulses of the various constituencies, and its ability and incentives to reflect the varying intensities of opinion over the population better than any other social organ of representative government. We know also to look directly to the organized and unorganized general public, particularly, the more vociferous members thereof for indication of what an appropriately balanced decision on optimal policy which would compare social preferences with social alternatives on the issues in question to select the best compromise, would be.

In the course of this review of the implicit norm-producing machinery of a model representative government we have begun to shed some light on the respective, appropriate roles of legislative and technical or administrative regulation in a model representative government, an issue which has troubled analysts of the regulation of public welfare-type scientific programs in the United States.[19] For although we have insistently denied that the choices of the legislature and the President automatically reveal the public interest, we have noted that these institutions normally are under some pressure to seek to maximize the achievement of the will of the community. It is therefore understandable that in stable societies their choices are regarded as temporarily binding if also subject to challenge and to change. On the other hand we can see that an appointed agency of experts and technicians or even of appointed administrators is in no position to specify society's values and objectives or to determine appropriate pure political choices in its purviews. Such officials have no inherent incentives to seek to effectuate the democratic social preference hierarchy comparable to the incentives implied by the regular subjection of the elected legislature and the chief executive to the polls. Thus, unless an appointed technical body can be presented by the representative legislature and the chief executive with at least a temporarily definitive set of specific instructions as to the executive's and the legislature's interpretations of the relevant sections of the social value and preference hierarchies or the social objectives on the issues in question, it presumably ought not to be given the power to make any important political choices either by its action or by default of its actions. It is not directly responsible to the electorate, and often the technical administrators' terms of office outlast the President's. When, to ease the burdens of decision making, it is deemed desirable to establish a regulatory agency, it is also desirable that specific instructions be given such technical administrative agencies. They should preferably contain simple identifiable, readily checkable choice rules of thumb for administrative decision making. Except for the few independent agencies, implementation of legislatively chosen policies by federal agencies is likely in most institutional arrangements to be heavily affected by the chief executive's vision of the relevant general social values and preferences and the optimal political and policy choices. Regular review of the activities of all regulatory agencies by the legislature to assure that the various constituencies of the legislators are being fairly treated and that the legislature's view of the appropriately chosen values and preferences and policy choices are being implemented is also necessary. Regular review intended to modify and correct these past choices in the light of experience, changed circumstances, changed tastes, changed political-power relationship or changed information as to the content of democratic social preferences is also obviously called for by both the executive and the legislature.

Thus it would seem that, ideally, major policy-making administrators and administrative regimes in weather modification and in other fields should be regularly designed to be responsible both to the chief executive and to the legislature.[20] In this way continuing efforts to maximize the achievement of the public interest as interpreted repeatedly by the legitimate processes of government, which are regularly subjected to public pressure, can be effectuated.

The Optimum Government Research Program
In Weather Modification

We turn from this somewhat abstract discussion of the aggregation of social-normative criteria out of individual values and preferences in an idealized representative democracy to discuss our first normative question with regard to U.S. Government policy: Should the society pursue a major social investment in weather-modification knowledge? Since we are not attempting a formal survey of social values and preferences of the United States, and indeed public discussion of this issue has probably not ripened to the point where one would be useful, this analysis will have to rely primarily on a priori logic augmented by some admittedly casual empiricism.

First and foremost, the United States does not exist in a closed political system. It is a member of an international system in which there are no important strong central forces maintaining international law and order, and each national state must primarily rely for security and survival on its own strength and that of the allies it can muster. As noted this may be an example of the need for a higher order (broader scope) of coercive government of an inherently communal activity than already exists or than is wanted on other grounds by the current set of legitimate decision makers in question. Thus an important national state has a rational national security reason for pursuing weather-modification technology. Given the fact that other important states cannot be trusted not to pursue it, each such state must pursue weather modification. If weather modification becomes a total weapon the traditional means of avoiding its use is by maintaining a first and second strike-deterrent capacity.[21] This means that not only weather modification but the technology of weather-modification reversal must be studied by all potentially affected states, or they must have allies who have studied it and will be willing to share with them reliably.

Since we assume a priori that national security and group survival are major social goals no matter how one aggregates the social value hierarchy—indeed they may well comprise the lexicographic primary goal of the society for which there are no conceivable trade-offs with other goals over many ranges of choice—our answer to our first normative question has been simple to reach.[22] Yes, weather-modification knowledge should be studied. But this only leads us to other more difficult questions. How much should be invested in this military technology compared to other military investments and the total military budget? Should weather-modification research be a strictly military program, or should a civilian-research program be attempted. Which should be dominant, if either? If there is a civilian program, who should run it, and how much of the overall budget for government-supported scientific research should be allocated to this program? We cannot answer these questions here; they could each be pursued in full-length studies. We can only sketch in our approach.

There is an ever-growing literature concerning the actual system of choice among alternative military investments in the United States. Cost-effectiveness studies by the Department of Defense have accumulated a modest history. The problem of budgeting investments among alternative demands for support, either of military or scientific interest, has been discussed but has not yet been solved operationally, though in formal, empty logic the nature of the optimized budget has of course been long understood, and the imposition of the Planning-Programming Budgeting (PPB) System in October, 1965 for the whole of the federal administration is an attempt to closer approach such rationalized budgeting procedures.[23] The facts that the benefits to be anticipated from investment in research have to be by their inherent nature unpredictable and that for both military goals and scientific goals no clear-cut means of achieving agreement as to the place of different specified goals and missions in an orderly hierarchy of goals has been determined, complicate efforts to develop an overall integrated, rationalized allocation of federal effort and funds in these spheres. Goals and missions tend to be regarded as noncomparable so that in PPB program procedures, cost-benefit estimates tend to be compared for alternative projects or programs aimed at the same goals rather than for the achievement of alternative goals.[24]

Even now the President and Congress have allowed the scientific community a major role in the direction of science policy. Scientists themselves have not seen fit or have not been forced to set up a firm hierarchy of priorities among research programs.[25] As Professor Waddington has suggested "...up to the present the American system is rich enough to allow all branches of pure science to develop at rates which are not so slow as to cause a major dissatisfaction to the scientists concerned."[26] Budgeting carefully at the margins is a phenomenon of scarcity.

A less affluent science budget would enforce the need to produce priorities on the President and the scientific community itself. There is no reason to feel that with the help of the National Security Council, Council of Economic Advisers and of his Science Advisor, and the other organizations which regularly offer assistance on these matters to the President, including the Office of Science and Technology, the President's Science Advisory Committee, the Federal Council for Science and Technology, the Bureau of the Budget, the National Academy of Sciences, and their National Research Council, the National Science Foundation, the National Aeronautics and Space Administration, the

Atomic Energy Commission, and the Department of Defense, the President could not force himself to determine more closely his view of the social priorities among competing projects, just as, indeed, he could impose his view of the appropriate objective, common social rate of discount for cost-benefit calculation purposes.[27] Both houses of Congress have several committees and other bodies which investigate science policy and the science budget and appropriations.[28] The results of their searching investigations, proposals, and decisions affect future public opinion and future administration policy choices as well as being important in the making of current policy and the setting of parameters for future science policy.

Thus the estimates of many specialized groups converge to assist in the making of operational United States' science policy. How rational can we expect it to turn out to be with reference to the democratic social preference hierarchy? This remains a difficult question to answer, again because we lack a precise objectified map of the democratic public interest.

European planners have long since devised techniques for estimating the relevant marginal rates of substitution between major social goals for planning purposes in part by interviewing important decision makers. There has been much discussion of how to determine such trade-offs in the United States.[29] But as noted earlier, such representations of the social preferences will always remain partial in a democracy in which all citizens' preferences count. In such a setting, there can be no simple, clear-cut, magic mathematical formulae for deducing information as to social priorities to be supplied to bureaucrats or technical-administrative agencies. Actual priorities are in fact revealed ex post by the complex administrative and legislative processes, and although, as noted, such choices can be rationalized ex ante in part, both by using PPB Program-type cost-benefit and other rationalizing studies and by consistent efforts to analyze the budget on the basis of the estimated preferences and priority scales of the most important decision makers, for whom the estimates are being made, residual conflicts as to the true content of the public interest are to be expected.

In logic this should suggest that all available analytical and evaluative techniques and means of informing choice in the Administration and in Congress should be eagerly grasped. An important question remains as to whether such aids to rational choice are really desired by political decision makers. They may create insecurity among vested interests.

63

They may often not promise to redound to the interests of some administrators and some legislators.[30] But, presumably, they are of interest to the President, whose constituency is the whole society. In sum we must expect heated conflict and political infighting as well as attempts at rational calculation to occur in the actual complex political processes of choice within the Administration and in the legislature. And as we noted above we must be prepared to find that the final outcome of such choice processes involving conflicting goals of conflicting social groups has not always appeared optimal or even rational and internally consistent. As one commentator on a review of intrinsically "irrational" post-war British fiscal policy has suggested, such experiences can themselves be instructive to technical advisers and political choosers, if only to teach them that difficult choices between mutually inconsistent goals usually cannot in fact be avoided and that therefore from the social point of view the development and use of means of identifying options and explicitly facing irreducible social choices is desirable.[31]

John Kennedy once suggested: "To govern, as wise men have said, is to choose." At present it seems clear that better use may be organized for technical information on competing programs of the PPB Program-cost-effectiveness type and for the technical advice of the scientists, better means of confrontation between the representatives of major administrative departments designed to achieve major competing national goals, better means of educating the public as to the implications of allocation choices and better means of surveying public opinion can be devised. Better use of all types of information can be organized within the Congress.[32] Ultimately, however, the decision makers, and that means first of all in the United States the President, as chosen chief executive for the whole society, must make the major policy choices. After the help of his technical and political advisers is collated he must determine his own hierarchy of social values and his own choices or trade-offs between major competing social goals. It is up to him to effectively convey his final preferences to his subordinates. He must take the responsibility for the system his administration devises and uses for determining (or for advising him so that he can most rationally determine) and for effectuating his choices of the major subgoals to be pursued within each category of major goals by administrative action. And the same is true for the subgoals and objectives within these, etc. In the American system, the Bureau of the Budget plays the strategic role in information gathering, including PPB System information gathering and digesting, in negotiating, in advising the President as to his alternatives, and in conveying the President's decision as to his preference hierarchy and his choices to his Administration by way of the critical budgetary processes.

If, despite all the analysis and advice, the President misreads or misconstrues important parts of the social value hierarchy and social preference scales of the electorate, mismanages his administration, guesses poorly, or has bad luck, he and members of Congress are likely to be subjected to mounting criticism from the public and the press, a process in which congressmen as vocal leaders normally partake. As noted above these are the constitutionally appropriate ways information as to actual social values and preferences of the electorate can be pressed on their necessarily imperfect representatives and administrators even in a model representative democracy. Such pressures can be expected to affect administrative and legislative policy choices. The final periodic ordeal at the polls gives the electorate its opportunity to express operationally its overall approval or dissatisfaction with the conduct of members of Congress and with the President, including, among many other things, the choices of effective priorities and goals which have resulted from the actual complex processes of social choice. For reasons already reviewed in the case of a model representative democracy and more relevant to an imperfect actual governmental mechanism, manned by at least partly self-interested humans, although society can attempt to further rationalize and lubricate the various necessary streams of information about actual alternatives and popular preferences which should illuminate difficult political decision making among exclusive alternatives, we cannot at present expect any aggregating computer to reveal the true democratic public interest and thus to substitute for or denature the hazards and responsibilities inherent in the roles of the decision maker in a representative democracy. As noted widely dispersed automated voting equipment might considerably change this situation in the foreseeable future.[33]

So much for the present complex American political processes of choice of science policy at the legislative and executive levels. Although all this suggests that the final decision as to the timing, direction, and scope of an optimal weather-modification research program must lie with these elected decision makers, yet we have stressed the importance of organizing informed, disciplined technical advice on alternatives, their relative feasibility and prospective costs and promise, to inform the complex political-decision process. What has been accomplished in the United States setting at the required level of competence and what does it suggest as to the promise of a major effort to understand weather modification?

Scientists have been reproached for offering little expert technical assistance in guiding the allocation of social resources for research among competing programs. Some criteria for scientific choice which could assist decision makers to rational decisions have been proposed by scientists and others as relevant even to necessarily political government decision in Big Science in which social support is called for on a large scale.[34] One typical approach is to evaluate scientific projects on the basis of both internal and external criteria. Internal criteria include such considerations as (1) is the field ready for exploitation? and (2) are the scientists in the field really competent? External criteria include the evaluation of technological merit, scientific merit, and social merit.[35] On such criteria what can be said about a major program of weather-modification research?

We leave to others more qualified the detailed evaluation of the promise of weather-modification research as a Big Science project on the basis of such criteria with but a few comments. First of all the fact of Weather Satellites and that an internationally sponsored World Weather Watch as well as a Global Atmospheric Research Program (GARP) is under way suggests to the layman that answers to the internal criteria, the readiness of the field for constructive work is likely to be in the affirmative. As to external criteria we have noted that a credible possibility exists that weather modification of various types is feasible and would become an important strategic activity. As such we concluded that in the current international system the national military decision makers have no recourse but to pursue the technology and to evaluate this alternative as they would any other important weapons system. We have asked if a heavily subsidized civilian-research program is also indicated, and we will indicate some apparently relevant suggestions on this issue. First and most persuasive it would seem that in the context of the current stress on the social and environmental problems of the cities that basic studies of the atmospheric sciences and of air pollution and of environmental control in general is being increasingly stressed as important, potentially socially productive foci of research interest.[36]

Weather-modification operations are currently undertaken by private parties for their own economic benefit and by federal mission-oriented departments in pursuit of their appropriate mission functions, which indicates that these agencies and individuals regard it as a productive activity. All indications in logic are that the use of weather-modification technology making it possible for man to free himself at least peripherally from the tyranny of nature, would be on balance very fruitful economically to society.[37] Presumably this will be assured if weather-modification activities are socially regulated in such a way that no modification is permitted unless it promises to produce a net social gain after all direct and external costs were considered. However it does not appear to be so regulated at present. Although half the states have some relevant legislation, no uniform evaluation, control or regulation policy exists. Reliance is still primarily placed on court-centered compensation. And as is well known most complaints of damages that have reached the courts have foundered on the inability of complainants to establish any convincing cause-effect nexus between weather-modification activities and the actual weather outcome. This suggests that, merely in order to estimate the prospects of gains and losses from weather-modification activities so that evaluation of anticipated net gains is possible, greater understanding of weather-modification phenomena is necessary. In order to establish a firmer cause-effect nexus between operations and outcomes so that the appropriate distribution of liability in weather-modification cases can be ascertained and the appropriate regulatory regime can be established to the end that only operations which are deemed on balance socially beneficial will be permitted, greater fundamental understanding is necessary of the dynamics of the atmosphere and the actual effects of utilization of the techniques and mechanisms of weather modification. In short an attempt at rational choice of overall policy and a policy instrument with respect to the social control of weather modification is not necessarily desirable at present without greater basic understanding of the phenomena to be regulated themselves. Since modification will be done for military reasons and is being pursued for presumed public and private benefit, this seems to suggest a strong case for a major program of nonmilitary fundamental research now.

Since the activity is already privately pursued, should government have to bear the major burdens of such a rationalizing basic-research program or should the government await private investment in such basic new knowledge? In general economists point out that large-scale governmental participation in basic research in addition to the likely level of private investment in such research can be justified in the case of weather modification as in other cases if (a) so much uncertainty exists as to the potentials of this research that individuals are incapable of estimating the value of private investments to themselves, but there is reason to feel that a substantial program emphasizing fundamental as well as applied research promises great social benefit or is necessary for public policy reasons, or (b) because so much research and development capital is necessary that no one company could afford to undertake research on the appropriate scale because no one company could expect to capture enough of the benefits of the increased knowledge achieved to make a return on this investment pay.[38] These conditions seem to apply to weather-modification research and strongly suggest that a public subsidy of a large-scale domestic research program would be necessary. In addition of course as a prospective utilizer of weather-modification techniques for various of its mission-oriented projects, the federal government and local governments as well may well have incentives of their own to support weather-modification research leading to a more fundamental understanding of the phenomena they wish to use and control, so that modification may be efficiently and safely pursued by them for the net benefit of society. We will not discuss here the size of an optimal federal program of research in the basic understanding of modification. This depends in part on the intensity of the various pressures for and desired speed of the new program, the alternative costs of projects of different speed, and the costs and benefits of alternative research programs and other calls for federal funds. We should note, however, that just as with private modification, government programs for operational or research purposes may cause losses to some parties; these must be treated as part of the total costs of such projects.[39]

One final argument for a vigorous civilian government-supported research program in weather modification has not yet been mentioned. The historic strategy of U.S. science policy has called for a major decentralized civilian science effort outside the military, pursued concomittantly in government laboratories, in quasi-governmental laboratories and research institutions, in private industry's laboratories, and in the universities, all receiving major support from the federal government, all pursuing new scientific knowledge and know-how together in research projects which have often paralleled each others' and the military's efforts, even in the expensive nuclear and space programs. Although it may have been primarily the result of the political convenience of decision makers in Congress and the federal administration rather than the result of strict rational choice this so-called "pluralistic" strategy of American science policy can be justified on political and technical efficiency grounds.[40] Reportedly competitive, slightly overlapping civilian-research programs assure that the multifarious varieties of civilian goals which, it is claimed, are often too varied for any one government agency to adequately pursue all important aspects thereof, will all be pursued and also that the search for new knowledge itself will be dynamic. Again this decentralized strategy is favored for political reasons—in other words, it reflects the division of powers, checks and balances philosophy of government so that no one administrative agency—and certainly not the military—will gain a monopoly over any one type of research or skill and thus gain potential capacity to dominate the others.

Again this raises questions for an organizational strategy for domestic weather-modification research. The current set of decentralized domestic programs has not produced basic understanding of weather phenomena and persuasive suggestions for a more centralized program directed toward basic knowledge have been made. How could a centrally rationalized domestic-research program be designed so that it effectively incorporates some of this dynamic competitive research strategy and services all the interested mission-oriented agencies adequately? Some combined program including both a centralized basic-research effort and continued departmentally-run mission-oriented programs might well be indicated.

These are difficult institutional strategy issues which we can raise but not really answer here. Fears of the stultifying effects of over-centralization of policy making are stressed even by those who urged a PPB program budgetary system for the whole administration.[41] The relative success of the pluralistic, overlapping, competitive U.S. science policy strategy with its heavy reliance on independent research contracts rather than on major integrated research programs in generating technical innovations in the context of an affluent society which could pursue many goals by many means has been noted by foreign observers. However some criticisms as to the biases of the resultant program, against basic research and in favor of development and against interdisciplinary and interagency programs, and some criticism as to the relatively modest showing of the program in the production of major new insights and intellectual "breakthroughs" have also been suggested.[42] In any case, to date fundamental understanding of weather-modification phenomena has not been achieved by the heavily mission-oriented approach to weather-modification research of the federal government. Some modification of strategy, perhaps by a reliance on a specified, unified dramatized weather-modification research program oriented to produce basic knowledge of weather mechanisms seems indicated.

We have discussed the types of criteria which, it has been suggested by scientists, economists, and others, a decision maker should apply to questions concerning the choice of scientific-research programs on weather modification or any other research area. We have noted that formally the rational decision maker should undertake programs which, because of externalities, will not be adequately supported by private enterprises and that in so doing he should equate the marginal expected social outputs per unit input from the various governmentally supported research projects chosen, insofar as they are calculable. We have noted that the content of such expected gains includes difficult to quantify but very important social, political, humanitarian benefits as well as expected total economic benefits, and that all net costs, including costs external to the calculations of any private decision makers involved must be included in the calculations. We have suggested that neither the social costs nor the social benefits of the search for new knowledge is likely to be precisely calculable in advance. Rough approximations or indications of the nature and importance of the new knowledge is often sought precisely to clarify the cost and benefit implications of possible new techniques. This appears to be the case with weather modification. Under the circumstances, actual emphasis is likely at best to be on estimating the costs of achieving the objectives of a project rather than on the comparative costs of achieving competing projects with different, not readily comparable goals. Thus new basic research goals are operationally likely to be chosen for major emphasis when they promise to yield dramatic payoffs or otherwise begin to look urgent from the social point of view.

Having said all this, we can suggest as our conclusion that there seem good reasons to support a major civilian federal effort which is reoriented so that it will seek to obtain basic weather-modification knowledge. This would contribute to the achievement of important military security, economic, social and political, and humanitarian values of the society not to mention the advancement of the specific goals of the mission-oriented agencies in addition to the prestige and exhiliration implied in the pursuit of new scientific knowledge. This would also illuminate the alternatives open for the rational choice of the optimal social regime for the regulation of weather-modification activities and help make reliable allocation of the responsibility for the results of weather-modification operations by the courts or by some regulatory agency more feasible.

The Regulation of Weather Modification Operations

The choice of the optimal regime for the regulation of weather-modification operations is what could be called a marginal constitutional-choice issue. It represents the parametric choice of a way of managing a new activity or a newly regulated activity in a complex, well-established, going governmental regime with an evolutionary, determined initial position on constitutional and other political issues. This is quite different from the rational choice of an initial constitutional bargain de novo. Among the major differences is the fact that whatever the voting rule chosen for the initial accession to the initial "social contract," marginal constitutional choices tend to be made by the going institutions of government on the basis of the going voting rules of the society, and thus normally, in the U.S.-type of system, on the basis of majority rule by qualified representatives, if the policy is determined in the legislature.[43] The basic conformity of the policy chosen with the constraints of the original constitutional bargain will be tested the way all such legislative choices are tested in the going system. In the United States this means by the testing of cases in the federal courts system and ultimately, if necessary, in the Supreme Court. Furthermore, unlike the usual convenient assumptions for constitutional-choice issues, the parties to the marginal constitutional choice tend to have some insight as to their preferences and interests in the status quo initial position and their interests in the activity, the future regulation of which is being designed; their alternatives and their positions can be assumed to be affected thereby. They can be expected to participate in strategic bargaining and coalition making.

Let us pose two questions for discussion: When and how much should local weather-modification activities be centrally regulated, and what is the optimal institutional compromise for achieving this regulation? Again we cannot answer these questions here. Again only the choosers can give a final answer, and they should do so after much information gathering as to the realistic alternatives. We will simply briefly discuss some of the elements of the implied constitutional calculus; other sections of the book will analyze important relevant institutional precedents.

It is to be recalled that in discussing the choices of a regime for weather-modification control we are again assuming the prior existence of a going, idealized democratic-type federal constitution with checks and balances and the division and separation of powers and regular elections of representatives and more than one political party and a set of entrenched individual rights, safeguarded by an independent judiciary. We will also assume a federal system and therefore the existence of a complex set of central, state, and local political choice institutions with executive, administrative, legislative, and judicial functions performed on several levels. We also assume an official, generally accepted political ideology, in general preferring local over centralized solutions to problems. Once again we assume the existence of a socially regulated workably competitive market sector which combines with the social system for the achievement of economic distributive and allocative choice with productive efficiency. The market and the social system together are expected to make interpersonal choices, selecting winners and losers in the economic contest. The results of these choice processes are corrected by sometimes quasi-technical but normally ultimately politically directed interventions for the achievement of major social macroeconomic, political, and international goals, such as economic growth, full employment, stability, and balance of payments viability, and for the achievement of socially desired income and welfare redistributions by tax and subsidy policy and by manipulation of the normal fiscal and monetary macroeconomic policy instruments. In general intervention is attempted to correct from the social viewpoint other defects and lacunae of the actually less-than-perfect market and the status quo-biased social systems and to modify market results so as to accommodate all other noneconomic goals as well, up to the point when their economic costs are viewed as too great.[44]

In order to discuss the alternatives we have to make some assumptions as to the content of the objectives of the society in re weather modification. We assume that the social aim is to maximize the net social benefit to be derived from weather-modification activities given the values and preferences of the members of society and their alternatives. We assume that the various component individuals aim for the greatest increase in social welfare consistent with the maximization of private welfare.

We must also ask: What would the current modifiers want? Presumably if they were maximizing their self-interests this would imply that they would prefer the minimum necessary coercive social interference with their business activities consistent with its secured prosperity. Would uniform federal regulation promise this?[45] There are indications that United States weather modifiers may think so.[46] Whatever they want on these issues, as importantly affected parties they can be expected to make their preferences known to the decision makers more forcefully than the apparently less intensely interested general public.

The relevant social value and preference hierarchies are to be aggregated from all these component individuals' values and preferences; they are to be aggregated by majority rule on the basis of one-man one-vote. The results of such aggregation may be unstable if no underlying consensus on values and no stable majority preference exists. In the social decision making apparatus the president and his major policy-making assistants and Congress together propose and examine the actually considered alternatives and finally make the actual institutional choices. As noted above, we assume that their incentives are such that they make their choices at least in part on the basis of their interpretation of the relevant social values and preferences of their various constituencies which may conflict or overlap. In so doing we will assume for this analysis that these actual decision makers seek to achieve a regulation of weather-modification activities which will promise to produce (a) equity, as defined by the legislature or the legislature and the president and the courts, interpreting the public will on these issues, (b) reasonable technical safety in modification activities, considering the costs and benefits of improving safety, (c) optimal efficiency in the use of weather resources of the nation, given the tastes of the society for output, and for weather, and the alternative output potentials of society, and (d) adequate consistency with attempts to achieve all other social objectives, such as economic stabilization, national security, etc.

We will briefly discuss how the decision makers might act to organize weather-modification activities so that society could be expected to maximize the achievement of these goals in the assumed decision-making context.

Given the going assumed constitutional predilections and compromises embodied in the political institutions and the political ideology of our model society, we can assume that the intention will be that weather modification continues to be pursued as far as possible as a local and as a private activity but that over time there will be pressure for it to be centrally regulated in an effort to assure the achievement of federal standards, especially of performance and safety and equity and,

73

also, potentially very important, in order to assure the containment and peaceful resolution of conflicts between jurisdictions competing for weather benefits and in general to achieve efficient weather policy from a national viewpoint. To date, as noted, in the United States private and local weather-modification activities have been locally regulated, if at all, with the pursuit of equity to affected parties primarily sought by way of the courts, which have in general failed to acknowledge a cause-effect link between weather and weather-modification activities.[47] Furthermore there will also continue to be a direct federal role in operations by the mission-oriented agencies focused on the provisions of inherently communal services and research and, no doubt, repeated pressures for a major governmentally-subsidized, organized-scientific research program.

We have assumed a constitutional bias in favor of decentralized market or decentralized government control. This reflects the traditional individualistic assumptions that each man knows what is best for himself, and should be allowed by society to follow these inclinations as far as his assets, luck, and the social rules will allow, that it is easier for local government to interpret and effectuate the wishes of a delimited group of local people, that local people are more likely to be alike and share common cultural, political, and social goals and norms, that it is desirable that local majorities decide issues concerning themselves for themselves rather than being submerged as perhaps frustrated minorities in the national arena, that centralization implies a great loss of information as to preferences and options and therefore a great loss of efficiency, as well, that the individual has more effective control over and knowledge about his local government than he would of a central government, and that a federal system offers alternative political power centers and political training grounds and opportunities for groups not in power in the central government and therefore promotes the viability of genuine democracy at the center as well. Any of these assumptions can be disputed and in fact most have been.[48] In any case, in practice, as the Civil War demonstrated, there has obviously been for some time considerable tension between the constitutional ideology favoring "subsidiarity" (the preference for the use of the most local, effective, suitable level of government) and the actual tendency in the United States of the central government to attempt to set an imposed centralized, humane, efficient social standards on the activities of lower levels of government, if not direct, centralized regulation on previously locally regulated activities.[49] This has been increasingly true

74

in such previously local matters as education and welfare assistance. It has been noted that the different standards achieved in different local and state governments have tended to reflect largely the different levels of achieved wealth of the local communities rather than any other aspects of differences in tastes and preferences, which those who justify decentralized choice on such standards have argued should be respected.[50] Many feel there are strong arguments for suggesting that different standards of achieved welfare should not be determined by divergences in ability of pay within one nationally integrated society.

Indeed, there has been some tendency on the part of some analysts to regard the state of the United States with its highly mobile population as increasingly anachronous. Yet the activities and expenditures of state and local governments together have grown approximately apace with those of the national government.[51] Furthermore there is some reason to expect that even if general norms and standards are increasingly set at the national level, the administrative role of the state and local governments will continue to grow, as it has. For although it is quite possible that a large nation need not be federalized in the sense that local norms and rules are chosen to regulate a specified sphere of social activities, yet, some genuine decentralization of administration seems inevitable.

A pure theory of constitutional choice by rational self-interested choosers of the appropriate level of government regulation on the basis of an individualistic calculus which would maximize the difference between the expected costs and benefits of participating in a coercive arrangement for the supply of a public good, like the regulation of weather modification, is possible, as we have noted earlier. It does not appear to be developed as yet to a state in which it can readily be applied to specific marginal constitutional choices.[52] Each activity could be rated by each individual participating in the constitutional calculus on the basis of the geographic extent of the parties affected importantly (which implies some scientific or technical knowledge of the distribution of effects including externalities and a judgment on what is a sufficiently important effect on others to be counted). This would help in the estimation of the geographic extent of the minimal technically efficient unit of regulation, given the goals of the regulation in question (which implies a judgment on the goals of regulation, which is importantly affected by the initial assumptions made as to whose judgment and goals are to be regarded as relevant in each case. Also required is technical information about the potential effectiveness of regulatory institutional alternatives in the cases in question). The static initial constitutional choice for the average rational individual, assuming he does not know his future specific interest on these issues, would presumably select out that partitioning of coercive decision making on each set of issues which would maximize the expected net benefits or minimize the expected net costs from participating in government on the issues in question. The decision rules by which this constitutional choice was to be aggregated would presumably make a difference as to its nature and its unique predictability.

An example of some of the problems raised by the search for a rational choice of a division of jurisdictional authority between various levels of government as either a question of original constitutional choice or of marginal constitutional choice in a going society may be useful. For example, in discussing the collective good, education of the young, who are the importantly affected parties in educational policy? Whose opinions are to count in running the process? The child and his parents and his local tribe or clan, to all of whom his traditional, cultural development may seem very important? Or his local school board district, or municipality or state which often invests heavily in supplying him with a costly education, which investment he may never repay if he moves from the district or state—or his nation, the security, prestige and material affluence of which depends importantly on producing a modern, technically well-educated, preferably mobile population base? And does not the whole human race share an important stake in each human's education up to his creative possibilities for the race? To assign the determination of educational policy to the appropriate level of government may be to importantly affect which of the various congeries of possible alternative educational goals is to predominate over all the others. It is a highly political question.

A complex strategy as, for example, in the United States, which assigns the choice of schools for the rich primarily to the parents and the choice of specific educational policy for the bulk of the people at the primary and secondary school levels, at least, primarily to local decision-making units with state and federal government imposing many standards relevant to their respective interests and regulating the process in general primarily by means of transfer and subsidy payments, which carry federal or state requirements with them, may be the necessarily institutionally complex way to achieve a many-layered complex set of educational goals. Such a strategy is rationalized in works on public finance by the observation that the federal government should contribute in this way for the benefit it receives ("spillover effects"). In return the central government should be able to specify standards of performance for the services for which it is paying.[53] This does not leave the ultimate locus of control over policy neatly clarified. If individual and local preferences were to be given less stress, either because the preferences, needs, and demands of the central government in re-education were deemed more important than the local interests, or because the federal government was deemed more efficient or less corrupt, less coercive or a better interpreter of social objectives, etc., and an alternative more highly centralized and homogeneous educational policy were sought, more clearly centralized institutional and policy control could be established by a ministry of education at the national level, as is the case in some countries.

Pressures toward uniform standards of social services have been increasing in the United States, partly to remove differences in achieved local services which were due largely to different financial capabilities, not different intrinsic values or preferences, or partly as a reflection of the belief that tastes are or should be quite homogeneous and that values and standards should be regarded as a national issue. Nevertheless the traditional choice in the United States' federal system for many traditionally local governmental activities has called for direct administration by local authorities and a division of decision making among the different contributing levels of government. It can probably be expected that weather-modification phenomena will in fact similarly be subjected to a multiple-level strategy of governmental regulation.

As far as weather modification is concerned then, a rational calculus made with a bias toward decentralization would no doubt suggest that purely local modification, insofar as this can be defined, should be primarily locally directed and operated; that modification which affected statewide, or more likely, multistate areas should be effectuated either by interstate cooperation or, if this involved many states or, as is likely, is found to be very cumbersome and ineffective or if the area of more than one national state was affected, it should be conducted under direct federal auspices or operations.[54] General standards could be set nationally by a federal regulatory agency.

Parallel overlapping regulation could exist at the different levels of government, with the higher level taking precedence in cases of conflict. Central government subsidy to local research or operational programs in which the federal government also shares an interest could be commonly used in part to effectuate the common standards. In any case since weather phenomena cannot be expected to respect states or national boundaries it would seem likely that at some time—at least by the time large-scale major weather modification became feasible, federal regulation of these activities would become unavoidable. In sum a mixed strategy of regulation and operations consistent with the already noted trend toward establishing uniform national standards and norms even for activities the conduct of which will be locally administered seems likely.

It would also seem reasonable, to achieve impartial regulation, that at the federal and state levels there should be a separation between operations and regulation. This would be in accord with some of the most ancient legal norms, in other words, that a man should not sit in judgment on his own case. Modern experience with the control of nuclear energy for example, suggests that this remains an important administrative concept. For an operating agency which could do so would be under great pressure to modify the relevant norms and operational standards to suit the demands of its planned activities. Thus where impartial regulation aimed at achieving the democratic public interest is desired a complete separation of regulation from operation seems desirable.

Let us focus now on issues implied by the achievement of the already specified objectives or norms for weather-modification policy at the federal level of regulation. In re safety standards we will simply pose the question for study and consideration. Is there any reason why the imposition of safety standards and of licensing of modifiers should be exclusively federal rather than local? Uniformity and general acceptability of standards would presumably replace numerous state and/or local safety and license standards. Is this desirable in a federal system? Is it necessary? It seems likely that federal regulation need not and quite possibly would not totally replace local licensing and safety regulation, which could be adapted to special local meteorological circumstances, for example. Nevertheless where purely technical requirements can be standardized it seems desirable to minimize interstate barriers and a multiplicity of licensing requirements. In general for interstate and federally regulated programs which might, in the case of major modifications, importantly affect the way of life of millions, it is likely that federal standards for operations, equipment, and insurance will be established. These types of standards should in logic be made to apply to federal government-supported operations or research whether undertaken under the aegis of the states or the national government as well as to private enterprises.

The appropriate social regulation of the equity of the outcome of a weather-modification program must be determined by representative decision makers, presumably on the basis of the distributive values and distributive institutional preferences of their constituency. It can be expected to have to be consistent with what we have called the basic constitutional bargain on distribution institutions and policy. We can explore these issues at least by pointing out what are the minimal assumptions as to such values and preferences, which would rationalize certain alternative outcomes. Let us assume that we are concerned with social policy towards incremental weather modification rather than with the search for the fair or optimal major weather switching pattern, since the former seems more likely to be developed technologically in the near future and policy concerning it seems more amenable to discussion on the basis of informed rational choice and going political institutions.

As welfare economics has emphasized, the only relatively simple case is the one in which the weather modifier gains (and therefore wants the right to keep on modifying) and no one is harmed. Then on very weak assumptions we can say that society is not harmed and probably gains. This is a variant of the so-called Paretian criterion for evaluating alternative social welfare positions. A Pareto optimum situation is one in which no one can be made better off without someone being made worse off.[55] On the probably acceptable assumption that something that helps one or some people and hurts none is a social gain in a society in which social welfare is composed of the aggregation of individual welfares, this type of activity should presumably be allowed by whatever system of regulation of the activity is adopted. The prior obtaining of a permit and public notice, to assure that anyone who fears he would be hurt could step forward and complain, would probably be called for. This type of case may hopefully cover a broad range of actual weather-modification cases.

If the weather modifier gains but does cause felt damage to others of a known calculable type, what criteria and policy instruments to use to determine when and under what circumstances modification should be allowed immediately becomes a difficult problem. There are two basic, distinct situations: (1) Compensation is possible out of the profits of modification because the total material gains from weather modification outweigh the total material losses to all parties. (2) Compensation is not possible because the total gains of the modifier do not equal the total losses of the damaged parties.[56] The simplest rule is to suggest that weather modification should not be undertaken in the second case because it represents an economically inefficient outcome from society's viewpoint and that modification should be undertaken and compensation should be paid in the first case if society wishes to protect the initial status quo distribution of welfare and property but still wishes to allow the pursuit of self-interested self-improvement and the pursuit of the maximum total output on the basis of private initiative.[57]

This is a common normative suggestion made by social scientists.[58] If fair, prompt, adequate compensation can be paid to all the damaged parties by the gainers directly or by the gainers indirectly with society acting as intermediary and, perhaps, taxing the gains to allow compensation (or compensation could be provided without the special financial participation of the gainers, if society so desired) then the situation after modification can be made in many senses comparable for all the parties to the situation before modification. The damaged party will be as well off as before. In logic, all parties can be brought to view the modification as a socially acceptable activity so long as they do not care importantly about their relative income situations. In such a case, the Paretian formula for arriving at a welfare optimum would be respected. Attempts to extend the Paretian formula (without resort to social-choice institutions capable of determining socially appropriate distributive outcomes); by compensation tests after which compensation is not paid have generally failed.[59] This leaves someone or some group worse off. Of course, society may legitimately choose to do this; but when one person or group is made better off, and another is left worse off, then the uninstructed economist as technician cannot say that society is better off or that output is unequivocably greater and that society should undertake the move.[60]

The Paretial formula requires unanimous agreement for a social change to be regarded as an improvement. Many would criticize such a standard as reactionary. Imposing the concordance of all damaged parties on all new activities or, indeed, on all activities, would very likely mean that few would be undertaken even though many would be characterized as socially useful by a majority of the people of the society. For although technicians may not be able to judge impartially between different distributions, society, using legitimate political-decision processes, regularly does this, constrained only by constitutional safeguards for damaged minorities.

Furthermore, the Paretian optimum which requires that no man be damaged, is biased in favor of the initial position and the initial distribution of welfare. The people who will benefit from modification are asked to pay the people who will lose therefrom. This implies that those who would lose have more right to their present welfare position than those who would gain have the right to improve their conditions in efficient ways. They may only do so if they can guarantee no adverse change to the prospective losers—if they can't do this they must acquiesce in losing their potential gain. It is important to remember also that losers in the market as a result of innovation are normally not compensated for capital values or income lost even though this may involve initially unforeseeable losses to the losers. Should they be? Market results are optimal only given the ex post distribution of income and wealth and the price ratios these imply. What this really means is that, for example, in the case of investment in innovation in the market, externalities are common, because the innovator does not include in his calculations the losses of those whose capital investments are being damaged. But ought society to count at least part of such costs as part of the total social costs of the innovation? A case for social aid (perhaps of the readaptation type) to those damaged by innovation can be made on such grounds and, indeed, socially subsidized area redevelopment and labor readaptation programs to aid the damaged sectors in the wake of technological obsolescence have gained increasing acceptance in Western welfare states.

One major reason actual compensation transfers programs between winner and loser have been so rarely arranged is that it is said to be difficult to implement such a policy operationally. It is difficult to estimate all the actual losses, psychic and material, which a loser sustains. Some compromise such as compensation only for clear-cut material losses is no doubt more operational, but it cannot promise to fully safeguard the losers from real, psychic loss, and remains difficult to calculate. Still another possibility is to rely on general social-welfare programs, such as full employment and decent income-maintenance programs rather than on specific compensations to damaged parties. This promises even less security to the losers. Clearly another problem is the financing of socially given compensation. Naturally the gainers can be expected to resist obligations to compensate as an unfair impost in favor of the status quo. If society decided to compensate losers itself, rather than requiring those who benefit to do so on the ground, perhaps, that material progress should be subsidized, then all taxed groups (or rather all groups who carry the costs of government—those who might lose from inflationary government financing should also be included, for example) bear the losses. This may appear a more reasonable distributive policy compromise if it is believed to encourage economic dynamism. There is, in any case, some rationale for arranging a partial social subsidy to cover the demands for compensation for pure windfall distributive losses.[61] But such redistributions must run the political gauntlet that all other redistributionary fiscal programs run. Such redistributions may be unlikely to be popular with the secure and fortunate, for example, who may often tend also to be the relatively more politically powerful group in society, and a social payment which must be voted on politically may reasonably appear much less secure or acceptable to the loser than the maintenance of his initial status quo property rights.

In all, the fact is that society has regularly failed to compensate the losers from social change and progress, but the fact that society may not have compensated those on whom it has imposed losses or allowed the uncorrected market to impose losses in the past is not necessarily binding on its future ethical choices. In general, modern social policy calls for mitigating the impact of the costs of progress on damaged groups. Furthermore it is probable that in most modern welfare states the basic underlying political bargain on distribution increasingly implies that no politically important groups should be forced to accept great losses to assist others or society. Furthermore property rights are among those protected by the Bill of Rights, part of the basic constitutional bargain of the United States system. U.S. and other nations' courts regularly adopt a status quo bias and levy on those who gain at the expense of others' property rights. If a property right to one's normal weather is established, it would be normal for the courts to grant compensation for the compromise of such a property right. Indeed it would prove legally very inconvenient for the courts to find that owners have a property right to their initial normal weather. For this would imply that without the owners' express agreement no modification would be legally possible except in cases of condemnation in favor of a government which would be required to pay full compensation after due process. We can assume that society would not want to put such a legal obstacle in the way of modifications which were likely to be desired by a majority and to prove efficient on the rough definition that total private and social gains outweighed total losses and a socially appropriate distributive result was to be achieved. Yet the capital value of a man's property undoubtedly is affected by its normal weather. To impose poorer normal weather on it will therefore normally affect the value of the owners' property and can be viewed as very much like an unauthorized taking of property. Owners are likely to be politically powerful. Indeed Maryland, Pennsylvania, and West Virginia have at times banned or heavily encumbered all modification efforts in response to such pressures. To require compensation, but not the express agreement of the owners to allow modification by private parties as well as governments whenever society favors it on balance would therefore seem a reasonable compromise of rights basically consistent with the constitutional guarantee of property rights. Yet it would allow society to choose to encourage economic flexibility, maximum output and growth on socially fair terms. For an activity as exotic and as potentially disturbing to the status quo of nature and the status quo distribution of property values in the society as weather modification is likely to be, compensation for losers may well be reasonable and desired. This is neither inevitable nor inevitably just.[62] But it seems a reasonable humane and politic policy choice.

The institutional means by which society chooses to assure compensation to losers—if it does so—offers another range of options. If more is learned of the physics and mechanics of weather modification and Congress wished to specify that compensation should be paid for losses imposed by private and by public programs of weather modification, court procedures could presumably give more acceptable results to claimed losers than has been possible in the past. These would often be only after losses were experienced, though injunction of anticipated weather modification would also continue to be possible. Public notification of an intention to modify made either to a local, state or federal weather modification district board could be required as a means of assuring that information would reach potentially affected parties before they suffered losses. A hearing outlining the planned operations and the prospective outcome before a qualified board or the relevant regulatory agency could be required before a permit to modify was granted especially if objections arose. Modifiers could be required to carry insurance to assure their capacity to pay damages.

Whether a modification district or an administrative agency, a regulatory agency or a court of law first handled the issue, as already noted, some policy choices are necessary if objections to a desired modification are raised on the grounds of expected losses. Whether or not compensation was to be paid, we have noted that it would presumably be social policy in general not to allow weather modifications which would result in a net social or economic loss and in general to allow net economically profitable modifications according to socially agreed concepts of gain and loss. The fact that, strictly speaking, there is no clear-cut way to compare two economic outcomes without making interpersonal comparisons must again be recognized, and then of course necessary comparisons and necessary choices have to be made as well as possible.[63]

If the legislature so decided it could instruct the court or weather-modification board or regulatory agency to calculate as the Flood Control Act of 1936 did and to add together economic losses and gains of different parties as if society were indifferent as to the distributive effects on the parties, whatever their initial income or welfare, to get a social total. If the sum was positive the project would be approved, if not it would not be.[64] Obviously such procedures require difficult careful cost-benefit analysis to be undertaken by the parties themselves, the expectant gainers and losers, or by the relevant weather-modification board or agency. The market system presupposes careful private cost-benefit-type estimates by the investors of his internalized costs. The costs to most of the losers are externalities in the market system, except for those categories of losers who are protected by a rule of law.

One way legislation could be designed to induce private or public modifiers to internalize all the costs generated by their modification activities and thus to undertake only projects which were socially profitable in an output sense would be to require them to provide compensation for all losses imposed by modification. This should tend to lead to optimal results if insurance rates the modifiers paid for liability insurance reflected real risks on the average and if the compensation-granting mechanism or institution (whether it be a local or central weather modification agency or the court system or each in turn) functioned effectively so that genuine losses tended to be reliably estimated and compensated. Presumably given this legal regime then, the decentralized choice by the modifiers would internalize all costs and yield economically optimal results if all benefits were also internalized by the modifying group. If benefits were underestimated because some were not internal to the modifying group, operations would be likely to be on suboptimal scale. Thus it would be useful to arrange that modification operations be organized primarily by weather-modification districts which are carefully organized and delimited so as to include all those who benefited or lost from modification.[65] The relative administrative simplicity of such a decentralized impersonal approach in which the parties are expected to be motivated principally by self-interest accounts for much of the historic prestige of relying principally on competitive market-generated outcomes in this society. In this case the principal alternative to leaving the matter essentially to local initiative by organizing appropriate modification districts and having the prospective modifier and his insurers primarily responsible for all net damages caused and therefore primarily responsible for estimating the probable internal and external benefits and costs likely to be generated and including these in their calculations before deciding to modify, would seem to be to call upon the regulatory agency itself to seek to locate the optimal choice for society. It could accept the primary burden for the attempt to estimate all the internal and external costs and benefits of each possible type of modification and alternatives to it before granting a permit to modify.[66] The possibility of granting permits principally on the initiative of the relevant properly constituted, externality-internalizing modification district, which has provided relatively simple procedures assuring the opportunity of prospective losers to object and to present their own estimates to the Board or District and has also provided securely for modifier responsibility for all losses, seems obviously more workable administratively.

Obviously such procedures would be predicated on the tacit assumption that the regulators of weather-modification activities are seeking to pursue economic efficiency, whatever the distributive implications, probably with assuaging compensation to damaged parties. What about society's many other goals? Should these also be considered by the relevant local, regional or central administrating weather-modification operating districts or by the state or central regulatory boards? We have noted that in order to reflect the democratic social preference structure in a consensual polity, society's various goals normally ought to be specified by the elected representatives of the citizens—the chief executive and the legislature, with the court system playing a very important role in interpreting and applying legislatively and constitutionally specified norms. Independent regulatory or administrative bodies should therefore be regularly supervised ultimately by such elected representatives and should be provided with clear-cut general and specific objectives and norms of administration. For ease and automaticity in supervision of weather modification regulatory and operative agencies then, it seems desirable to give them simple instructions with a relatively clear-cut, measurable, preferably one-dimensional goal. It would seem logical to make that goal the one which is most directly affected by the operations in question. In weather modifications aimed generally at increasing output or welfare it would seem reasonable that such a prescription should call on the agencies to seek maximum economic efficiency, including compensation to losers when necessary to make this goal meaningful from society's point of view. At least, the prospective complexities of asking the numerous multilayered operative and regulatory agencies from local to central to make weather modification policy choices which also further other governmental goals, such as a fairer distribution of weather, income and opportunity, full employment, or stable prices seems obvious.

This choice is again not inevitable.[67] If Congress or the President wished to specify other economic or social-policy aims which should be pursued and the necessary tradeoffs between them when the achievement of one tends to conflict with others, such policies could presumably be designed and pursued even by local and, probably more readily, by central agencies administering or regulating weather-modification activities.[68] It would however probably be difficult to predict, much less to monitor or control centrally, the type and level of attainment of the various economic and other goals that could be expected from the far-flung efforts of innumerable local operative agencies. The attractiveness from the point of view of a central independent regulatory agency supervising a network of operative agencies and from the point of view of the Administrative and Parliamentary bodies which in turn monitor its performance of a simple, one-dimensional criterion seems obvious. Furthermore, if greater output were achieved pursuant to this policy of regulation of weather modification, in theory fiscal policy and incomes policy measures could be used to directly achieve many of the other social goals out of the profits of pursuing efficiency, meaning maximum output.

It remains true, however, that an automatically achieved redistribution for example, is often much easier to get politically than one that has to be voted on. The same is likely to be true for the pursuit of the governments' other economic objectives, such as stability, full employment, balance of payments viability; they may be politically more difficult to pursue specifically by policy instruments designed to effectuate them than as fallout from programs which are acceptable or profitable for other reasons. Sometimes also, society prefers to give subsidies in kind or in employment rather than in income. Thus, for example, it is possible that society might choose to give the poor better weather in which to become self-sufficient rather than a financial subsidy, even if pure efficiency criteria would suggest another choice of weather distribution. Thus we must leave the question of the range of goals to be pursued at least at the central level of weather-modification policy regulation for further study. The advantages of a simple set of one-dimensional objectives, such as "pursue 'efficiency' with compensation" to be applied normally at the local operating level, unless specific instructions to the contrary are delivered by superior authority, seems persuasive.

There is another important interdependent normative question that we have occasionally touched upon which needs to be discussed. In general who should pay for weather-modification operations and research? This clearly depends in part on the distributive policy which the weather-modification machinery is directed to further. If it is agreed that the national weather-modification regulatory board should principally aim for maximized economic efficiency rather than at seeking to redistribute welfare as part of its policy objectives then it would seem reasonable to generally expect to finance weather-modification activities on a benefit basis. On the other hand, if a desirable redistribution is part of the aim of regulation itself, then taxes and subsidies which favored the groups society wished to favor might be called for. Alternatively if it were social policy to favor the utilization of weather modification, such activities might be subsidized rather than entirely self-supporting.

There are obviously problems with achieving any socially desired incidence of costs and benefits which result from the nature of weather-modification operations as a public good.[69] If the good or service in question were simply marketable to those who benefit from its use and there were no likelihood of externalities involved, there would probably be no special need to have government regulation or intervention in its production and marketing. Some form of government intervention or regulation is likely to be necessary in weather-modification activities precisely to assure that all who benefit pay. As noted if efficiency is an aim it is also likely to be necessary to assure that all appropriate costs and benefits are attributed to weather-modification activities so that only programs which yield a net social benefit above all such costs will be undertaken up to the appropriate scale, whether or not compensation for all losses is also required.

We have been assuming all along that one useful way to attempt to assure that externalities are covered and that the socially desired policy on incidence of costs and benefits is achieved would be to establish what could be called weather-modification districts for the whole of the region principally affected by a modification project. The prospectively affected members of such a district might be asked to decide by a majority rule whether and when to undertake a modification program at all.

In general such districts are often given limited power to tax for specified purposes. In view of our earlier discussions such a district could normally be expected to apportion taxes on a benefit basis and therefore presumably tax even some of those who originally were in the minority which did not favor the modification, as well as those who would have liked to receive external benefits without paying for them. It could arrange for compensation from a district-supported compensation fund or an insurance pool, perhaps actuarily realistic, or partly socially supported, partly supported by modifiers, if such subsidy to modification was deemed desirable.

For some programs the district might allow private initiators to suggest, evaluate, submit, and carry out approved projects probably only after affording prospective losers the opportunity to object and after presenting proof of financial responsibility. Or it might be called on to study and compare alternative projects for the district and calculate the foreseeable losses and benefits thereof, and perhaps to undertake or supervise operations itself, subject, of course, to general standards established by state and federal regulatory agencies. It would in any case presumably permit effectuation only of projects promising to yield some net social benefits.

We have noted that under ideal circumstances, the efficient level and types of modification should result automatically from such a system of local control. This would be likely in a competitive system if entrepreneurs were reasonably well acquainted with prospective weather-modification opportunities; if all who benefited were induced by the district to contribute fairly, including those outside its boundaries; if all risks of losses were covered by insurance or other proof of financial responsibility and if the compensation mechanisms or institutions did normally realistically evaluate and compensate losses fairly and insurance rates were fair and were socially subsidized to the extent that compensation was made for pure income transfers, if society so decides that such pure transfers should be socially supported.[70] Of course, the local district need not rely on insurance to assure liability coverage, and that all costs are internalized, but this seems definitely the simplest suggestion.[71]

In sum we are thinking of an overall system in which the regulatory, allocative, and operational functions can be conceptually distinguished. In general the regulatory functions (registry, licensing, etc.) would be performed centrally at the appropriate national or state government level. General allocation between competing regions and major uses for statewide or multiregional areas would tend to be made at the statewide or national level by the decisions of the relevant weather-modification regulatory boards among competitive projects. These could be appealed from to the courts. General legislative guidance on the norms to be applied would exist and legislative and executive pressure could likewise be expected to be brought to bear on the weather-modification Regulatory Board's policies if they seemed too inconsistent with pressure group interests or with the mission interests of the Government mission-oriented agencies or with the general interest. The results of such pressures would depend in part on the design of the relationships between the Board, the President, and Congress. This is a matter worthy of careful attention.

Purely local aspects of allocation and operations could be locally organized, at least at the first stages and only in cases of conflict or disagreement with the policy of the modification district would local allocation issues be likely to be brought for contest before the central regulatory machinery or finally before the state and federal court systems. In general emphasis in this system would be placed on primary reliance on decentralized decision making, in which central government action focuses upon regulation and upon programs aimed at creating weather-modification knowledge and providing certain desirable social services and acquainting the relevant local entities with the opportunities, while allowing them to pursue their local self-interests in such a way that the results satisfy the local majority and at the same time conform to the general interest.

In any case it seems quite possible for society, after due investigation, to decide on its general normative policy in re the regulation of weather modification, and it seems possible for the representative legislature to establish an institutional regime which will tend to accomplish it. This could entail that the legislature establish and instruct a central regulatory agency on this general policy for weather-modification decisions in specific enough form so that the agency could adopt conformable procedures for the regulation of private and public modifiers and so that the work of the agency could be readily supervised by the chief executive and readily reviewed by the legislature. One plausible simple, relatively clear-cut set of instructions would call on the regulatory agency to seek efficiency, equity and the general interest by requiring operating agencies and other modifiers to aim to maximize total output whatever its distribution and to adopt procedures assuring the compensation of losers, while generally allocating costs on a benefit basis, unless other valued social goals are specifically deemed to take precedence over normal policy.

What about major weather switching changes? Should the representative legislature allow an independent body like a state or central weather-modification board or a central weather-modification district if one were created or a department of the federal government to determine and administer policy on this basic structural issue?

If a country could select its weather what would it choose and how? Starting from scratch? Starting from some initial weather status quo? How would such decisions be made? As we all know, agreement would not be easily forthcoming. Some people like the changes of seasons. Some like, or think they like, an eternally moderate climate (some like it cold—some hot, etc.). Should decision on the social-weather choice be by majority rule? If so, should there be a unitary climate strategy for the whole nation or should there be a federalized multiple choice established with different weather regions set up to accommodate different types of preferences for weather? Obviously short of a unanimity of tastes there is no single correct a priori answer to the question of the socially optimum distribution of good weather that could be reached by a regulatory agency or an administrative board applying such legislatively determined instructions as "maximize output and compensate." These instructions are at best suited to only marginal changes so that for example, implied changes in relative prices on which calculations for a social maximum are based are somewhat meaningful. However the output and welfare implications of different weather structures could presumably be explored by a central regulatory agency on some modified cost-benefit calculus which somehow estimated changes in the structure of relative prices and income distributions implied by alternative widespread major climate-pattern changes. But clearly many alternatives are likely to exist, and major aspects of the welfare of millions of people are likely to be importantly involved. The only right answer to such major structural choices can be determined by the values and preferences of the relevant parties—in a democracy, again this implies the majority decision on weather choice of the populace or at least the decision of their duly selected representatives, on such major political matters. The political choice of a marginal constitutional bargain on weather for the nation is required. If tastes and interests are so different that no majority bargain can be hammered out in the legislature, the courts may have to be relied upon to determine the weather outcome as they have at times decided on the division of the waters of disputed rivers, in part on the basis of precedent and the general institutional and other tie-breaking norms of the society. Either their verdict will be regarded as binding or internal social strife could be expected. It is possible that the capacity to actually achieve major weather modification would be too much for the consensual fabric of many societies. Fortunately we are apparently not yet faced with such potentially revoluntionary capacities in weather modification.

Summary

We can conclude this discussion by suggesting that, if the plans for and the operation of government research and operational programs in weather modification pass the tests of satisfying the scientists, the military, the Bureau of the Budget with its centralized collection of cost-benefit information, the domestic mission-oriented agencies and ultimately and most important, the President and the legislature, and if local government programs meet comparable standards in those local political arenas, and are consistent with central government programs and if private weather-modification operations pass the tests of the market and both private and public operations pass the hurdles established by administrative regulation set up by the central and local governments to effectuate their specified normative policy purposes, then we can feel that the level and types of weather-modification activities achieved is likely to be roughly optimal, *given society's operational values, aims and chosen choice rules and institutions.* Nevertheless, as always, continued questioning, criticisms, exploration, and review of the goals and operations and outcomes of the system by interested, informed private and public parties remains essential, as part of the process of disciplining policy, if it is desired to keep the general outcome relatively close to that implied by maximizing the achievement of the decentralized democratic social values and preferences.

Notes

1. A formal theoretical answer to this question (which comprises a major issue in the theory of rational constitutional choice and is important to the rational choice of a division of power in a federal

system) would probably call for the average man (who is assumed for this purpose not to know with what side of future issues his best interests will lie) to calculate the normal expected benefits to the average individual over time of dividing decision-making power into coercive political-choice units in such a way that all important externalities are internalized by the political units in question. In other words he would evaluate the net gains of dividing governmental jurisdiction so that each unit will be able to capture all the benefits and losses generated by the activity in question. These net benefits would be counterpoised by him against the normal expected net costs over time of acquiescing in such coercive choice processes by the externality-internalizing political units. In some cases because of prospective high costs of acquiescing to government control of the activity he might choose control by a lower level of government than the one which could internalize all externalities—sometimes perhaps with some subsidy payments from the higher level of government, which might result in a sharing of control between levels of government. The ideal political structures will be those which maximize his expected satisfactions or minimize his expected costs from participating in compulsory choice processes. We discuss the closely related issue of the optional allocation of jurisdiction among levels of government in a federal system below.

For this type of an approach to a rational constitutional choice see, for example, James Buchanan and Gordon Tullock, *The Calculus of Consent,* (Ann Arbor, Michigan: University of Michigan Press, 1962); for an application of some of these principles to planning the optimal control regime for public water quality management see A.V. Kneese and B.T. Bower, *Managing Water Quality, Economics, Technology, Institutions* (Baltimore: Johns Hopkins Press, 1968), p. 303; for rationalizations of a federal system see materials cited below at notes 48 and 52.

2. If we apply the criteria of the last note to weather-modification activities, it is obvious that there are good reasons for suggesting that the whole world is the appropriate size decision-making unit, since only that way would all externalities be internalized in the political-choice units. It would seem that all humanity should be thought of as the relevant set of decision makers. All are likely to be affected meteorologically, economically, and politically by the success or failure of the development of weather-modification technology. If the new technology would allow major weather-switching contests among nations it could quite possibly lead to a final war. For a survey of this type of prediction see, Rita Taubenfeld and Howard Taubenfeld, *The International Implications of Weather Modification Activities* (Dept. of State, External Research Office, June, 1968); see also Rita Taubenfeld and Howard Taubenfeld, *Some International Implications of Weather Modification Activities,* International Organization Vol. XXIII, No. 4 (1969). Such a prospective political cost would weigh heavily against the rationality of choosing to pursue weather-modification technology

without changing the current international political system. Even if no such major weather-switching capacity was predicted, the expected costs and benefits of weather-modification investment from a world point of view would have to be evaluated in relation to the prospective costs and benefits of other possible ways to invest from the point of view of humanity. For example, more immediate development projects would have to compete with investment in weather-modification knowledge. But the considerations of the highest welfare of humanity remain externalities given the present world political system in which all major decisions are taken by the subunits called national states.

3. For an excellent survey of recent attempts to define the "public interest" see Peter O. Steiner, "The Public Sector and the Public Interest"; Joint Economic Committee, *The Analysis and Evaluation of Public Expenditures: The PPB System,* 91st Cong., 1st sess. Joint Committee Print, (Washington, D.C.: U.S. Government Printing Office, 1969), Vol. 1, pp. 13-45. This 3-volume Joint Committee Print will hereafter be cited as Joint Economic Committee, *Analysis and Evaluation of Public Expenditure,* Vol. I, II, or III.

Without retracing all the relevant issues, we have suggested that it can be argued that the present national state system is probably no longer the optimal world political institutional choice because it no longer internalizes decision making on major world-survival issues, and such failures must be viewed as potentially very significant in anybody's calculations. However the classic rationalization for the continued maintenance of the current decentralized world political system, that the nation is the largest political unit in which sufficient consensus of group values, including group political values, can be obtained with adequate security for the rights of the dominant internal majorities, remains powerful, too, and reflects the risk of extreme possible costs to many or most current national communities of acquiescing in an effective, coercive world political authority in which they might easily be placed in the position of an exploited minority. Thus the continuation of the inherently unstable international system of order can quite possibly still be rationalized on the basis of an individualistic rational choice calculus.

For a brief discussion of the inherent instability of such an international system which fails to internalize the pursuit of the world-wide interest in public order see Wm. Baumol, *Welfare Economics and the Theory of the State* (2nd ed.; London, 1965), ch. 8.

4. For a discussion of this point see R. Taubenfeld and H. Taubenfeld, op. cit.

5. See, for example, Louis De Alessi, "Implications of Property Rights for Government Investment Choices," *American Economic Review* (March 1969), pp. 13-24, and note other sources cited there.

6. In some cases minor aspects of direct democracy like the initiative and referendum are included in the Constitution.

7. For a pioneer treatment of the social welfare function see A. Bergson, "On the Concept of Social Welfare," *Quarterly Journal of Economics*, Vol. 52 (February 1938), pp. 316-334; for a review of later developments see J. Rothenberg, *The Measurement of Social Welfare* (Englewood Cliffs: Prentice-Hall, 1961).

The idea that representative democracy is likely to lead to dangerous deviations between the democratic public interest and the actual choice is not new. Thus Rousseau said "In any case, the moment a people allows itself to be represented, it is no longer free: it no longer exists." He supported the existence of small city-states. The Social Contract, III, XV. Translated by G.D.H. Cole, Everyman Library ed.

However, of the sources of divergence between actual social choices and the social preference structure discussed in the text below, several would apply also to the objective choice processes of a direct democracy. Thus, for example, direct democracy remains subject to Arrow's paradox of voting.

8. For the famous paradox of voting in the democratic choice of social preferences (or in any other democratic choices in which the same assumptions as to the voting rules and incompatible preferences of the parties apply) see Kenneth J. Arrow, *Social Choice and Individual Values* (2nd ed.; New York: John Wiley and Sons, 1963).

9. Indeed there has been some debate as to their existence. See, for example, Buchanan and Tullock, op. cit. Certainly they do not exist in the sense that no actual aggregation of individual preferences is made. However, it is sometimes predicted that the technological capacity for direct democracy by means of automated voting will be achieved by the year 2000. See T.J. Gordon and Olaf Helmer, *Report on a Long Range Forecasting Study*, The Rand Corp. Study P-2982 (Santa Monica, Calif., 1964). Even now the democratic social preferences can be said to exist as a conceptual construct designed to allow us to evaluate the output of democratic choice mechanisms. Ultimately evaluation norms must always be assumed to exist; we have simply made one set of standard assumptions and assumed that the relevant norms in this case are deduced from the values and preferences of all the members of society, democratically aggregated without opportunity for bargaining or vote trading, and the outcome of these putative aggregation processes we have labelled the social value hierarchy and the social preference structure. For a review of some proposed ways of estimating the content of various types of social preference structures see Steiner, op. cit. Also see A. Myrick Freeman, III, "Project Design and Evaluation with Multiple Objectives," in Joint Economic Committee, *Analysis and Evaluation of Public Expenditures*, I, pp. 565-578.

10. See for example, S.K. Nath, "Are Formal Welfare Criteria Required," *Economic Journal*, 74 (Sept. 1964), pp. 548-577; but see I.M.D. Little, *A Critique of Welfare Economics* (2nd ed.; 1957, Oxford Paperback, 1960) for an earlier but still relevant criticism of this view. Little notes that the claim that whatever the government does is optimal is like saying that the place you happen to be in is optimal when you happen to be motoring through it. Also see J.S. Coleman, "The Possibility of a Social Welfare Function," *American Economic Review*, LVI, 5 (December, 1966), pp. 1105-1122 for an attempt to define perfectly neutral political choice machinery.

Clearly, the attraction of past choices is that they provide objective data. Unfortunately, they may not have been or may no longer be optimal choices.

11. Arrow demonstrated that under reasonable assumptions and constraints on the outcome a unique, internally consistent, transitive group preference hierarchy not dominated by any dictator or subgroup cannot be produced by majority-rule processes among individuals whose values or preferences differ greatly. (In Arrow's case all possible orderings are included within the population, and no two persons have the same preferences.) Essentially this demonstrates the importance of the existence of a fundamental consensus on values or overwhelming loyalty to the outcome of legitimate decision processes among the members of a democratic society if democratic social choice is to be stable and to avoid inconsistent cycles of choices or the imposition of dominance by one minority subgroup over the decision processes. It is important to note that the paradox of voting applies to all majority rule processes, not only aggregation of the social-welfare function. It has been shown that logrolling, bargaining, and vote trading by tieing issues together can allow stable democratic choices to be achieved despite *initial* Arrow-type preference structures. Arrow has argued that he happens to be interested in aggregation of the constitutional choice after all such trades have taken place and alternative "social states" are being compared. See Buchanan and Tullock, op. cit. See Arrow, op. cit. (2nd ed.); p. 109. On the paradox of voting see also J. Rothenberg, *The Measurement of Social Welfare*, 1961, and bibliography cited there. See also Gordon Tullock, "The General Irrelevance of the General Impossibility Theorem," *Quarterly Journal of Economics*, Vol. 81 (May 1967), pp. 256-270.

It should be noted that since the paradox of voting as a logical construct applies to all types of simple democratic choices, in logic it does apply to the aggregation of subjective individual values or preferences into a set of social values or preferences whether or not these lead directly to readily empirically verifiable processes and choices. And despite Arrow, op. cit., ch. VIII, aggregation of the social-value structure and the social-preference structure are not the same thing as the aggregation of the social-constitutional choice, which is normally interpreted to mean the process of rationally selecting the optimal set of legitimate social-choice rules and constitutions given the future expectations of the choosers. If they are decided by one-man one-vote majority rule and Arrow's constraints are applied, both types of issues are subject to the paradox. For a political scientist's treatment of the paradox as applied to democratic choice in general see Wm. Riker, "The Paradox of Voting and Congressional Rules for Voting on Amendments," *American Political Science Review,* Vol. 52 (1958), pp. 349-366. Also see Wm. Riker, "Arrow's Theorem and Some Examples of the Paradox of Voting" in *Mathematical Applications in Political Science* (Dallas, Texas: Arnold Foundation Monograph, 1965), pp. 41-60.

12. For a summary of the literature on the restricted types of preference structures which will yield a stable internally consistent social-preference function on Arrow's assumptions, see A.K. Sen, "A Possibility Theorem on Majority Decisions," *Econometrica,* Vol. 34, No. 2 (April 1966), pp. 491-499; see also O.E. Williamson and T.J. Sargent, "A Probabilistic Approach," *Economic Journal,* Vol. 77 (December 1967); see also, Gordon Tullock, "The General Irrelevance of the General Impossibility Theorem," loc. cit. and Gordon Tullock, *Toward a Mathematics of Politics* (Ann Arbor, Michigan: University of Michigan Press, 1967).

As Arrow has pointed out, Tullock has shown that "if the distribution of opinions on social issues is fairly uniform and if the dimensionality of the space of social issues is much less than the number of individuals, then majority voting on a sincere basis will be transitive. The argument is not, however, applicable to income distribution for such a policy has as many dimensions as there are individuals..." See Kenneth J. Arrow, "The Organization of Economic Activity: Issues Pertinent to the Choice of Market Versus Nonmarket Allocation," in Joint Economic Committee, *The Analysis and Evaluation of Public Expenditures,* Vol. I, pp. 47-64 at p. 61.

13. For analysis of the implications of distributive conflict for democratic choice mechanisms see Benjamin Ward, "Majority Rule and Allocation," *Journal of Conflict Resolution,* Vol. VI (1962), pp. 379-389.

14. It is possible to exaggerate this contrast between pressures on the legislature and the executive. Pressure group and sectional interests are pressed upon the president as well. In certain circumstances he may find it useful to make (tacit) bargains with them for the support of a major block of states, for example.

15. Although it has been mentioned, we have not discussed the intensity of feeling on public-issues problems. Some may barely care about an issue; some may care desperately. Obviously the one-man one-vote majority-rule choice formula we and Arrow have chosen for

the social preference hierarchy masks such intensity differences.

In actual voting the introduction of political processes such as vote trading and logrolling reintroduces intensity weights. See Buchanan and Tullock, op. cit. It is to be noted that the intensity weights that can be expressed in the legislature are determined by the initial distribution of decision-making power in that body which is likely, in fact, in actual legislatures to be very unequal as among different representatives and thus to offer members of different constituencies very unequal importance in the weight-making process. Indeed in many imperfect democracies some groups of the population are virtually or totally disenfranchised from participation in the choice of representatives. The values and preferences of these excluded political "pariah groups" are not reflected in the social weight-making or the decision-making processes at all. Society normally bars explicit vote selling, and vote trading is often disapproved. One major problem with vote trading is that although both parties to a freely made trade can be presumed to be better off as a result thereof, others who are not parties to the trade may be hurt thereby. In that sense the trade should not be thought of as facilitating a move to a Paretian optimum. Many alternative social bargains and outcomes are likely to be possible in legislation. The one the eventually winning coalition chooses can be given no special properties from society's point of view. The win may be only testimony to the superior bargaining skills or power or luck of the winners. Thus, the legislatively derived expost weights are unlikely to be socially optimal in any sense applicable to the social value and preference functions. How to correctly correct the social value and social preference functions aggregated on the basis of one-man one-vote majority rule on nontradable subjective values and preferences for genuine differences in the intensity of feeling of the members on different issues is unclear unless at some stage in the aggregation process some All-knowing, All-judging Aggregator could assign the socially "correct" weights to the votes of the component parties; but we lack access to the revelations of such a metaphysically correct mind. The adoption of the one-man one-vote majority rule may imply that since we do not know how much each man should count on each issue that such differences in intensity of feelings should not be counted in the final vote, perhaps because the socially correct weights are unknowable and "a man is a man for that."

16. Giving weight in the choice processes to divergent intensity of feeling on issues can be desired as a safeguard for.the individual and the minority in cases in which the democratic majority might combine to exploit the individual of the minority in democratic-choice procedures. It is likely that members of the minority will tend to care much more intensely than members of the majority on many issues and that good arguments can be made that this should be reflected in the choice processes. Of course either the majority or the minority can care intensely about retaining its privileges, including the right to exploit

other minorities or politically powerless majorities. Partitioning a society federally so that local minorities in the central legislature can become local majorities in their decentralized legislatures does promise additional safeguards on the limited range of issues which are reserved to the local jurisdictions, to the local majorities. The local minorities (or politically powerless local majorities) retain the usual problems of possible subjugation to a possibly tyrannous local-power majority. And they may lack effective counterbalancing weights they might have in the central legislature where they could possibly coalesce with other groups to protect themselves. They might also be less protected in their civil and individual rights than they would be in the central government. In sum, even ideal democratic decision processes can at best be a compromise between the needs for security of the minority and the rights of the majority to be counted as equally important per man. One possible compromise would be to encourage intense feelings to be expressed as part of the process of educating the decision makers on the issues in question even if in the last analysis, one-man one-vote equal weightings majority rule is regarded as the only appropriate set of final decision weights and rules at least for aggregating the social preferences. Obviously other mechanisms than weighted voting (or qualified majorities, which is another device often proposed) may be used to reassure the individual and the minority against the overwhelming power of the majority. One of the most important of these are entrenched individual and sub-group constitutional rights buttressed by a largely independent court system.

17. De Alessi, op. cit., passim, stresses this point in re government administrators, for example, p. 18. He uses this as an explanation of "why governments in fact do undertake investments which are too long-lived by market standards," p. 21.

18. Only the choice acts of a nonexistent, perfectly neutral, simple direct democracy composed of fully self-aware calculating, rational individuals with complete knowledge of and unrestricted choice among unrestricted alternatives and mutually consistent and preferably equally intensely-felt well-integrated preferences could be expected to optimize the achievement of a well-integrated, internally consistent set of democratic social preferences, given their alternatives, until the circumstances changed.

19. See National Academy of Sciences, National Research Council, Waste Management and Control, *A Report to the Federal Council for Science and Technology by the Committee on Pollution* (Washington, D.C.: 1966), Appendix 6.

20. The appropriate role of the so-called technician turns out to be more complex and difficult. It cannot be adequately examined here. It does seem likely that insofar as he is simply an employed problem

solver, loyalty to the objectives of his employer—be he an administrator or a chief executive or a member of the legislature itself—has traditionally been expected, qualified, of course, by the requisites of intellectual discipline and honesty. Yet since Nuremberg it seems clear that even under "superior orders" a technician may not convert people into lampshades or aid in a conspiracy to commit war with impunity. It does matter to whom a technician hires himself out, and it does matter what job he is willing to undertake. He is responsible for respecting certain minimum human moral laws. At some point, if his own vision of the relevant social values and preferences or his own opinion on what is right diverges from the legitimate decision makers for whom he performs, he should no doubt step down. But it would seem that unless he was instructed to do so by a President and legislature and given appropriate guides as to how to do so, he is not in a position to attempt to make "technical" decisions which are operational for society—in economics or any other discipline—on the basis of his own vision of the social preferences, much less on the basis of that partial section of the social value and preference systems which his discipline has traditionally stressed—such as, for example, economic efficiency. However, both the moral and technical advice of technicians may be sought by decision makers. Obviously all such advice should be appropriately labelled with the normative and distributive assumptions underscored. As such it is undoubtedly a desirable and necessary source of information to the legitimate decision makers as to social options. The importance to this process of exploring aims and options and hence to a democratic society, of maintaining relatively independent university-based social-science specialists who regularly foreswear the role of "pure" technician and regularly seek to explore questions on the basis of their own specially technically informed visions of the relevant social values and preferences should be clear.

21. For a discussion see R. Taubenfeld and H. Taubenfeld, op. cit.

22. See, for example, the words of President Johnson from the 1966 Economic Report of the President: "National Security, of course, has first priority on the budget and the first claim on production." Reuben E. Slesinger, *National Economic Policy: The Presidential Reports* (Princeton: D. Van Nostrand, Co., 1968), p. 77.

23. For observations that no one and no country has found the operational solution to the problem of achieving an ideal allocation of national budgetary resources among competing projects with essentially noncomparable ends, see Organization for Economic Co-operation and Development (OECD), *Reviews of National Science Policy, United States,* Paris 1968, passim, for example, p. 10. (hereafter cited as *OECD, Review, United States*); also see Clarence H. Danhof, *Government Contracting and Technological Change,* (Washington, D.C.: The Brookings Institution, 1968); on PPB see the same OECD study, pp.

151-161. See also, Joint Economic Committee, *The Analysis and Evaluation of Public Expenditures: The PPB System*, 91st Cong., 1st sess. Vols. I, II, III (Washington, D.C., 1969); also see Fremont J. Lyden and Ernest G. Miller (eds.), *Planning, Programming, Budgeting: A Systems Approach to Management* (Chicago: Markham Publishing Co., 1968); for one specification of a formal budgetary optimum for government investments in research and development in a static, certainty model see Frederic M. Scherer, "Government Research and Development Programs" in Robert Dorfman (ed.), *Measuring Benefits of Government Investments* (Washington, D.C.: The Brookings Institution, 1965). In this formulation "utility is maximized by maximizing the Lagrangean function: $L = U^i (q_{i1}, \ldots, q_{im}, Q_i, t_i) + \lambda [R - C^i(q_{i1}, \ldots, q_{im}, Q^i t_i)]$," where U represents the government's utility function, and in the ith research and development program expected utility, Ui, is a function of $y=1, \ldots, m$ end product quality variables, q_{ij}, the quantity, Q_i of units eventually to be produced, and the time, t_i, at which the R & D effort will be completed so that useful end products can be produced, R represents the total budgetary constraint and C represents the expected total cost. It turns out that λ equals $\partial U^i / \partial C_i$ or roughly speaking, the increase in utility afforded by the last dollar spent on increasing quality variable, q_{ij}, or on any other quality of quantity or time variable. In other words λ reflects the marginal utility of resources allocated to program i. Therefore "For an optimal allocation of resources, the λ's for each program must be equal, assuming one common utility function to be maximized and one common scarce resource to be economized" (p. 21). For a criticism of the relevance of this static, certainty constrained choice model see Edwin Mansfield's "Comments" in the same volume p. 58-61. See also Burton Klein, "The Decision-Making Problem in Development," in Universities National Bureau Committee for Economic Research, *The Rate and Direction of Inventive Activity* (Princeton: Princeton University Press, 1962), who emphasizes that the problem of carrying out R & D resembles a problem of sequential decision under uncertainty rather more than a problem like that of the maximizing consumer satisfactions under static certainty.

24. On PPB, the OECD report states "Nothing in the method proposed makes it possible to define a single order of priority between expenditures or types of research. There is also great difficulty in this field in assessing the indirect effect, in putting a money value on various direct or indirect results (knowledge, health, power, etc.) and in choosing a cash-flow discount rate for the cost-benefit comparison." *OECD, Review: United States* p. 159. On the potentials, then-current status and limitations of PPB see the already cited study for the Joint Economic Committee, *The Analysis and Evaluation of Public Expenditures: The PPB System*, especially Vols. II and III.

25. For a survey of the very complex mechanism of making science

policy in executive and legislative branches of the United States Government see *OECD, Review: United States*. At the request of the Sub-Committee on Science, Research and Development of the House Committee on Science and Aeronautics (The Daddario Committee) the National Academy of Science Committee on Science and Public Policy reported on *Basic Research and National Goals, A Report to the Committee on Science and Astronautics, U.S. House of Representatives, By the National Academy of Sciences*, (Committee Prints, Washington, D.C.: March 1965) (hereafter *Basic Research and National Goals*). This report took the form of several individually signed essays. It did not produce a clear picture or even a few alternative clear pictures of the general priorities of the scientific community of the United States. Many of the documents did suggest a strategy of allocation among competing science goals which suggested different criteria of choice for "big" science and "little" science. A quotation will display the tone of the report with regard to the merits of the decentralized individual project-based grant system normally followed by U.S. Science policy for "little science." The report states "allocations within 'little science' or, almost synonymously," academic based science, "should be made by the free play of the scientific market place of ideas . . . The total allocation within 'little science,' broadly is the sum of innumerable individual judgments by individual scientists. Such a self-equilibrating system of allocation is almost the only one that can ensure continued long-term viability for our preciously individualistic 'little science'." p. 18. On the other hand, decisions regarding allocations within "big science," because it "may affect a large sector of science," for years ahead "must be centralized at a high level in Government" and reflect, in addition to the type of internal and external scientific criteria, the government's "scientific priorities for many years ahead." p. 19.

26. C.H. Waddington, *Science Policy, Research and Universities*, in *OECD, Review United States*, pp. 369-415 at 386.

27. For one suggestion as to the appropriate rate discount stressing the President's point of view see De Alessi, op. cit., p. 15, note 10; for a different, more traditional suggestion and a discussion of the appropriate discount rate see W.J. Baumol, "On the Discount Rate for Public Projects," in Joint Economic Committee, *The Analysis and Evaluation of Public Expenditures*, op. cit., Vol. I, pp. 489-503. Former Secretary of the Interior, Stuart Udall, has testified to a House-Senate economic subcommittee on the military budget and national priorities that neither President Kennedy nor President Johnson had "any institutionalized way whereby there was a forum where you could intelligently argue domestic priorities versus military priorities." Joseph A. Califano, a Johnson adviser testified that "Until the Congress and the executive have the means to make informal judgments on military and domestic needs, side by side, just as they now make choices among

competitive weapons systems, they cannot fulfill their responsibility to our people." Udall suggested that perhaps the most useful way a President could determine budget allocations was to "Take everybody up to Camp David for a few weeks and have a slam-bang argument." See the *Dallas Morning News,* 7 June 1969, p. 14A.

28. Included among these are the various appropriations and committees and the House Committee for Science and Astronautics and its Subcommittee for Science Research and Development, the Subcommittee for Research and Technical Programs of the House Government Operations Committee, the Senate Committee on Aeronautical and Space Science, the Government Research Subcommittee of the Senate Government Operations Committee, the Joint Committee on Atomic Energy among others.

29. For a discussion of the early technique in Holland using "imaginary" interviews see Jan Sandee and C.J. van Eijk, "Quantitative Determination of an Optimum Economic Policy," *Econometrica,* Vol. 27, No. 1 (January 1959), pp. 1-13; for excerpts from the United States' Presidential and Council of Economic Advisers' Annual Reports, which frequently discuss the major economic goals of the nation and the need to make rational trade-offs between them, see Reuben E. Slesinger, op. cit., passim.

30. For a discussion of the problems of and resistance to the application of PPB, Systems-type analysis with its reliance on cost-benefit rationality in a political organization like the federal government see James R. Schlesinger, "Systems Analysis and the Political Process," *The Journal of Law and Economics,* Vol. XI (October 1968), pp. 281-298. Schlesinger points out that self-interested bureaucratic and legislative incentives are such that this type of rationality is not really wanted. Despite this and the genuine technical difficulties in applying cost-benefit analysis to many choices he remains hopeful that the attempt to impose such calculations on the federal government will be fruitful.

31. See G.D.N. Worswick, "Fiscal Policy and Stabilization in Britain," *Journal of Money Credit and Banking,* Vol. I, No. 3 (August 1969), pp. 474-495; and see also the comment by Karl Brunner which follows this article; see also, Herbert Stein, "Where Stands the New Fiscal Policy," in the same journal issue (pp. 463-473) for a discussion of some of the actual political problems of social goal and policy choosing and pursuing in the complex American political setting involving both division of powers between the Administration and Congress and an independent regulatory system, the Federal Reserve System, and concerning issues in which the relevant technicians' knowledge and tools are so far quite modest.

32. For a call for better use by the Bureau of the Budget and by

Congress of information generated by the use of PPB System see House of Representatives *1969 Joint Economic Report, Report of the Joint Economic Committee, Congress of the United States, on the 1969 Report of the President,* 91st Cong. 1st sess. (April 1969). The report states "substantial progress has yet to be made by the program-evaluation system in bringing this information to bear on budget-allocation decisions" (pp. 35-36). And "The impact of competent analysis is negligible if it is not brought to bear directly on the bargaining process through which public decisions are made." (p. 36). This report also urges Congress to undertake "formal study of national goals and priorities with a view to establishing guidelines for legislation and expenditure policy" (p. 33). For other evaluations of the impact of the PPB System see Jack W. Carlson, "The Status, and Next Steps for Planning, Programming and Budgeting," and other studies in Vols. II and III of the Joint Economic Committee study, *The Analysis and Evaluation of Public Expenditures: The PPB System,* op. cit.

33. See above, note 9.

34. For suggested criteria see, for example, *Basic Research and National Goals,* pp. 18, 19; see also Alvin M. Weinberg, "Criteria for Scientific Choice," in Sanford A. Lakoff, *Knowledge and Power* (New York: The Free Press, 1966), pp. 406-419. Although he discusses them and applies them casually, Weinberg does not offer any detailed statement of how these criteria can be objectively applied. In this discussion "technological merit" includes estimation of the technological feasibility and value for other technological problems and for society of investing in the technology required to fulfill the scientific project. For "scientific merit" Weinberg suggests that emphasis be placed on the relevance of the field to "neighboring areas of science"; "social merit" focuses back on the effect of the project on the values of society and on "relevance to human welfare." In this he claims that scientific achievements produce national prestige and can help increase international understanding and cooperation at least among scientists in the same field. We must also note that they can also increase tension and competition and competitive technological, scientific, and arms races. For another discussion of why the federal government should support basic research and presumably therefore implicit criteria for evaluation of such research, see Harvey Brooks, "Future Needs for the Support of Basic Research," in Lakoff, op. cit., pp. 432-468, who stresses cultural, economic, social, and educational reasons including the widespread sense of identification with the adventure of intellectual exploration into the unknown, the maintenance of the nation's position of leadership in scientific exploration, the importance of technological innovation in economic growth, the relevance of scientific exploration to the solution of pressing social problems such as those associated with public health and industrialization, etc. In sum, general social criteria to be politically evaluated are important in the choice of the politically

103

optimal Big Science program to be supported.

35. Weinberg, op. cit., pp. 410-411.

36. See, for example, Brooks, op. cit., p. 446, who concludes cautiously "The degree of federal responsibility in these areas will always tend to be a matter of public debate, but there is greater consensus that the federal government has a responsibility for seeing that the foundations of knowledge are laid in these areas than there is that it has an operational responsibility."

37. For some preliminary studies attempting to indicate the types of economic gains to be expected see the various studies in W.R. Derrick Sewell (ed.), *Human Dimensions of Weather Modification,* National Science Foundation (Washington, D.C.: February 1969).

38. See James A. Crutchfield, "Investment in Weather Modification Research: Objectives, Incentives and Applications" in W.R. Derrick Sewell (ed.), *Human Dimensions of Weather Modification* (Chicago: University of Chicago, 1966). Other reasons, such as insufficient availability of capital for research and development due to capital market imperfections or simply lack of foresight, could also suggest the need for a governmentally subsidized research effort.

39. To date of course federal modification and research have been pursued on an unintegrated and largely unregulated basis by many competing federal mission-oriented agencies and their grantees. Federal agencies enjoy limited liability to be sued. They cannot be effectively sued for damages except under the limited provisions of the Tort Claims Act under which they cannot be sued for so-called discretionary functions or for actions taking place outside the United States. If, as seems likely, there would seem to be no reason for society to decide to treat such governmentally imposed losses as essentially different from those imposed by private modifiers, some modification of federal liability provisions vis-à-vis weather modification may be called for.

40. See *OECD, Review, United States, passim;* see also Sanford A. Lakoff, "The Scientific Establishment and American Pluralism" in Lakoff (ed.), *Knowledge and Power,* 1966, p. 377.

41. See Roland N. McKean and Melvin Anshen, "Limitations, Risks, and Problems" in Lyden and Miller, *Planning, Programming, Budgeting,* (Chicago: Markham Publishing Co., 1968), pp. 337-357; see also Aaron Wildavsky, "The Political Economy of Efficiency . . ." in the same volume, pp. 371-402; see also the four critiques in Section A, pp. 801-898 of Vol. III of the Joint Economic Committee Study, *The Analysis and Evaluation of Public Expenditures.*

42. *OCED, Review, United States,* passim, for example, p. 377.

43. It has been claimed that as the freely made bargain by which the "free individual" submits to coercive social decision making, the constitutional choice, should be made on the basis of a unanimity rule. See Buchanan and Tullock, op. cit., p. 14-15; see also Douglas W. Rae, "Decision Rules and Individual Values in Constitutional Choice," *The American Political Science Review,* Vol. LXIII, No. 1 (March 1969), pp. 40-56, who argues that even for the initial constitutional choice, majority rule is the rational choice of the average individual (who is uninformed as to his future preferences or options but is choosing a decision rule by which these choices will be made) since it minimizes the number of times he can expect to *not* be in the winning coalition.

44. It is clear in logic that such corrections of the market outcome should be made ultimately politically; if made by economic "technicians," that these parties should be carefully instructed politically, and their actions should be subject to regular political review in order to assure that the legitimate, constitutionally-chosen political decision makers will be empowered to fill their legitimate role as representative choosers among social values and alternative social options, so that these inevitable, political choices will not be arrogated by so-called "apolitical" technicians, not responsible to any political constituency. Not all economic policy-making institutions have been so designed. For example, for criticism of the independence from direct, immediate accountability to the democratic processes of the Federal Reserve Board, see, for example, E. Ray Canterberry, *Economics of a New Frontier,* (Belmont, Calif.: Wadsworth, 1968).

45. It has sometimes been suggested that federal regulatory agencies which are presumably designed to provide disinterested regulation for the benefit of society have tended to become captured by the industry they are regulating. See, for example, E. Ray Canterberry, op. cit., passim; see however, Emmette S. Redford, *The Regulatory Process* (Austin: University of Texas Press, 1969, ch. 7), which notes some adoption of private industry's goals by the regulatory agencies studied, but nonetheless gives federal regulation of commercial aviation a relatively favorable evaluation, from the general public's viewpoint, while pointing out room for improvement.

46. See the various mimeographed reports, recommendations and policy statements of the Weather Modification Association which has proposed a model of state legislation for weather modification and has suggested that an independent, federal regulatory commission be established, perhaps along the lines of the Federal Power Commission. Their suggestions have stressed in particular that federal regulation should be vested in an "independent" commission, which is not involved in operations as well, presumably to assure its impartiality. Such a separation between the regulatory and operational functions by government seems reasonable from the point of view of defending the

public interest impartially, as well, and we shall assume regulatory policy is designed to achieve this separation.

47. See, in general, Taubenfeld, *Weather Modification: Law, Controls, Operations* (NSF 66-7) and study by Ray Jay Davis, infra herein.

48. See, for a generally favorable evaluation of local government in the United States as a means of minimizing and "denationalizing" conflict and making democracy at the center more manageable, Robert A. Dahl, *Pluralist Democracy in the United States: Conflict and Consent,* Rand McNally (1967), ch. 7; for other generally favorable treatments of the potentials of federalism see Arthur W. Macmahon (ed.) *Federalism, Mature and Emergent,* (Garden City: Doubleday 1955); but note the generally unfavorable essay included therein by Franz L. Neumann: "Federalism and Freedom, A Critique"; see also George C.S. Benson, "Values of Decentralized Government," in George C.S. Benson (ed.), *Essays in Federalism,* Inst. for Studies in Federalism, Claremont Men's College (1961); see also the essay by Proctor Thomson in the same collection: "Size and Effectiveness in a Federal System: A Theoretical Introduction"; for recent generally unfavorable analysis of federalism see Wm. H. Riker, *Federalism, Origin, Operation, Significance,* (Boston: Little, Brown and Co., 1964).

49. There has obviously always been competition between the valued social goal of maximum local self-governing independence and the valued social objective of achieving fair, uniform standards of an efficient, well-integrated society.

50. See R. Dahl, op. cit., p. 183.

51. Ibid., pp. 174-180.

52. There do not seem to have been many formal attempts to focus on the optimum allocation of jurisdictional responsibility among governmental units, although consideration of what is involved in the choice is clear. See, for example, Gordon Tullock, "Social Cost and Government Action," *American Economic Review,* Vol. IX, No. 2 (May 1969), pp. 189-197, who says: "In general, as the size of government unit is increased the number of externalities internalized is increased but the adjustment of the government activity to the desires of any individual voter is decreased." (p. 193). Mancur Olson, Jr. has attempted to draw out the implications of rational choice on these issues in a model in which the rational choosers are assumed to aim at producing a distribution of responsibilities among different levels of government which will yield allocative economic efficiency given the distribution of wealth and welfare. He does not adequately justify this assumption as to the aims of the rational choosers, and in general his is a highly oversimplified model which assumes in addition, for example, that

every collective good affects some clearly delineated group or area and that there is no complementarity in production among different public goods so that a different government for production of each social good would be an efficient choice. He also assumes that costs and benefits should be allocated on a benefit basis. Even then there seems no clear reason to feel that some unique allocation of function is implied. It seems likely that many different allocations of functions could be arranged to yield governments which could devise a set of taxes and subsidies to achieve these aims posited. Thus the specific assumption that the lowest "efficient" level of government should be chosen remains necessary as an assumption in this model, too. See Mancur Olson, Jr., "The Optimal Allocation of Jurisdictional Responsibility: The Principle of 'Fiscal Equivalence'," in Joint Economic Committee, *The Analysis and Evaluation of Public Expenditure,* Vol. I, pp. 321-331.

53. See George F. Break, *Intergovernmental Fiscal Relations in the United States,* (Washington, D.C.: The Brookings Institution, 1967), passim, for example p. 78. On the division of jurisdiction Break suggests that the locus of ultimate governmental control and direction of an activity should always be with the governmental jurisdiction which internalizes the preponderance of benefits from an activity so that externalities will always be less important than internalities; see p. 78 note 26. Even if this could be neatly specified, it clearly involves a powerful political assumption, which may conflict with the results of the choice calculus implied for the rational individual constitutional choosers who, as noted, are expected to weigh the varying prospective *costs to themselves* of coercive government at the various levels in question as well as the technical factors Break stresses.

54. As might be expected, interstate compacts have generally been found to be an unwieldy, inflexible, and poorly financially-supported devices for achieving voluntary multistate cooperation. See for example, Weldon V. Barton, *Interstate Compacts in the Political Process* (Chapel Hill: University of North Carolina Press, 1965).

55. See V. Pareto, Manuel d'Économie Politique, 2nd ed., pp. 617-18. Note that this criterion normally neglects the fact that people may care about their relative positions so that improving a social competitor's welfare may make his envious neighbor feel worse off. This is an important difficulty with the Paretian formula in the case of national states. National power, for example, turns out to be just such a relative concept. Leaving the U.S. as well off as before in absolute terms and raising the material welfare of the Soviet Union will not normally leave the U.S. as powerful or as secure or indeed as well off as before in the important relative sense.

56. A third case, important in the theoretical literature cited below in

note 59, and not considered here because it does not seem likely to be common in practice, occurs when compensation is possible because the gainers from a proposed move could compensate the losers but, once the weather modification was made, a proposed change back to the initial position would also pass the same test. The losers from the first move could now compensate the prospective losers from a return move to the initial situation. To avoid or handle such situations dual compensation tests were suggested in the literature, and, later, social judgments as to the socially preferable of the two distributions were suggested. See the readings of note 59; see also I.M.O. Little, *A Critique of Welfare Economics,* Oxford, Eng., 2nd ed. (1957); also see J. de V. Graaf, "On Making a Recommendation in a Democracy," *The Economic Journal* (June 1962), pp. 293-298. Such paradoxes arise because different distributions are involved, and they imply different output streams and different valuations of output. It would seem consistent with the spirit of a common approach to cost-benefit analysis (see below note 63) which normally seeks to maximize the (strictly speaking noncomparable) value of national product, if one were to compare the size of the two possible sets of bribes and to choose the one which would imply the larger (noncomparable) total national product, presumably paying the requisite compensation to any net losers, if this were the social policy on compensation.

57. The prospective losers from modification could afford to bribe the prospective gainers not to modify and still be better off. Note they do not do so, of course; therefore this is a case in which compensation to those who lose because society stays at the status quo is not paid and again, the alternative income streams being compared are not strictly comparable (see notes 59, 60, 61). Furthermore society might want to modify in this case even if it could be labelled "inefficient" on productivity grounds if the income distribution generated were sufficiently superior. However economists would probably suggest that other means be sought to improve the income distribution without incurring "inefficiency." For example, see J. de V. Graaf, ibid.

58. See especially the welfare economists. For a review of the literature see S. Rothenberg, *The Measurement of Social Welfare.*

59. See the "New Welfare" economists and their critics. For example, see Nicholas Kaldor, "Welfare Proposition in Economics," *Economic Journal* (September 1939), pp. 549-552; N. Kaldor, "A Note on Tariffs and the Terms of Trade" *Economica* (November 1940); J.R. Hicks, "The Foundation of Welfare Economics," *Economic Journal* (December 1939), p. 706; T. Scitovsky, "A Note on Welfare Proposition in Economics," *Review of Economic Studies* (November 1941), pp. 77-88; P.A. Samuelson, *Foundations of Economic Analysis* (Cambridge, Mass., 1947), p. 251; P.A. Samuelson, "Evaluation of Real National Income," *Oxford Economic Papers,* New Series, Vol. 11 (1950), pp.

1-20. For a summary discussion see J. de V. Graaf, *Theoretical Welfare Economics* (Cambridge, Mass. 1957), ch. V.

60. The value of real output in two different situations cannot be unequivocably compared when one is including different persons' income streams and using the different relative prices these imply. See de V. Graaf, *Theoretical Welfare Economics* (Cambridge, 1957), ch. V and XI. Yet the market system does not provide compensation to those not chosen for a good job or a large order. Society may well choose to compare different output-distribution situations this way, but unless society has specifically done so, as it has for the area of market choice, despite noncomparabilities, the "technician" is in no position to do so.

61. See note 70 below.

62. For a much more complex set of suggestions as to when economists should suggest that a policy change should be made and compensation should be paid in a democracy, after the "efficiency" and popularity of a move has been ascertained see J. de V. Graaf, "On Making a Recommendation in a Democracy," op. cit. These suggestions which would require in some cases that pure redistribution without any other social change be made, seem unsuitable as a guide to policy to be carried out by a technical, apolitical administrative body focusing on the regulation of weather modification. However a modification of them which required the technical agency not to make such a change but to report all cases in which redistribution itself was principally desired to the executive, legislature, or the courts seems potentially more suitable.

63. Strictly speaking because a different distribution is implicit for each total output, there is no clear-cut a priori way of comparing the efficiency of two different economic outcomes with two different income distributions, whether or not the points being compared are both optimal, except where voluntary exchanges can be arranged on the assumptions that there is no coercion and all these imply that all parties and society are better off. See E.J. Mishan, *A Survey of Welfare Economics, 1939-59, The Economic Journal* (June 1960); also see E.J. Mishan, "A Reappraisal of the Principle of Resource Allocation," *Economica* (1957), p. 324.
    The only exception is the situation (in which two different economic outcomes can be compared consistently on the basis of efficiency criteria alone) in which the preferred situation is superior to or preferred to the less desired situation in all conceivable distributions. This is the Samuelson criterion. See P. Samuelson, "Evaluation of Real National Income," *Oxford Economic Papers,* New Series, Vol. 2, No. 1, p. 1.
    However economists regularly do make such essentially noncomparable, value-loaded "efficiency" comparisons in fact, ignoring, for

example, the interpersonal comparisons implicit in the distributive differences in two GNPs or assuming, as Meade does explicitly, that the welfare weights implied are the same for all members of society. See J.E. Meade, *Theory of International Economic Policy, Vol. II: Trade and Welfare* (Oxford: Oxford University Press, 1955). Of course, society can adopt techniques for making such comparisons acceptably, hopefully remembering their limitations. If society is interested in assuring that some impersonal social maximum physical output be achieved without respect to who gets what, then cost-benefit analyses can be made which in effect would help society evaluate the several essentially noncomparable alternative total streams of social outputs implied by alternatives irrespective of who gets them, very much like evaluators in a market system are supposed to impersonally calculate their alternative options. These comparisons would customarily be made in terms of the monetary units which would be expected to emerge in the alternative cases preferably given the initial and expected final price structure. The fact that different parties would be spending different incomes and generating somewhat different price structures, outputs, and values depending on their needs and tastes can be ignored as relatively insignificant from society's view for computational purposes in all cases in which only marginal changes are expected in the price structure. In short the inherent noncomparability of the alternative total figures can be ignored and the macroeconomic totals or at least the benefit-cost ratios can be compared as if they were comparable. The higher of the two totals or the alternative yielding the higher benefit-cost ratio can be labelled more socially efficient in this restricted physical output sense (or, indeed, society can be thought of as adopting equal welfare weights for all individual income changes). This is the common type of approach to interpersonal comparisons implied in cost-benefit studies as used by the federal government. The question of compensation or alternative distributive rights is generally ignored. Pure redistributive gains and losses are not counted in the benefit-cost calculations at all. The choice by implication, at least, goes to the policy that appears to generate more total output, as well as this can be analyzed given the inevitable noncomparabilities involved.

Thus the Flood Control Act of 1936 authorized federal participation in flood-control schemes "if the benefits to whomsoever they may accrue are in excess of the estimated costs." On benefit-cost analysis see in general A.R. Prest and R. Turvey, "Cost-Benefit Analysis: A Survey" in *Surveys of Economic Theory*, Vol. 3, American Economic Association and the Royal Economic Society (London, MacMillan, New York: St. Martin's Press), pp. 155-207. Richard A. Musgrave, "Cost-Benefit Analysis and the Theory of Public Finance," *Journal of Economic Literature*, Vol. VII, No. 3 (September 1969), 797-806.

64. Zero sums imply purely redistributive results and present special problems for a technical agency. Should the potential gainer or loser be favored if the gainer expects to gain $25 and the loser to lose $25?

65. This would be more difficult to do if for technical reasons such operative districts had to cross state lines. Federal operating districts subject to the federal government might well be preferable to multistate entities for which there is also some precedent, like the Port of New York Authority. If some who benefit cannot be included in the modification district, the optimal efficiency solution implied might be closely approximated if those on the outside who benefited were taxed for their contribution to the costs of the joint effort and the partial district undertaking the operations was subsidized to the same extent. This type of situation is sometimes offered as a rationalization for many types of federal grants in aid to state and local governments. See Break, op. cit., supra, p. 64.

66. Since uncorrected externalities are assumed to be involved which might detract disproportionately from the socially best alternatives it might be dangerous for it to merely examine the external costs and benefits of proposals set before it, leaving to the relevant local government or private initiative the burden of seeking out and proposing the socially best alternatives.

67. For example, suppose a policy promises to greatly improve the distribution of income but implies some losses in economic "efficiency" in the sense that the value of total output would be lowered— or suppose the reverse, it promises to greatly improve income but the final distribution implied is much less desirable, how should a decision of the desirability of such a policy be pursued? What weights should be given to the improvement (or debasement) of the distribution as compared to the increase in social output?

68. The literature exploring the inclusion of multiple objectives in an objective function is extensive and growing. See Musgrave op. cit. for discussion and citations. For other recent discussions see the papers by Weisbrod, Haneman, Freeman and Mushkin and Cotton in Joint Economic Committee, *The Analysis and Evaluation of Public Expenditures*, Vol. I.

69. Of course a government can legitimately choose to intervene in the market for many reasons. We agree with Steiner that the concept, public good, need not be limited to so-called classical perfect collective goods, but that collective goods arise whenever "some segment of the public collectively wants and is prepared to pay for a different bundle of goods and services than the unhampered market will produce" and that when "the coordinating mechanism for providing a collective good invokes the powers of the state it is a public good." P.O. Steiner, "The Public Sector and the Public Interest," op. cit., p. 17. Weather-modification activities are likely to be quite classic public goods requiring at minimum public regulation. This is because externalities are likely to exist in that both benefits and costs of weather-modification activities

are likely to be generated which are not received or borne by the parties responsible. Thus, for example, modification may affect an area outside that of the commissioning party. Some landowners are likely to receive benefits for which they do not pay or suffer losses not automatically chargeable to the modifying parties. Thus public intervention is required to share the costs of providing it, so that it is produced up to the optimal efficient level of supply given the distribution of assets and income. Also public intervention is required to correct the inefficiency implied by the existence of external costs which are not calculated in the costs of operation and possible to compensate the losers. As suggested earlier, also, the search for basic weather-modification knowledge is likewise a classical type public good, since up to the optimum point society must subsidize the search for all knowledge which can be expected to yield generally useful or valuable information to society that could not be supported by or exploited by any one subscriber because it is expensive and the benefits are diffused, but are likely to become very valuable.

70. Note that normally compensations to all losers are demanded, not just for losses normally counted in cost-benefit estimates, which normally exclude consideration of redistributive pecuniary windfalls. If there are such purely redistributive losses and they are counted at least in the case of the initial status quo position then presumably total losses on some chosen projects could exceed apparent total gains to the extent of the net purely redistributive loss. Presumably if society wished to encourage initiative, rather than to burden all alternatives to the status quo, the financing of compensation for such windfall losses should be supported by social subsidy of some kind rather than out of the profits of modification. This would justify mixed support for compensation. The macroeconomic effects of such a social subsidy would as usual depend in part on how the subsidy was raised. Presumably this could be tailored to the needs of the times as well as other fiscal policy is.

71. Actually it is difficult to conceive of society compensating all parties for opportunities foregone because their projects for self-improvement via modification were not chosen, perhaps because others promised to generate greater output. Yet without compensation such parties are damaged for the "social interest." Since compensation for all losses of prospective gains would place an impossible burden on any choice it would seem that compensation for such "losses" could best be approached by general income maintenance and fair distribution policies.
   The local, regional, or central weather-modification district could use various financial devices, for assuring that external costs were internalized, depending on the scope of its roles and its basic philosophy about incidence. Instead of relying upon insurance it could sell the right to modify to the highest bidder within the district so long as

the bid plus any social subsidy deemed appropriate at least equalled the total expected external costs (or losses to be imposed on others whom it would compensate), or it could simply tax the modifier for at least an amount equal to the losses involved less any social subsidy deemed appropriate. This would involve the district in cost-benefit estimation.

To show the types of calculations implied, let us assume the gainer's calculation suggest he will gain $20 and the loser calculates that he will lose $25 from the modification in question. We are assuming a competitive equilibrium price structure exists. The loser cannot pay society not to modify because this would drive his costs above the equilibrium price and he would be losing money. The prospective gainer as usual, could not pay society $25 to cover the losses so that the modification would not be permitted. Ceteris paribus, the monetary value of total social output will be higher because the modification was not permitted. If the gainer expected to gain $25 and the loser to lose $20, then the gainer could pay society over $20 (up to $25), and he and society would be better off in this limited monetary sense if he modified.

4   Some Problems and Objectives of the Federal Effort in Weather Modification

Peter H. Wyckoff

In discussing the present status of the national weather-modification program, it is wise to recall that scientific efforts at modification began only in the post-World War II period. Following the success of early demonstrations of a capacity to modify weather under some circumstances in the late 1950's and early 1960's, a surge of optimism prompted many opportunists to take advantage of the situation and to promote schemes of weather control which had only minor basis in scientific fact. Conflicting claims and lack of proven success not only produced confusion in the minds of the public, but discredited the legitimate operators and alienated the very scientists who were needed to place this promising field of resource management on a sound scientific basis.

A widespread feeling of confusion and concern prompted Congress to create an Advisory Committee on Weather Control in 1953 to make an impartial study of the fact and to report to Congress and the public. In 1957 the Committee reported that scientific evidence to support these claims of success was lacking but that there did seem to be reason to believe that under favorable conditions it was possible to induce an increase of 10 to 15 percent in precipitation from winter and spring storms which occurred over mountain areas. The Committee recommended that a federal agency be assigned lead responsibility to initiate a program of scientific investigation which would uncover the scientific evidence needed to resolve this problem and lay a scientific foundation for beneficially influencing the weather. In 1958, Congress directed the

NSF to establish a program of research into the scientific basis of weather modification. In the ten years from 1959 to 1968, research into the scientific basis of weather modification was sponsored at both academic and profit institutions, and by the mid-sixties much was learned concerning the mechanisms of atmospheric processes which affected the weather. It became evident, however, that the processes of precipitation formation, fog dissipation, lightning and hail suppression, and severe storm modification were extremely complex and that in order to influence the weather it would become necessary to establish a much stronger basis of understanding of how the atmosphere functions before man could routinely intercede in these processes to influence them beneficially. Much of the new knowledge was tested in the field through programs of research by the Department of Interior, Department of Commerce, Department of Agriculture, Department of Defense, and other federal agencies who required a means of environmental management in order to achieve their mission objectives. The commercial sector of weather modification was also rapidly undergoing a change in the degree of sophistication utilized in application of weather-modification techniques. The entrance of highly qualified scientists into the area of commercial rain augmentation, hail suppression, and fog dissipation supplemented the basic studies of the federal scientists. Through the influence of professional societies, including American Meteorological Society, American Geophysical Union, Weather Modification Association, and others, forums were established for the exchange of scientific information and field-observational data which has been invaluable in supplementing federally sponsored conferences in compiling a growing body of knowledge needed by all who seek to improve man's environment. The field of weather modification has been unique in the coordination which has occurred at the working level between the scientist of the federal agencies and the scientist in academic and commercial institutions.

In 1966, the Panel on Weather and Climate Modification of the NAS and the NSF's Special Commission on Weather Modification issued reports concurrently on the status of weather modification and concluded that the evidence available at that time justified an optimistic outlook for achieving an operational capability in some aspects of weather modification in the reasonably near future. They also emphasized the need to increase the national efforts to achieve a better understanding of atmospheric processes which determine the ability of man to intercede in the natural-weather processes. The reports also stressed the imminent need to recognize the impact of our growing capability for atmospheric management upon the social, economic, ecological and legal structure of society, and urged that studies be initiated immediately to incorporate these problem areas into the plans for future research efforts.

In 1969, the ICAS was requested by the President's Science Advisor to review again the status of weather modification and to suggest a plan for a coordinated national effort which would insure that the major problem areas of weather modification are being approached in the most effective manner and that the opportunities for applying the knowledge gained over the past 20 years will be promptly used for the benefit of society. That plan is due to be issued in the spring of 1970.

In brief, the plan is aimed at formalizing the cooperative nature of the national effort in weather modification and confirming certain national objectives designed to produce maximum benefits through the application of knowledge and expertise gained over the past 20 years of research. It is readily acknowledged that there is much yet unknown about the mechanisms of the atmosphere; it is also recognized that considerable field experience has been acquired in specific areas of weather modification which could now be put to useful social and economic purposes through a cooperative national-program effort. While the present programs of the various mission agencies are expected to continue as before, by selecting certain problem areas common to all agency interests, it should be possible to focus a portion of the ongoing governmentally supported activities toward a coordinated attack on the most urgent problem areas which offer opportunities for the most immediate implementation. It is hoped that through a coordinated approach among the interested agencies on a specific number of important problem areas all scientific groups will be enabled to achieve their common goals more effectively and more promptly.

Some Problems and Challenges Facing Weather Modification Research

If the difference between art and science is the capability of science to express itself in numbers, the growing capability of the atmospheric scientist to describe the atmosphere in terms of mathematical models is evidence that weather modification is approaching the status of a science. Today, many of these mathematical models are crude and are based upon observations of cause and effect rather than upon a sound understanding of the atmospheric mechanisms involved. Crude as they

117

are, these models have been of great value in guiding researchers in the field as to the proper time, place, and manner to apply a modification procedure to obtain a desired change in the atmosphere. High-speed electronic computers are now becoming an indespensible part of field operations and are providing much of the decision-making information needed by the field director at the time and place where the operating decision must be made. The success of these initial computer applications to both field and laboratory experiments indicates the need to incorporate a computer facility in all major field weather-modification efforts. Computers are expensive, however, and require programming by experts who have not only programming knowledge but access to the large volume of data which has been acquired by many researchers in the past. Certain centers of excellence in the programming of atmospheric models presently exist in which computer facilities are available to handle a field problem in real time. The feasibility of connecting a remote computer facility with an operating field site by telephone transmission lines has been demonstrated in the past few years. One major problem area confronting the field experimenter is that of assuring that every major field experiment will have access to such a central computer facility on a real time basis to provide prompt decision-making information to him. The results of each major field experiment must also be fed back into the computer model to continuously upgrade the quality of the model and insure that the benefits of the experimental results can be made available to all future users of the facility. This implies some type of national computer facility and a data bank which would be available on a national service basis. Nowhere within the present federal structure has a decision been made to establish such a central weather-modification facility which would be available to the scientific community regardless of whether their work is supported by federal, state, municipal, or private funding.

Most weather-modification experiments are seasonal operations and require an intensive period of field operation for a limited number of months, with the bulk of the time during the year being spent in the laboratory analyzing data. Field experiments are extremely costly and require the use of large radars and instrumented aircraft to obtain the required data. Under the present limited budgets available to weather-modification experimenters, considerable ingenuity must be exercised by experimenters in converting surplus radars designed for aircraft tracking into weather radars and in instrumenting light aircraft with home-made or inexpensive sensors which have limited capabilities to perform under adverse weather conditions. Once the experimenter has completed his field program, the aircraft instrumentation must often be removed from the aircraft before its return to the rental firm. This is a highly inefficient method of operation. A real need exists for a national source of instrumented aircraft of a size and performance characteristics which would permit obtaining atmospheric data safely and accurately with provision for telemetering the data to the ground computer which would form the basis of the decision process in real time. At the present time only the largest federally funded projects can approach this capability. There appears to be a need for a national source of supply, on a loan basis, complete field observing systems to experimenters which would include modern weather radars, properly calibrated instrumented aircraft, telemeter systems, and interface equipment suitable for linking with and displaying information from a central "on line" computer facility mentioned previously.

Moreover, atmospheric sensors used in the field today require considerable improvement to measure the necessary parameters of the atmosphere which require measurement. Laboratory and field tests of condensation and ice forming nuclei have recently revealed that side-by-side tests of different nuclei-measuring devices may differ by three orders of magnitude in their readings. At the present time there is a need for improved sensor capable of being carred on an aircraft which will measure and transmit over a telemeter link readings of liquid-water content, drop-size spectra, temperature, and humidity within a cloud. Present mathematical models are based upon the mean values of a large mass of data, and considerable art and experience must be employed by the modeler in selecting and smoothing out these data. If weather modification is to be considered a science rather than an art, this measurement capability must be improved. The ability to measure and monitor cloud and weather parameters over a finite volume from a distance by indirect probing will be necessary in order that weather modification can be placed upon a firm operational basis. Radar has been the only feasible approach at the present time, but the ambiguities present in even the most advanced techniques require that instrumented aircraft or balloons provide calibration and verification of the results obtained. A new and more powerful approach to the indirect probing technique is required.

Our knowledge of the structure and behavior of the atmosphere is incomplete but improving. Weather phenomena occur in all scales of magnitude from local fog in a valley to global circulations which affect entire continents. Small-scale phenomena, such as local thunderstorms, are superimposed upon large movements which affect the weather of entire regions. It is not known how much coupling exists between these small-scale phenomena and the larger scale mass movements in which they are imbedded. Atmospheric scientists are approaching the study of this problem by computer simulation and through large-scale observations made possible by meteorological satellites and large-scale probing in such international efforts as BOMEX and GARP. The possibility that weather-modification operations in one location can produce changes in another location cannot be discounted at the present time. Until answers are available through actual observations of a more detailed nature over a larger area, it cannot be determined whether the "down wind" effects reported in several instances by experimenters are real or fortuitous. It is obvious that answers to this problem must be found if the effects of either experimental or operational weather modification are to be assessed on either a scientific basis or on the basis of their social, economic, ecological, and legal impact on our society.

The evaluation of weather-modification efforts continues to remain one of the major problem areas in the application of weather-modification techniques. Unlike problems in physics, mathematics, and space flight in which the variables can be defined and controlled, the weather is a vast and complex machine in which many of the important variables have not yet been defined or possibly even recognized. In the past, it was assumed that the weather was so far beyond comprehension that only statistical analysis could account for the random variables and point out those variables which were significant.

Over the past 20 years we have accepted the fact that all weather-modification research must be randomized, and that from five to ten years often must pass before an acceptable confidence level can be achieved in the results. The results achieved by these randomized tests have mostly succeeded in producing controversy and have produced very little progress unless they were stratified in accordance with a physical model of a recognized atmospheric mechanism. It is apparent that a short cut is needed to demonstrate the effect of a weather-modification technique which will be significant in one to three years' time and which will provide specific insight into some atmospheric mechanism which can be measured and modeled. It is possible that our present knowledge of the atmosphere will permit us to design atmospheric experiments around a crude mathematical model, and to test the effectiveness of a modification technique by the actual verification of a forecast made by that model. In some of the more simple cases of cumulus convection and fog dissipation this technique has shown considerable promise as a tool of verification. There is a need to develop such a verification technique for the future which can be more generally applied to more complex field situations without the need for randomization and long periods of data taking. We have many instances where valid observational information exists which did not fit into the usual randomized statistical testing format, and we have been forced to ignore it. It is probable that we know much more about the atmosphere than we think we do, if we can only organize what we know into a physical and mathematical model. The evaluation of weather-modification techniques remains one of our more challenging problem areas.

In the past five years, atmospheric scientists have become aware of the fact that the presence of man on this planet has had a significant impact upon both the local and possibly global weather patterns through the pollution of the atmosphere, the conversion of open fields and forests into surfaces of asphalt, concrete, and steel, and by the emission of large quantities of heat from highly localized urban areas. It is possible that this inadvertent weather modification has produced more changes in our weather patterns already than all of the intentional weather-modification activities carried on to date by the atmospheric scientists. It is extremely important that these changing weather patterns be recognized as quickly as possible and that means be established immediately for monitoring the weather-related components of the atmosphere to establish benchmarks for future comparison. There is a need to initiate large-scale studies, both in the field and on the computer, to determine the basic mechanisms of these inadvertent weather changes and to discover whether they are irreversible or whether the trend can be reversed. It is conceivable that means can be found to scavenge some of the pollution burden from the atmosphere by artificial-treatment techniques until an abatement of the sources can be achieved. It is unfortunate that leadership in the field of inadvertent weather modification is so diffuse at the present time. A truly national approach to this problem must be developed in the near future.

The encouraging results which have been obtained in augmenting snowpack over the mountains and the years of experience in the treatment of thunderstorms to reduce lightning-caused fires in national forests brings up the possibility of operational programs in the near future. We must now answer the question as to whether we are prepared to justify these programs on a sound economic basis and to assess their impact upon the social and political values of society. Since we now recognize that the atmosphere is not limitless and that ecological balances must be preserved, we must be prepared to understand more fully the interaction between weather and the ecological system and be prepared to manage the atmosphere on a continuous basis for the enhancement of society as a whole. We must also develop the regulatory and legal framework which will insure that benefits will be maximized and that those who suffer loss or inconvenience for the benefit of the majority will be compensated in some way. An effort must be made to interest the social, economic, ecological, and legal scholars in this problem and provide a means for inserting their recommendations into the decision-making process.

Beside these broad problem areas which face the application of weather modification to the benefit of society, there are many problems which face the scientific community today. Most of these center about the dynamics of convective cloud precipitation processes, the generation and role of electricity in clouds, the development of cloud systems on a macroscale basis, and the dynamics of severe storms. Much has already been learned in the laboratory and in the field about the microphysical processes in clouds, and several impressive mathematical models have been developed to explain and predict these processes in the atmosphere. They are, however, far from perfect and require considerable refinement. The incorporation of these microphysical models into the dynamical structure of a convective cloud system, however, is a challenge which will require considerable research in the field, in the laboratory, and on the computer.

In summary, some basic problems which must be faced and some important knowledge gaps which must be filled so that weather modification can be practiced securely for the benefit of society are listed as follows:

1. Social acceptance of weather modification as a program of weather improvement for the benefit of society and the practical approach to the social, political, ecological, and legal problems which accompany it. No matter how feasible the technique of weather modification can be demonstrated to be scientifically, it must pass the test of social and economic acceptability first before becoming operational. It must fill a social need of society which no other alternative solution can do.

2. An improved, more accurate, and faster means for the evaluation of weather-modification experimentation in the field.

3. A vastly improved capability to measure atmospheric parameters within clouds both directly from air and indirectly from the ground.

4. A national approach to computer-modeling capabilities with central data handling and field computer use available to qualified scientific investigators.

5. Adequate sources of modern field equipment, such as weather radars, instrumented aircraft, telemeter systems, computer interface equipment etc., to be available to qualified scientific investigators. Included should also be a national calibration facility to provide standardization of results.

6. A more complete understanding of the consequences of a local weather modification act upon the environment locally and some finite distances away from the target area.

7. A more complete appreciation of the effects of inadvertent modification upon the changes in natural weather patterns and how these effects may be accounted for in improving the weather for the benefit of society.

8. A more adequate understanding of the dynamics of convective cloud systems on both a large and small scale.

9. A more adequate understanding of the microphysical processes taking place within a cloud.

10. A more adequate understanding of the generation and role of electricity in clouds.

The Federal Objectives

Weather-modification science has been developed over the years as a means of providing society the capability to improve its atmospheric environment. In developing this capability, certain national objectives were recognized as desirable, and the thrust of the federal effort has been directed toward their achievement. These objectives are as follows:

1. The increase of national clean-water resources in areas where water reserves are marginal.

2. The reduction of the incidence and duration of drought.

3. The reduction of the damage produced by severe storms, winds, floods, excessive snow, hail, and lightning.

4. The reduction of hazards to transportation through the dissipation of fog.

5. The protection of agricultural, water, and forest resources through frost reduction and boundary-layer control in the lowest layer

of the atmosphere immediately adjacent to the surface of the Earth.

6. The reduction in climatic extremes of temperature and humidity.

7. The understanding and appreciation of the causes and effects of inadvertent weather modification.

Most of the effort in weather modification to date has been devoted to meeting the first objective of clean-water augmentation. Years of experience have now been acquired in increasing the winter snowpack over the mountain ranges of the Rockies in Colorado and the Sierras in California. In the spring this snowpack melts and provides the run-off for the river-basin areas which provide water for irrigation and electrical-power generation. The meteorological circumstances under which seeding will produce snowpack increases over the mountain have now been reasonably well identified, and in several locations this knowledge is well enough established to justify the initiation of pilot or pre-operational tests directed toward obtaining answers to the economic aspect of water increase, operational procedures, and ecological consequences of such augmentation.

The augmentation of water from summer convective cloud systems has been tested in areas such as Florida, Arizona, and the midwestern Great Plains with mixed, but lately encouraging results. Due to the fact that precipitation from these cloud systems is not confined to any particular ground-water system and normal precipitation patterns are so variable on a seasonal and annual basis, it is difficult to evaluate either the economic or the ecological impact of any potential artificial augmentation. With the development of more adequate evaluation techniques, it would appear reasonable to expect a capability to establish a pilot project in one or more of the meteorologically favorable areas in the very near future. It should be pointed out that there have been a number of municipally or privately sponsored operational cloud-seeding programs in effect throughout the country for many years which are supported by nonfederal funds. While the success of these projects in augmenting natural rainfall is obscured by statistical uncertainties, their sponsors clearly regard them as economically feasible and worth supporting.

In addition to the possibilities of stimulating increased quantities of precipitation from existing cloud systems, there is also the distinct possibility of diverting precipitation from areas receiving adequate water supply to those in need of additional precipitation. This might take the form of suppressing the formation of precipitation on the

124

upslope of a mountain system and stimulating rainfall on the down-slope, thus eliminating the effects of the natural rain shadow and achieving an entirely different watershed distribution. Research is still in the exploratory stages, but there is reason to believe that it will eventually result in a practical form of management of water resources.

The second objective, drought reduction, is in the distant future since it implies the ability to divert large air-mass movements over the target area against the existing global circulation patterns. It is closely allied to the objective of reducing climatic extremes of temperature and humidity. Present studies are being performed largely through computer simulation based upon world-wide data supplied by satellite, aircraft, ship, and ground-network observations. The establishment of large areas of land with modified thermal response to solar radiation or the change in ocean currents to produce changes in sea-surface temperature are examples of the type of approach being so simulated. Progress is slow because of the complexity and physical extent of the problem and the need to examine minute detail in weather patterns over such large areas of the globe. Projects such as BOMEX and GARP will add to our knowledge of these energy-exchange processes, and the development of a new generation of computers is required.

The third objective, the reduction in the damage produced by severe storms, has shown some promise in several specific areas of research. A long series of experiments in Montana directed toward the reduction through cloud seeding of lightning-caused fires which occur in "dry" thunderstorms over the national forests has yielded an impressive set of statistical evidence indicating that fewer lightning-initiated fires are started under seeded situations. While very little understanding exists as to why the seeding of dry lightning storms (releasing relatively small amounts of precipitation) should reduce the incidence of the long-duration lightning strokes which produce most forest fires, the statistical evidence indicates that a pilot experiment might now be justified over an extended forest area. The seeding of clouds to produce precipitation for the purpose of putting out forest fires is being tested in Alaska, but results at present are inconclusive.

The reduction of the maximum wind strength by seeding the eye wall or rain band in a hurricane has been studied in computer models over the past five years, and last year's Hurricane Debbie was seeded from aircraft on two occasions a day apart. The reduction in maximum wind strength of 30 percent during the first seeding follows the prediction of the computer model and provides some hope that hurricane modification may become an operational practice in the near future. Project scientists do not feel that one successful test is sufficient for operational application and expect to continue the modeling research and to experimentally seed additional hurricanes when the opportunities may arise. The complete elimination of hurricanes is not desired, since these storms provide a large percentage of the yearly rainfall in the eastern coast of the United States. The project is designed to reduce wind speeds but leave the precipitation intact if at all possible.

The reduction or suppression of hail in thunderstorms is presently the object of intensive study under federal sponsorship in Colorado, South Dakota, and Illinois. The Soviet Union reports that an operational hail-suppression program is now successfully in progress in that country, but the mechanism of hail production in severe storms is still poorly understood. Usually insurance statistics are quoted as proof of suppression claims, and a more scientific method must now be developed. Evidence in this country indicates that there are at least two separate types of hail-producing storms which have been observed and that the treatment of each may have to be somewhat different. Success in suppressing hail on an operational basis has been reported by commercial operators in North Dakota, Texas, Alberta (Canada), Kenya, and other areas, but the problem of evaluation is still open to further refinement. There is need to develop a more adequate evaluation technique for hail suppression before it can be considered ready for a pilot type of test which might occur within the next five years. While the suppression of hail may appear possible by massive overseeding of small growing convective cells to destroy their growth, this is not considered an acceptable solution if the end result is a deficiency in regional rainfall. More sophisticated techniques are now being developed which are based upon mathematical models which will stimulate rain production at the same time that hail is suppressed.

The suppression of tornadoes is tied to the study of severe storms, and tornado funnels are of such a transient and random nature that little practical consideration can be given at this time to performing field experiments on their modification. It is felt that the knowledge of severe storm structure gained from hurricane and hail-suppression research will eventually provide the necessary understanding to design a modification technique to suppress tornado funnels. Most of the tornado-suppression research at the present time is confined to computer simulation and to laboratory experiments in rotating water tanks

126

or wind tunnels. The probability of devising a field procedure for testing tornado suppression is small for the next three to five years, and will be determined to a large extent on the studies of the severe storm mechanisms, which are part of the hurricane and hail-suppression programs.

The fourth objective, reducing hazards to transportation, has been largely directed toward the improvement of visibility in fog, especially at airports where hazards are especially severe. The dissipation of fogs containing water droplets below freezing temperature (supercooled fog) is reasonably well understood today, and operational supercooled fog-clearance programs are already in progress in over 20 commercial airports in the United States during the winter months. The technique most successfully employed is the dropping of dry ice pellets into the fog from a light aircraft. The armed services are also well along in the development of an operational supercooled fog-clearance system for military airbase use. The dissipation of fog where the droplets are warmer than freezing is not as well advanced. There are many studies of warm fog in progress utilizing large quantities of heat along the runway or the use of hygroscopic nuclei, such as common sodium chloride, to dry out the water vapor in the fog and produce dissipation. Several of these schemes have been successfully demonstrated from time to time, but economic considerations or the possibility of corrosive contamination have prevented their consideration on a full operational basis. The use of helicopter down wash to clear a finite hole in a ground fog has been tested by the armed services and has been given limited operational tests in theaters of military activity with some success where a relatively dry layer of air is found to lie above the fog bank. U.S. airlines have tested various warm fog-dissipation techniques using hygroscopic nuclei, polyelectrolytes, or surfactants, but it is still being approached on an experimental basis. The lack of adequate scientific-measurement instrumentation for fog and cloud measurement and the need for a better evaluation system precludes the possibility of an operational application of these warm-fog techniques in the immediate near future. It is not unreasonable to expect that sufficient progress will be made in the next five years to justify the establishment of a warm-fog dissipation pilot project.

National objective five is concerned with techniques for modifying the microclimate of the atmosphere from tree top level to the ground. It has been practiced for many years by the erection of snow fences in the winter and the planting or selective cutting of tree stands to act as wind breaks. Artificial water fogs stabilized with a nonevaporative chemical such as hexadecanol have been used successfully to protect orchards from temporary frost situations as have the well-known smudge pots which, however, produce excessive atmospheric pollution. In some orchards, large fans are used to mix warmer air into the surface layers to prevent frost. In arid areas, ponds and reservoirs are covered with a molecular thin film of organic chemical which inhibits water evaporation but permits the free exchange of oxygen. These practices will continue to be improved as our knowledge of the surface layers of the atmosphere increases and our engineering and agricultural knowledge continues to grow.

Objective seven is tied directly to our incomplete knowledge of the effects of pollution on the atmosphere and how these may affect the weather patterns both locally and on a regional or even a global scale. Many field observers have reported the growing increase of glaciated clouds in the vicinity of thickly populated urban areas, and pollution plumes have been observed by researchers to trigger snow showers over the Great Lakes in the winter. The anomalous rain fall at La Porte, Indiana downwind of the Gary, Indiana industrial complex has been reported in the scientific literature, and the correlations between rainfall and steel mill operations have been quite interesting. The burning of sugar cane slash in Tasmania has been correlated with the reduction in rainfall in that area, and a similar phenomenon was noted by research workers in the Philippines. While no scientific body of proof exists to confirm these observations, the increasing number of cases of correlations which are coming to light indicate that a serious study of this problem is necessary. It is a well-known fact that air temperatures in large cities are at least five degrees higher than in the surrounding suburbs and that rain showers are often triggered over cities during the hot summer months by the rising convective column of air produced by the absorption of solar energy on asphalt, concrete, and brick surfaces. It is conceivable that cities act as thermal mountains to divert local air-mass motions and produce changes in the local climatic patterns. The ever increasing burden of carbon dioxide in the atmosphere was believed to be responsible for a general warming trend in the lower atmosphere until approximately ten years ago when a cooling trend began to emerge. It is hypothesized by many atmospheric scientists that this reversal of temperature trend was due to the overpowering effect of the increasing pollution of the atmosphere due to smoke particles and dust. The need to scientifically monitor and

128

understand the magnitude of this problem is an important national objective. Also needed are studies of the ways pollutants are scavenged from the atmosphere by precipitation processes or coagulative fall out.

Summary

In summary, in certain specific areas of weather modification, 20 years of effort have been rewarded, and we are ready to put our knowledge and experience to the test of social and economic benefit. In other areas, we are almost ready or will be within the next few years. In any event, however, a continuing research effort will be required to improve and update these operating techniques and to assure that the necessary interpretive and productive model of the atmosphere are developed and that evaluation of modification experimentation and operations is made more accurate, more comprehensive, faster, and more secure.

Then, we will be even better able to make the social decisions necessary to assure that the maximum social benefit is derived from the management of our vital and scarce atmospheric resources.

5 Federal Organization for Control of Weather Modification

Ralph W. Johnson

This study is designed to explore the alternative institutional structures that might be adopted by the federal government to manage weather modification. Should all federal weather-modification activities be managed by a new department? Should these activities be carried out by one of the existing mission agencies or by a new one; should the various weather-modification functions of research, operations, data collection, monitoring, coordination, comprehensive planning, project review, regulation, licensing, and indemnification all be carried by one federal agency, or should they be scattered among a variety of agencies; should some be assigned to new entities not yet created?

These are some of the questions explored here. No attempt will be made to design the ultimate form of federal organization that might most effectively carry out these various functions. Rather an attempt will be made to analyze the effects that a variety of alternative institutional arrangements might have.

One threshold question is that of definition: What is meant by the term "weather modification." Some activities clearly fall within the term, such as the following:

The author is indebted to the rest of the Task Group for their helpful criticism in completing this study and to other experts who reviewed the study in draft form and gave their insights toward its improvement: George Shipman, Freemont Leiden, and Gilbert White. Needless to say, the final product is the responsibility of the author and not of any of the above.

1. Cloud seeding from either air or ground generators or other devices for the purpose of increasing or decreasing precipitation over a given area. Also included would be the laying of a large area of asphalt to increase the absorption of solar energy in an attempt to stimulate cloud formation to increase rainfall.

2. Hail damage suppression through cloud seeding.

3. Lightning suppression through cloud seeding.

4. Fog removal at airports (either cold or warm fog).

5. Climate modification through cloud seeding or other intentional activities.

6. Hurricane modification through cloud seeding.

7. Reducing destructiveness of severe thunderstorms and tornadoes.

The difficulty with the above list is that it tends to exclude certain activities that have similar effects to those on the list, and for a complete understanding of man's effect on the weather they possibly should be included. Some perplexing questions may be raised as to whether to include or exclude the inadvertent weather modifier, such as a pulp mill or steel mill, which in its normal operation may put wastes into the air that cause a seeding effect much like a ground generator or the commercial jet airplane that creates a contrail and starts the formation of a widespread cloud layer which reduces solar energy reaching the ground growth of a large cloud formation. Other illustrations can be thought of, although they may not be as important, such as the farmer who puts out smudge pots to warm his orchard, uses lightning rods to reduce lightning strikes, or who plants a row of poplars to reduce the wind speed near his farm house.

Needless to say, the definition of weather modification must turn upon the purpose for which the definition is to be used. If the purpose is to control inadvertent modification as well as intentional modification then the definition should include both. To date the definitions used in various bills and proposals has vacillated on this point.

The definition that appeared in S. 2916 was that "the term 'weather modification' includes any intentional or inadvertent artificially produced changes in the composition, behavior, or dynamics of the atmosphere."[1] This definition is also found in a number of departmental and industry drafts.[2] This definition is explicit about the inclusion of inadvertent modification. However the definition that appeared in S. 1182 did not include inadvertent modification.[3] The theoretical desirability of including inadvertent modification in the definition can be little doubted. If the weather is inadvertently being

132

modified we should know it and be prepared to control the modification the same as we would intentional activities. The problem is a practical one. The task of reporting, monitoring, and managing intentional weather modification is feasible with a modest effort at the present time. But the task of reporting, monitoring, and managing all inadvertent modification is a much greater task and will require a very great effort indeed. It is, possibly, more of an effort than the federal government is willing to undertake at present. Furthermore, to undertake this responsibility would require careful consideration of the roles and activities of the Federal Air Pollution Control Administration which is engaged in a program that bears a direct relationship to the problem. For these reasons it may be well to keep in mind a flexible definition of weather modification for the present. The term may be defined differently under different circumstances. It may, for example, be desirable to consider both intentional and inadvertent modification in connection with regulation or indemnification; it may be desirable to consider both types of modification from time to time in connection with program planning.

Another threshold question is whether, in fact, the weather can be modified. The initial surge of enthusiasm of the early 1950's was followed by disillusionment and doubt in the late 1950's and early 1960's. Recently a new, albeit cautious confidence has returned. The NAS and NSF reports of 1966 both attested that the weather was modifiable by man; a host of other scientists acting individually have come to similar conclusions. Very much, indeed, remains to be learned about the subject, but for the purpose of this study we need not know all the answers to all the questions; we need only know that the weather is now modifiable to some extent by man and that in the not too distant future it will probably be significantly modifiable, if not entirely controllable by man.

At the same time we need be aware that, for the most part, weather modification in this country is still in the research and experimental stage and that although many nonfederal privately financed programs have been conducted on an operational basis no federal programs have yet reached that stage. The recommended federal institutional structure must therefore be designed to accommodate a continuing period of research and experiment as well as the management over time of those programs that gradually become operational. Considerable flexibility is required because different aspects of weather modification will phase from experiment to development to operation at different times.

133

Is federal management essential? Clearly so with reference to certain weather-modification functions as will be explained later. Some activities clearly have effects beyond the local area, and even the state area, and thus must necessarily be managed at the federal level if they are to be effectively managed at all. Some cloud seeding for precipitation augmentation and for hail or lightning suppression will have an interstate effect and thus must be managed or at least reviewed by the federal government. An analogy can be found in the water field where some problems are handled locally, some at the state level, and others, such as the control of large interstate rivers at the federal level.

Many questions concerning the proper place for management can only be answered after we have more knowledge. We still do not know, for example, the total geographic reach of the so-called small or medium size cloud-seeding operation. All weather is so closely interrelated that a change at one location inevitably has effects at other locations. The question is, where does the outward reach of those effects become so small as to be inconsequential? Also some so-called "small" cloud-seeding operations may have negligible effect at a given distance under certain circumstances but have substantial effect in other circumstances. One theory extant suggests that certain projects, even though small, may trigger consequences that reach far beyond the local area.[4] If this is true then federal management or review will certainly be appropriate for such projects. In fact if it is found that such triggering is possible then it may be necessary to bring all weather modification under federal management to assure that only desirable triggering occurs. There is also the possibility that the combined effects of many small projects may cause substantial consequences beyond the immediate locale of the projects and that some overall federal management may be essential.

These organizational questions cannot yet be answered because we do not know enough about weather modification to fully understand the consequences of our efforts. As this knowledge is acquired we should be able to develop appropriate organizational patterns. In the meantime we should keep our management system as flexible as circumstances will permit.

In order to consider where control of weather modification should rest, it is essential to break this activity down into separate functions. For purposes of this study ten of these functions have been identified as follows: data collection, research, monitoring, operations, coordination, comprehensive planning, project review, regulation, licensing, and

134

indemnification. As this classification is used throughout the study I would like to describe each one briefly.

1. Data Collection. In order to manage, coordinate, and plan for weather modification it is essential that some central information bank be created to gather and classify all data on all weather-modification activities throughout the nation. It should also gather what data are available from outside the country. Such a bank of data will also be vital for research and experimentation; for example, those conducting research will have to know who is modifying what weather, else they may interfere with each other's activities. It seems unlikely that such data gathering can be done properly at the state level. Experience has shown that (a) some states won't take the trouble to collect and organize the information, and (b) those states that do collect it will not have it in any standardized form, thus making it difficult if not impossible to use, and (c) no single state will have the data on weather-modification activities that are interstate or international in their effect.

The precise information to be gathered will vary under different circumstances, however it would be important to know (a) what modification is planned; (b) data concerning the effect the modification attempt actually had on the weather, so far as that can be ascertained; and (c) methods used and other research information.

2. Research. This function can be carried on at all levels of government as well as in the private and semipublic sector. However, certain research activities must necessarily be under surveillance, if not actual control, by the federal government for a number of reasons; for example, the project might have an effect on large areas of the nation. Such projects might involve attempts to affect hurricanes or to affect the climate of regions. Also whenever the research will have an effect beyond the borders of a single state, some federal interest would be involved, at least unless an interstate agreement had been consummated by the affected states. If the experiment will have an impact on federal lands or installations then the federal government should be involved, and if the experiment has any potential international implications either on the high seas or on some other land area then the federal government must necessarily be interested in overseeing it.

3. Monitoring. This label actually covers two functions: policing and "primary data gathering." The first is closely allied to that of data gathering. Data gathering would result from the sending of data by various modifiers to a central data collection agency. Policing would go

one step further and would assure that the planned modification was in fact carried out in the manner indicated. Presumably with the general growth of weather modification there will be an increase in the numbers of operators with an increase in potential conflicts, both between modifiers and between those clients or members of the public who want one kind of weather and those who want another. It seems likely that some type of monitoring system will be required to assure that standards of operation are met and that planned modification, once approved by the appropriate government agency is carried out in the manner approved.

A second aspect of monitoring concerns primary data gathering in connection with inadvertent modification. An analogy can be made to stream guaging. If you want to know whether more or less water is in a stream now than 20 years ago or whether the water is more or less polluted than 20 years ago, you must have records of the amount and quality of water for the previous period. The same is true for weather modification. We need to monitor the weather to find out what effect man is having on it.[5] The weather bureau has observed and kept records on the weather for years, and these records would be helpful. Also, the Air Pollution Control Administration is now gathering data on the quality of air in various places in the nation, although only on a modest scale at present. However certain other types of data must now be gathered in order to ascertain man's effect on the weather. There is no apparent agreement among the scientific community as to exactly what data on inadvertent modification ought to be gathered, although there is agreement that a closer examination should be made of the subject and a decision be made as to the additional information that would be useful. Very possibly the monitoring should note the amount of condensation and ice nuclii as well as the concentrations of certain gaseous and particulate pollutants in the atmosphere so that we might have some means of telling what levels are being added either through intentional seeding operations or through inadvertent modification.[6]

There is little doubt that such monitoring would have to be undertaken by a federal agency. To be useful the information would have to be standardized, and the location of the monitoring stations would have to be carefully selected throughout the entire nation. One obvious possibility for the handling of this function is the Weather Bureau. A carefully selected network of its existing stations might begin to collect certain additional data.

4. Operations. This function can be carried on at all levels of both

the public and private sectors. There seems to be no reason why a variety of weather-modification operational activities cannot be carried on outside the federal government. On the other hand, some operations would most appropriately be handled by federal agencies.

Operational activities that might desirably be carried on by the federal agencies include lightning suppression over national forest or grazing lands, precipitation augmentation or storm control over federal lands or areas where the added water would flow into federally operated reservoirs, weather modification in furtherance of U.S. defense programs, and modification efforts that have an impact over large areas involving more than one state. Within the next five years or so probably two important operational programs that may be carried on by federal agencies are lightning suppression program of the Department of Agriculture, over national forest lands, and the precipitation augmentation program of the Department of the Interior over public and private lands in the Southwestern United States.

5. Coordination. Coordination can be effected by voluntary exchange of information and cooperation, or, at the other end of the spectrum, by outright control by' a single government agency. For purposes of this analysis I have used two categories: coordination and project review. Coordination means voluntary exchanges of information and cooperation. Project review, which will be discussed later, means endowing some agency with legal authority that can be used to require compliance with an overall plan and national objectives.

The coordination function is one that will need to apply to all levels of weather-modification activity, private as well as public. Certainly it will be essential for all experimenters and operators in a given area, whether individuals, firms, universities, local, state and federal agencies, or others to coordinate their activities so they do not interfere with each other. Some of this coordination will occur naturally and informally; however, as more modifiers enter the scene, some organized method of coordination will be required. Such institutional coordination can be located at the local, state, or federal level, or even in some nongovernmental entity; however, as projects become more numerous and larger and as more federal agencies become involved, there will be an increasing need for some federal institutional means of coordination.

To date coordination between federal agencies has been performed largely by the ICAS with an assist from the annual Inter-Agency Conference on Weather Modification.[7] This was formerly sponsored by NSF, but now is sponsored by ICAS.[8]

6. Project Review. This function must be compared to comprehensive planning. If a new department of weather modification were created, comprehensive planning might be accomplished by such a department; however in view of the diversity of goals for which weather might be modified, such an organizational centralization seems unlikely. If weather modification is carried on by a variety of departments, as it is now and as it probably will continue to be, then planning will probably occur to some extent in each of these departments. Nonetheless some kind of review of departmental projects seems desirable, if not essential, to assure that institutional enthusiasm remains consistent with the best interests of the nation. The project review function is not now performed in the weather modification field, except through the standard review processes of the Bureau of the Budget and of Congress.

As used here project review means some kind of outside, nonmission-oriented departmental review of projects, both experimental and operational, to determine if they are in the best interests of the nation and are the most efficient means of achieving the goals sought. Ideally this review might best be effected by an entity separate and apart from the mission-oriented operating agency carrying out the project; such entity could have the political as well as legal power to require changes in the project or even its cancellation. Such a review entity was recommended for the water field in the 1949 Hoover Commission Report.[9] Another was recommended in the 1955 Hoover Commission Report.[10] There were also recommendations in the 1950 Cooke Commission Report and by numerous political analysts.[11] The same arguments that favor a review board for the water field speak for one here, possibly even more persuasively, as will be indicated below.

Project review for the federal agencies must of necessity occur at the federal level. Also, if state sponsored or operated projects are to be reviewed, such a review would probably have to occur at the federal level, although it might be possible in some states to obtain an effective review at the state level, either through another state agency or through a private-research organization.

7. Regulation. This function is well known and is the standard function performed by a host of federal agencies at present, for example, the FCC, ICC, and CAB.[12] As more weather modification occurs the need for regulation will increase. In particular, standards of operation will be needed, for example, to assure quality performance of cloud seeding, especially where larger operations are involved or where any interstate or specific federal interests are involved. If a regulatory

system is created the coordination function as between nonfederal entities would probably occur through that system. Regulation of the federal agencies would also be possible through an independent federal regulatory agency; however, whether such regulation would be politically possible is an open question. The analogy of the water field suggests this might not be easy, although the possibility should certainly be considered as one of the institutional alternatives. In the same way the project-reivew function, even for the federal agencies, could occur through a regulatory agency and should be considered as one possible institutional arrangement.

A regulatory agency might also perform the monitoring function assuring that standards of operation were being met by both intentional and inadvertent weather modifiers. The licensing function would also be a natural function for such an agency to handle; this is considered further below.

Regulation of weather modification now occurs in a number of states through a variety of state agencies. It is conceivable that for those operations having a limited geographic effect, regulation at the state level could continue. It seems likely, however, that as weather modification becomes more widespread the overall effect of a multitude of small operations might be so pervasive as to require a single-management system. Such a system would necessarily have to be located at the federal level. Certainly as to those projects having an interstate or international effect there will have to be regulation at the federal level.

8. Comprehensive Planning. Some entity of federal government might be specifically assigned the responsibility for preparing and keeping up to date a comprehensive plan in the weather-modification field, identifying national goals, and methods for achieving them. Of course the Office of the President, and Congress perform this task regularly in many areas, often with the assistance of such outside entities as the NAS and the National Academy of Engineering, as well as various ad hoc commissions, such as the 1953 Advisory Committee on Weather Control.[13] The more recent Special Commission on Weather Modification appointed by the NSF also provides assistance.[14] The President might, by executive order, assign the responsibility for such comprehensive planning to the Office of Science and Technology as he has done with other new technologies. Alternatively, Congress might assign the responsibility by statute (as prepared in S. 2916 (1966) which would have placed it in the Office of the President). Such an assignment might occur with the implied understanding that the

planning would actually be carried out by the Office of Science and Technology, probably through ICAS, with an assist by the Department of Commerce. S. 2875 was more limited in scope, being concerned only with atmospheric water resources.[15] Comprehensive planning for this activity would have been assigned to the Secretary of the Interior.

9. Licensing. As more operators come into the field this function will become essential to assure that the operators are competent to perform as weather modifiers. Similar licensing functions are performed by numerous other federal, state, and local agencies and even by nongovernmental entities, such as Bar Associations and Medical Associations in some professional fields. So long as the weather modifier is operating on a limited scale and performs no act that has an interstate or international effect, there may be no need for federal licensing. However, as weather modification becomes more widespread, it seems likely that the need, or at least the desirability of a federal licensing system will increase. Not only might it be desirable to assure standards of competency for interstate and international operators, but it may also be desirable to assure that incompetent operators do not cause harm in states that fail to design adequate licensing systems.

10. Indemnification. This function concerns the indemnification of persons injured or damaged by weather-modification activities, both for the purpose of those injured or damaged and to encourage research. To what extent should this responsibility be carried by the federal government and to what extent by private-insurance carriers, state and local governments, and others? Should the federal government attempt to regulate the indemnification activities of nonfederal modifiers in the field? S. 2875 would have adopted the approach of the Atomic Energy Act of 1946 as amended in 1954.[16] S. 2916 would have studied the question and reported on it at a later time to Congress.[17]

Identification of Goals

Although weather modification is a new technology it does not pose any truly novel problems of governmental organization. Because it is new, however, and has not yet become fully institutionalized it provides an opportunity for applying our best wisdom to its management. In recent years much thought has been given to governmental organization in the water field, a field that has many similarities to weather modification, and some useful analogies can be found there.

One critical threshold question is whether this activity is important enough to be an "organizing" idea for the structuring of government.

That is, is it important enough to justify creation of a department or special agency for the explicit purpose of carrying out weather modification?[18] It should be remembered in this connection that the basic problems to be solved are not weather-modification problems, but rather are problems of agricultural production, forest protection, airport safety, and quality of environment and that weather modification is merely one of a variety of means of achieving these diverse ends. Weather modification has little, if any, value in itself, except as it is designed to achieve one or more of these broader goals.

An analogy can be seen in the water field where some years ago it was thought that water resources was the logical place for an organizing idea and that those federal agencies that carried water-resources responsibilities should give them up to a new agency that would encompass all such activities. Professor Fesler criticized this view however, saying that there was no agreement on the problem to be solved by such a water-resources administrative organization, and that inasmuch as administrative organizations are designed to solve human problems, not merely to regulate resources, it would be exceedingly difficult to organize a government around water.[19] Fesler pursued the water example by observing that those who analyzed the question further usually realized that although water is valuable in the channel where it flows, for navigation, flood control, and recreation, much of its value exists only in relation to the land on which it is used, for irrigation, pollution control or other purposes, and that this fact requires a shift in the organizing idea from water to natural resources. (Other analysts of government have shifted away from water to the drainage basin as an organizing idea.)[20] Carrying this analysis a step further he argued that natural resources have, in the past, been used as one means of bringing about economic development and that possibly the organizing idea should be shifted more in this direction. In recent year man's use of natural resources seems to be shifting again as he becomes more interested in the quality of environment. Economic development and quality of environment are now sometimes competitors for the central role in the use of these resources.

One of the major constraints that must be worked with in any such analysis, is the fact that a well-established government system already exists, built around organizing ideas deemed important at some earlier time. Thus we have Departments of Agriculture, Commerce, Interior, Defense, and others and subdepartments within those organizations. It is true that our notions of organizing ideas have changed from time to time over the years (see creation of ESSA); however, they do not change easily and will undoubtedly persist as is unless compelling reasons for change can be put forward.

It is also appropriate to note explicitly that weather modification is a new technology that does not serve merely one purpose but rather a whole range of purposes. It can be used in theory, for example, to augment or reduce rainfall, to clear fog from airports, to reduce hailstorms, to reduce lightning, and possibly to make climactic changes over a whole region. The principal similarity between these different activities is the technology involved, and even this can vary substantially. Certainly the same human goals are not served by all these different activities. One approach that ought to be considered is to see whether the human goals to be achieved are already being served by existing agencies of government and whether the particular weather-modification activity should be located in those existing agencies as merely another means of achieving those goals.

The Alternatives Concept

The question of identification of goals is vital to an analysis of federal organization for management of weather modification. Not many years ago national policy concerning natural resources was concerned primarily with finding the most economic means for their development. However,

> events of the recent past reveal that social objectives considered desirable by society have been significantly broadened and that certain objectives desired by society may not be consistent with the most economically profitable use of resources. The public interest in recreation, quality of environment, and aesthetics implies a willingness to forego opportunity or to spend money in a way that does not necessarily yield the highest benefit-cost ratio as we are now able to compute it: The public is willing to pay for intangibles.[21]

One of the factors that makes the question of government organization for weather modification complex is the fact that it serves many goals, including the intangibles of aesthetics and quality of environment.

As a general approach to governmental organization for the accomplishment of a given goal, responsibility should be assigned so as to encourage consideration of the broadest possible range of alternative

142

approaches to the problem.[22] If, for example, the goal is the economic production of food then ideally the government agency charged with responsibility for that activity would have jurisdiction to consider food production from (a) irrigated agriculture in the southwestern United States, (b) nonirrigated agriculture from the Middle West or East, (c) hydroponics, (d) importation of food from other countries, (e) other food sources. Such an ideal organization can seldom exist however, because a variety of other human goals constantly contend for priority in the design of governmental institutions and require that compromises be made. Thus the agencies actually created can seldom consider more than a limited number of alternative approaches to their goal. The result is the mission-oriented agency, with its sometimes too limited approach to the human goals it is intended to serve and its sometimes overenthusiasm for its assigned mission. The Bureau of Reclamation was designed to aid in providing water for irrigated agriculture in the West. A variety of other goals might be articulated which the Bureau has attempted to serve, such as food production, employment, economic growth, and preservation of the quality of environment. The Bureau has been distinctly limited, however, in the means available to it to achieve these goals and has often been accused of using something less than the most efficient means—because it used the means legally available to it.

Such problems of organization will never be susceptible of total solution because of the contending goals that must be considered in designing the framework of government. Nonetheless, recognition of this organizational problem may assist in designing the optimum form of governmental structure for management of weather modification and provide a basis for analysis in this study.

Existing Institutional Structure

Over 20 years ago, in 1946, Irving Langmuir, Vincent H. Schaefer, and their associates proved that certain rain and fog clouds could be modified. Although legislation was introduced as early as 1948 concerning federal participation in weather modification, the disagreement among the scientific community concerning the feasibility of weather modification was so serious that no major federal program was practicable. In 1953 Congress enacted P.L. 83-256, creating the Advisory Committee on Weather Control, whose purpose was to conduct a complete study and evaluation of experiments in weather control.[23] Following a modestly favorable report on the potentials of weather

143

modification by the Commission in 1957, Congress enacted P.L. 85-510 under which the NSF was authorized and directed to

> "... initiate and support a program of study, research and evaluation in the field of weather modification, giving particular attention to areas that have experienced floods, drought, hail, lightning, fog, tornadoes, hurricanes, or other weather phenomena, and to report annually to the President and Congress thereon.[24]

This appeared to be the first attempt at designing or encouraging the design of a federal program. Considerable disagreement has arisen over the intent of this legislation, specifically over whether NSF should have been more aggressive in moving from its historic research mission into a mission concerned more with operational engineering aspects of weather modification and with overall coordination of the efforts of other federal agencies.[25] In any event NSF did not so conceive its function and only partially moved into these other activities.

Between 1958 and 1966 NSF gathered data on weather-modification research and operations on a voluntary basis. Then in 1966 it issued regulations requiring advance notice of all weather modification, the maintenance of records, and the submission of reports from all commercial and private weather modifiers. Such records were kept by NSF from 1958 to 1968 when Congress terminated this authority in the apparent expectation that it would be assigned to another agency during the same session; however, no authorizing law was enacted in 1968 locating this responsibility and the only agency now collecting data is NSF which has continued to obtain voluntary reports.

NSF also undertook a modest effort at coordinating of various federal programs by organizing an annual, two-day Inter-Agency Conference on Weather Modification where scientists and others from the different departments get together to discuss their projects and exchange ideas and data.

NSF has, of course, continued its support of basic research in the field of weather modification as have a number of other federal departments and agencies. As early as 1947-1951 the three military departments jointly sponsored a variety of field experiments; the Department of Agriculture has supported Project Skyfire, a research effort into the possible reduction of lightning over national forest land; the Departments of Commerce, Navy, and Air Force have supported Project Stormfury, designed to learn whether hurricanes can be modified; and the Department of the Interior has been conducting research in precipitation augmentation in the Colorado River Basin and else-where in the western states. Only one federal program now appears to be preparing for operational activity—namely the Department of the Interior pilot precipitation-augmentation program for the Colorado River basin.

In 1966 all of these efforts cost the federal government the modest sum of about $7 million.[26] This figure has grown to only about $11.3 million in 1969, and 11.8 million in 1970.[27]

Coordination of weather modification among federal agencies has occurred to date largely through ICAS, currently chaired by an Assistant Secretary of Commerce. ICAS is under the Federal Council for Science and Technology and is composed of representatives of all the federal departments and agencies involved in research, development, and operations in weather modification. It is interesting that although ICAS is under the Federal Council of Science and Technology and thus potentially wields a piece of the Executive Office's power toward coordination, it is chaired by an assistant secretary from the Department of Commerce, one of the operating departments in the field. Apparently this coordination effort has been reasonably effective to date, possibly in part because of the modest and widely dispersed efforts of the various federal agencies in the field.

No federal institution is currently charged by Congress with the responsibility for preparing and keeping up to date a comprehensive national plan for weather modification. Within the Executive Department the President's Special Assistant for Science and Technology has by letter recently authorized and directed the Chairman of ICAS to design a national program in the field.[28] Such an effort is now under way. Outside the federal government the NAS is also working on recommendations toward a national program. Although it was initially thought this NAS report might be forthcoming in September 1969, the forecast now seems to be that it might not be available until well into 1970.

Licensing of operators has been undertaken by a number of states but has not been attempted by any federal agency. Nor has any federal organization yet become involved in regulation, monitoring, or in-demnification.

Proposed Federal Institutional Structures

A variety of proposals have been made for the institutional structure of the federal government to manage weather modification. Some of these have reached bill stage, and some have even gone through committee hearings. Others have been or still are being considered by different agencies of the federal government or are being proposed by respected private individuals or organizations.

These proposals are analyzed here not to record their historical existence but rather to demonstrate analytically several of the more plausible ways that the various weather-modification functions can be grouped among existing and proposed federal agencies. They are important in this respect in that they were the most nearly politically possible and contain themes that will undoubtedly be given most serious consideration as this question arises again.

The first serious attempt at structuring the federal government for managing weather modification came in 1966. Two principal bills were introduced at that time, S. 2875 and S. 2916. Before commenting on these, however, it is appropriate to note briefly an earlier and much more modest bill introduced in the Senate, S. 1020.[29] This bill directed the Secretary of the Interior, in cooperation with NSF, to initiate and carry out a program directed at increasing precipitation in water-short areas of a nation. The governors of the states affected were to have a power to veto any proposed program for their state. Studies and investigations of precipitation-augmentation possibilities were to be made at not less than five different locations in the nation. The bill provided for a $20 million authorization over an eight-year period from 1963 to 1971.

S. 1020 produced extensive hearings and was introduced again in 1966 as Sen. 23, at which time the Secretary of the Interior testified against it, pointing out that it was identical to S. 1020 and that subsequent to its earlier introduction the Department of the Interior had greatly expanded its atmospheric water-resources program under the general authority of the Reclamation laws, that Interior was doing this in close cooperation with NSF, and that it was operating under a budget of $1,126,000 in 1965, $2,980,000 in 1966, and planned $3,000,000 for 1967, substantially more than the amounts envisioned in S. 23.[30] As the purposes of S. 23 had already been met within the existing law, there was no need for passage of a new one and the bill died.

S. 23 (and S. 1020) made only a partial attempt to handle the functions of research operations and coordination and made no attempt to handle the functions of data collection, monitoring, comprehensive planning, project review, regulation, licensing, or indemnification. These bills were designed simply to beef up the Bureau of Reclama-

146

tion's research and operational program in precipitation augmentation in cooperation with the ongoing research effort of NSF. These bills also would have explicitly removed any geographic limitation on the Bureau of Recalamation's operations, giving it authority to perform weather-modification operations anywhere in the United States.[31]

S. 2875 and S. 2916 were much more ambitious, calling for substantial assignments of various weather-modification functions to some old and some newly created federal agencies.

S. 2875 authorized and directed the Secretary of the Interior to formulate and carry out a comprehensive program of scientific and engineering research, experiments, tests, and operations for increasing the yield of water from atmospheric sources throughout the nation. In the conduct of this comprehensive program the advice and participation of other federal agencies would be required. A central scientific and engineering facility and regional research and operations centers would be established. General contract and grant authority would be provided, and the Secretary of the Interior would be required to make an annual status report on the program to Congress. Compensation for damages as well as licensing authority over all activities affecting U.S. atmospheric water resources would be provided in the same manner as in the Atomic Energy Act of August 30, 1954. S. 2875 would also provide that except for licensing authority the bill was not intended to give the Secretary of the Interior authority over research conducted by other federal agencies under other laws.

The bill was criticized by a number of other departments and agencies, the gist of the criticism being summed up in the comments on the bill by the Bureau of the Budget.[32] These comments indicated that there was a broad need for further research and development in the whole field of weather modification and that research was now being conducted throughout the federal establishment by a variety of different agencies. It then criticized S. 2875 because the bill dealt with this multitude of problems by granting the Secretary of the Interior broad leadership responsibilities in the whole field in order to advance the nation's capability to use modification techniques in only one, albeit critical aspect of this field, in other words, precipitation augmentation.[33] Bureau of the Budget argued that due to the breadth of national interest and federal effort in weather modification, it would appear unwise to subordinate all federal weather-modification activities exclusively to the water-resources problem.[34] In addition, the regulatory and indemnification matters dealt with in the bill were said to be of great importance and complexity, and most of the issues involved should be thoroughly studied before comprehensive legislation is enacted.

The second major bill introduced in 1966 was S. 2916. The revised version of this bill that finally passed the Senate was called The Weather Modification Act of 1966 and would have established the Department of Commerce as the leading federal agency on weather modification. The major responsibility for a research and development program would be in the Secretary of Commerce. Each of the other agencies with missions that might be aided by weather modification were given responsibilities for research and development allied to those missions. The Secretary of Commerce was authorized to issue regulations governing research, development, and operations of private business concerns that conflicted with federal research and development programs. The Secretary was to report within a year after passage of the Act on the need for additional legislation concerning regulation of weather modification.

The bill authorized the President to establish national goals for weather modification through the Office of Science and Technology. The Secretary of Commerce was authorized to engage in international activities but only with the prior approval of the Secretary of State. The bill required the President to inform specified congressional committees of any federal agency weather-modification program that was intentionally designed to affect the atmosphere more than 150 mi. from the source of such activity and required any federal agency conducting weather modification *operational* activities to obtain prior approval of Congress unless already authorized (the FAA was so authorized by Sec. 201 [e] [2] of the bill). It also authorized the Secretary to engage in a study program to determine the extent to which the U.S. should be liable for damages including indemnification of contractors and grantees, and to report to Congress within one year. Further the Secretary of Commerce was instructed, in cooperation with other agency heads, to conduct studies and investigations on the social, economic, biological, and ecological effects, deliberate and inadvertent, of weather modification, and to report to Congress in two years.

The bill was criticized by the Secretary of the Interior's representative among others because it would have given substantial leadership in the field to the Department of Commerce in contrast to S. 2875 which would have put that leadership in the Department of the Interior.[35] Others pointed out that the Department of Commerce's claim to weather modification, had in the past demonstrated a marked coolness toward the activity.[36] Secretary Udall argued that S. 2916 was really only a starting point and that definitive congressional action could only come after the studies envisioned in the bill were completed. He urged that the bill might be construed as a "blank check" for the Department of Commerce; that the President, rather than the Secretary of Commerce should be responsible for conducting studies and reporting to Congress on the need for further legislation; and that the bill should authorize all relevant agency heads, not only the Secretary of Commerce, to cooperate in appropriate weather-modification international activities (with the approval of the Secretary of State). He also wanted to change the provision requiring Congressional approval before new agency programs could become operational and urged that this restriction might, if left in the bill, take too much time in the event of a drought where cloud seeding might provide some relief. Instead the President should establish regulations to be followed by all federal agencies in carrying out weather-modification programs.[37]

The NSF and others criticized the 150-mi. provision, arguing that it would, in effect, require a specific act of Congress approving the activity and that this would "seriously impede some of the best current research on large-scale storm systems, as well as present efforts on hail suppression, lightning suppression and hurricane modification." Instead, NSF urged that prior reports of such activities be made to the President through the Office of Science and Technology for the President's approval.[38]

The bill gained substantial support through compromises made during the 1966 session; however, it passed only the Senate a few days prior to adjournment and did not pass the House.

S. 2875 contained no explicit provision for handling the data-gathering function, although the authority granted to the Secretary of the Interior in Sec. 100 to formulate and carry out a comprehensive program of research and operations re precipitation augmentation, in Sec. 101 to require participation by other federal agencies working in the field, and in Sec. 202 to license all operators in the field, federal, state, public, and private, was no doubt broad enough to empower the Secretary of the Interior to require full reporting both before and after any and all precipitation-augmentation experiments and operations in the nation. Whether such a function was being planned by the Secretary of the Interior in the event of passage of S. 2875 was not clear from the Senate hearings on the bill, although some sort of effort in this direction might be implied from the responsibility to issue licenses. Presumably no data gathering was envisioned for hail or lightning suppression or other weather-modification activities not having to do with precipitation augmentation.

S. 2916 also does not explicitly mention data gathering but seems to grant ample authority to the Secretary of Commerce to carry out this function, both as to federal agencies and other public and private entities. Certainly if the President assigned the Secretary of Commerce the responsibility for preparing his annual report to Congress on all federal and nonfederal weather modification, the Secretary would be expected to gather the relevant data to prepare such a report. Presumably the one-year study on the need for further regulation called for in Sec. 205(b) of the bill would also include the question of the need for further data gathering.[39]

The regulatory function was provided for to some degree in Sec. 205(a) of S. 2916 in that private weather modifiers could be regulated by the Secretary of Commerce where their operations might conflict with or impede federal programs. The bill also provided for a one-year study by the Secretary of Commerce of the need for additional regulatory power. S. 2875 did not provide for any regulatory power, although Sec. 202 did require other agencies involved in precipitation augmentation to first obtain a license from the Secretary of the Interior. Conceivably regulations might have issued to effectuate this power, in spite of the limitation in Sec. 204 of the bill that the Secretary of the Interior was not to have any authority or surveillance over other federal agencies.

Sec. 202 of S. 2875 would have given the Secretary of the Interior authority to control through the licensing power all "activities intended to affect, or determined by the Secretary to be likely to affect the atmospheric water resources of the U.S." Because of the atmospheric interrelationship of all weather modification this provision might have given the Secretary effective licensing authority over virtually all weather modification in the nation. One can even postulate that he might, through this clause, have jurisdiction over inadvertent weather modifiers, such as industries whose waste burning might inadvertently cause cloud seeding and "affect the atmospheric water resources." Needless to say this licensing authority is much broader than the mere authority to determine the professional credentials of the modifiers; it would seem to grant the power of review over every federal, state, local, or private entity or person operating in the field. The review function aspects of this power will be taken up later. Suffice it to say that the

150

Secretary of the Interior would, under this provision, have authority to establish a system for licensing all operators and for determining their professional credentials if he believed it wise to do so. S. 2916 made no explicit reference to licensing, although it did give the Secretary of Commerce sufficient power to undertake this responsibility as part of his regulatory function if he deemed it appropriate to do so.

Both bills left the research function in the various mission agencies concerned with the particular activity, although each provided for a focal point for research, in Interior or Commerce respectively. S. 2875 especially would have put Interior in the central role regarding all precipitation-augmentation research and any other research that might affect it; as the same techniques are used for hail and lightning suppression and various other weather-modification activities, this could have put Interior in the leading role in the whole research effort. S. 2916 provided that each mission agency would continue research relevant to its mission and directed the Secretary of Commerce only to coordinate these programs.

S. 2875 placed all authority for operational precipitation augmentation in the Secretary of the Interior (Sec. 100-105). Other weather modification operational programs were to be carried out by appropriate mission agencies. S. 2916 authorized only the FAA to conduct operational-weather modification at that time (Sec. 201(e)(2)). New operational programs would have to be approved by Congress.

The coordination provided for under S. 2875 affected only precipitation augmentation. For the Secretary of the Interior would have licensing power, and thus presumably some coordinating power, over all other federal agencies operating in this field. The bill did not provide specifically for coordination of research or operations of hail or lightning suppression or other types of weather modification, although some coordination would probably have resulted naturally from the leadership role given to Interior in precipitation augmentation and other activities affecting it. ICAS might well have continued to play a role here also, although probably a less important one. S. 2916 provided more explicitly and broadly for coordination, placing this responsibility in the Office of the President with the apparent understanding that the President would use the Federal Council for Science and Technology and the ICAS for coordinating research and the Federal Coordinator for Meteorological Services and Supporting Research or some similar entity in Commerce for coordinating operational weather modification.[40]

S. 2875 provided for the development of a comprehensive program by the Secretary of the Interior but only regarding precipitation augmentation. All other programming for other types of weather modification and for other agencies was left to those other agencies. Of course, because of the importance and pervasiveness of precipitation augmentation the development of a comprehensive program for that activity would be a significant move in the direction of programming for the entire field. It would, however, suffer the defect of starting from a single focal point rather than from an overview of the whole field.[41] S. 2916 explicitly provided for comprehensive planning and establishment of goals for the entire weather-modification field, placing this responsibility in the President and authorizing him to consult with the NAS and others on "scientific and technological development and new opportunities for the beneficial application or weather modification."[42]

International cooperation was not mentioned in S. 2875, being left to the normal processes of government through the Department of State and the various mission agencies whenever their programs made such cooperation appropriate. S. 2916 expressly authorized the Secretary of Commerce to "cooperate in any international activities relating to weather modification" but only with the approval of the Secretary of State; any actual negotiations with foreign countries or agencies were to be carried on by the Secretary of State.[43] The Secretary of State was directed to designate the Secretary of Commerce or his designee as a member of the delegation attending all international meetings or conferences relating to weather modification.

The indemnity function was provided for in S. 2875 by a brief but comprehensive provision, stating that the U.S. would compensate for the taking of property or rights or for damage, injury, or for other just claims arising out of execution of the comprehensive program in the manner provided in the Act of August 30, 1954, an Act to amend the Atomic Energy Act of 1946.[44] S. 2916 used a more cautious approach, providing that the Secretary of Commerce should study the entire indemnification question for both the U.S. and private parties and report to Congress not more than one year later.[45]

S. 2875 provided partially for the project-review function by placing the Secretary of the Interior in a position to require other agencies participating in the comprehensive precipitation-augmentation program to do so on the basis of agreements with him and by giving the Secretary licensing power over both federal and nonfederal entities engaged in weather-modification activities "intended to affect, or determined by the Secretary to be likely to affect, the atmospheric water resources of the U.S."[46] This coverage is, of course, very broad and might have given the Secretary of the Interior licensing and thus reviewing authority over virtually all weather-modification activities in the nation, whether or not directed specifically at precipitation augmentation, because the Secretary of the Interior might determine that they are "likely to affect the atmospheric water resources of the U.S." Criticism of his approach in recent years has been based on the notion that the reviewing function, to be effective, must not be performed by a mission agency that is itself operating and competing for projects and funds in the field. Such review it is said, should be conducted by some independent entity, such as the FPC, ICC, or FCC.

S. 2916 was not so explicit about the project-review function. It placed general responsibility in the President for establishing goals, resolving priorities between different federal agencies, and coordinating federal programs. In many ways this was merely an explicit statement of the responsibilities already carried by the President in connection with all departments in the executive branch. S. 2916 also provided for a one-year study of the need for further legislation concerning possible additional regulation; this study might well have included the question of the need for some kind of independent review board. Essentially, however, S. 2916 did not envisage a project-review function other than that normally performed in the Executive branch through the Office of Science and Technology and the Bureau of Budget.

It will be seen from the above analysis that the approach of 2875 was one designed to place the Department of the Interior in the lead position regarding weather modification, but on the basis of only one activity, precipitation augmentation, rather than on the basis of an overall weather-modification program. This limitation on the Department of the Interior's authority applied to all other functions too, such as comprehensive planning, coordination, regulation, licensing, and indemnification. The Secretary of the Interior could perform these functions only as they related to precipitation augmentation. S. 2916 undertook to cover all weather-modification activities, including precipitation augmentation, hail suppression, lightning suppression, fog removal, etc. It placed the Secretary of Commerce in a leading role in the field, although placing in the President the specific responsibility for coordination, comprehensive planning, and reporting to Congress. Coordination would probably have been effected by the ICAS of the Office of Science and Technology and by the Federal Coordinator in the Department of Commerce. Overall planning would probably have been effected by the Department of Commerce and the Office of Science and Technology. The general approach of the bill was considerably more cautious than S. 2875, providing for one- or two-year studies of the need for regulation in the field, the need for additional research facilities, the indemnification question, the social and economic effects of weather modification, and the biological and ecological effects of weather modification.

At least five different proposals have been made since 1966 that would change or affect the existing federal institutional structure for management of weather modification. One, H.R. 8977 would entirely prohibit intentional weather modification anywhere in the nation. It would not affect inadvertent weather modification.[47]

A second proposal, S. 1182, the Weather Modification Commission Act of 1969, takes a study approach to the subject, recommending that a nine-member Commission be appointed by the President from the state and federal governments, universities, and private industry to study the need for regulation and coordination in the field and the appropriate areas of responsibility for the federal agencies. It would specifically study the "development of an organization plan for a federally sponsored permanent commission designed to carry out a regulatory program consistent with the purposes of [the] Act."[48] The Commission's report is to be transmitted to the President and Congress within two years after the Commission's first meeting.

This Bill caused concern among some government and other people in the field who feel that it would unnecessarily delay the development of weather modification. A number of studies have already been completed of the scientific, institutional, and legal aspects of weather modification and another study of these same issues would not necessarily add anything and might well delay action for another two years or more. There are, of course, aspects of the problem that all agree need further study, but S. 1182 does not distinguish these and lumps everything together in the study responsibility for the new commission.

A third proposal, made by the Weather Modification Association, Weather Modification Act of 1969, is one of the most comprehensive yet designed. It would create a weather modification Commission "in order to provide for the general purpose of monitoring and regulation . . . of both federal and nonfederal activities in the field of weather modification."[49] The Commission would be composed of five members appointed by the President with the advice and consent of the Senate and would have authority to study and review all relevant data, enunciate national policies, develop a national organizational plan, and conduct whatever regulatory and monitoring functions are required.[50] The idea is apparently to develop regulations for those few aspects of weather modification that now justify regulation and design a national organizational plan for the future for those areas where greater organization and regulation may be required in coming years. Included in the proposed Commission's regulatory authority is an explicit power to set up a certification system to determine the qualifications of weather modifiers throughout the nation, thus evidently taking this function away from the states that have already initiated such certification programs.[51] The Commission would also "promote the research and development programs of other agencies of federal and local government as well as weather-modification interest and activity in universities and in private industry."

The proposal provides that the various federal departments and agencies now involved in weather modification, the Departments of Commerce, Interior, Agriculture, HEW, the FAA, and NSF are all authorized to consider weather modification as an appropriate vehicle for carrying out their existing missions.[52] However while each of these departments is authorized to carry out a weather-modification program relating to its particular mission, the Secretary of Commerce is more specifically authorized to carry out a "Comprehensive program in the field" to "include a specific program designed to control or modify tornadoes, hurricanes, or other severe storms."[53] This difference in authority is similar to that reflected in S. 2916 (1966) and would apparently put the Department of Commerce in somewhat of a lead position in the field, although with no authority over the activities of the other departments and agencies. Interestingly the Defense Department is not mentioned in the bill.[54]

The Commission would make a report each year on its own activities as well as on the activities of the other federal agencies. It would study and report to Congress on the need for legislation in the area of international cooperation. In the meantime, each federal agency would be authorized to cooperate in international activities in the area related to their respective missions and with the approval of the Secretary of State.

The NSF would sponsor and convene an annual Interagency Conference on weather modification as it does now and make an annual report to Congress on the information elicited at the Conference.[55]

Indemnity for the taking of property or rights, or for damage, injury, or for other claims arising out of execution of the comprehensive weather-modification program would be provided in the same way as in the Act of August 30, 1954, an Act to Amend the Atomic Energy Act of 1946.[56]

This bill would give the new Commission authority to carry out the data-gathering and monitoring functions. Research and operations would be carried out by the various mission agencies in accordance with their missions. NSF would also be involved in appropriate basic research. The crucial functions of comprehensive planning, project review, coordination, regulation, and licensing would all be carried out by the new Commission. The indemnification provision of the bill is the same as that in S. 2875 (1966).

Some criticism of this proposal has come from those who believe that, although such a new and independent regulatory agency may be appropriate some time in the future, it is not yet time for its creation. It is appropriate to note also that this Commission would have full regulatory power over all the mission agencies in the weather-modification field with the exception of the Defense Department and that the mission agencies have not in the past taken lightly to the notion of such regulation. The Commission's authority would also include reviewing of agency projects and programs. This particular idea has been suggested repeatedly in the water field, in other words, that some independent reviewing agency be created to review all agency projects and proposals but has met with such vigorous opposition from the water-oriented agencies and others that it has never been adopted. It seems questionable whether it would gather enough support to be adopted here.

The indemnification provision of this proposal is the same as that in S. 2875 (1966) and is therefore subject to the same criticism, in other words, that it may be too comprehensive for the knowledge we now have available. In 1966 insufficient study had been given to the implications of such a provision to justify its adoption, and no study has been forthcoming in the intervening years; thus, it is said, the same criticism applies today.

The fourth of the 1969 proposals is still informal but is one that has the support of a number of individuals with whom the author spoke in Washington, D.C. recently who are closely associated with weather modification in the federal government. It would be similar to S. 2916 in assigning relevant weather-modification activities to the various mission agencies consistent with their ongoing programs but placing in the Department of Commerce a leadership responsibility for carrying

156

out a comprehensive program in weather modification.[57] The most significant innovation of this proposal would be the creation of a new weather-modification Panel within the Office of the President, responsible for continuous coordination in the field.[58] The membership of the Panel would consist of representatives of each of the mission agencies involved in weather modification, Commerce, Defense, Interior, Agriculture, HEW, Transportation, NASA, and NSF; the chairman would be the Director of OST. The Panel would be responsible for "review of weather-modification activities" of the various agencies and departments and "for making recommendations to each department or agency for coordination or cooperative interagency programs that will avoid waste and duplication and will foster maximum productive efforts. . . ."[59] The Panel chairman would have authority to call meetings whenever necessary to accomplish the work of the Panel. In addition, the Panel would sponsor and convene at least once annually an Interagency Conference on Weather Modification (until now sponsored and convened by NSF) at which each agency would present a comprehensive review of its program. The Panel then would compile the information thus presented into a report which the President would forward annually to Congress.[60]

Each agency involved in weather modification would be authorized to cooperate in international activities relevant to its own program, but only with the approval of the Secretary of State.

The Secretary of Commerce would obtain and keep up-to-date complete information on all weather modification in the nation, whether performed by public or private persons or entities and would be authorized to promulgate regulations to do this.[61]

Indemnity was provided for in a rather lengthy section authorizing each agency to enter into agreements of indemnification with contractors or grantees. These agreements would require appropriate financial protection to persons who might be injured or damaged and would provide for excess insurance for losses greater than the required coverage.

Studies would be called for similar to those provided for in S. 2916 (1966). The Secretary of Commerce would study the need for further regulation and report to Congress within two years; NSF would study the social and economic effects of both deliberate and inadvertent weather modification and report to Congress within two years (In S. 2916 this study was to be done by Commerce.); and the Secretary of Agriculture would study the biological and ecological effects of weather modification and report to Congress within two years (In S. 2916 this study was to be done by Commerce).[62]

This proposal thus would place the data-gathering function in the Department of Commerce. Although the monitoring function is not explicitly provided for it would seem that the data-gathering authority given the Department of Commerce is broad enough to include this. In any event the Secretary of Commerce through the Weather Bureau probably already has sufficient authority to set up a monitoring system throughout the nation. What is needed is not further legal authority but money to pay for performance of this function. Research and operations under this proposal would be carried on by the relevant mission agencies, with NSF carrying forward its role in basic research. Comprehensive planning is not specifically provided for and presumably would be expected to result naturally from the composite efforts of the mission agencies and the weather-modification Panel. This Panel would be specifically charged with responsibility for coordination and project reviewing. Although it would have no regulatory authority over other federal agencies, its charge to make recommendations to each department or agency for coordinated or cooperative interagency programs, combined with the fact that its chairman would be from OST and not from a mission agency would give it considerable authority and weight in bringing about essential coordination.

The last of the 1969 proposals is now being considered by some ICAS members. It is a compromise proposal designed as a bare minimum bill in order to glean enough support for passage this year. It would do two things: (1) provide for the data-gathering function by placing this responsibility in the Secretary of Commerce, and (2) provide for the dissemination of this information through channels available to the Department of Commerce. The bill would thus only take care of the data-collection function and would leave all other functions to be considered at a later time.

Optimum Institutional Structure
for Different Functions

In examining the possibilities for different institutional structures, it is essential to consider the state of the art. If weather modification were either actually or immediately to become a full-blown operation activity in government or private industry then it might be well to establish an independent regulatory body for its management. The reasons for this are more apparent than in some other fields. Here the

158

potential effect on large groups of the public is obvious. Very often the particular modification activity would not and could not be limited in its effect to a well-defined geographical area or to a particular group. People not intending to participate in either the costs or benefits will be affected. There will be, in the economists' terms, externalities that will make the control through "market place" a virtual impossibility. Too many individuals will receive benefits who have not paid for them, and too many who are not being compensated will bear the cost. Even the weather-modification activities of government agencies may have such a pervasive and widespread effect that they will have to be regulated. An analogy might be drawn to the communciations field where the FCC was created to regulate the use of radio space in a situation where the externalities were so great that the market place could not possibly provide adequate controls.[63]

But weather modification is not yet a full-blown operational activity, and in its present stage of development the creation of an entirely new and independent regulatory agency for its management would seem premature. At the same time we know that the organizational pattern established now is likely to have a substantial effect on the patterns of the future. Care must therefore be taken to assure that the optimum patterns are created now.

In spite of the length of time, some 22 years, since the first weather-modification experiment, we are still just emerging from the experimental stage in many aspects of weather modification, such as fog dispersal, precipitation augmentation, hail suppression, and possibly lightning suppression. There is still widespread disagreement among the scientific community as to how advanced our technology is in these activities. All would agree, however, that in respect to climate modification and severe storm control we are very far away indeed from any operational stage. At the same time we must be aware of the increasingly wide agreement among scientists that the weather can be modified in significant respects and that within a few years almost certainly will be operationally modified as our knowledge continues to grow. Recent visits by U.S. experts to the USSR indicate that a major operational hail-suppression program is already under way in that country. And there is strong political pressure in this country for operational precipitation augmentation in the Southwest and for hail suppression and fog control in other areas. To sum up, it seems likely that we will be moving into a more operational phase of weather modification reasonably soon and that we should think seriously about

159

the governmental organization that will be most appropriate when that occurs.

We could, of course, consider weather modification as merely another technique for accomplishing the various goals of the mission agencies and regulate it no more or no less than the other activities of those agencies. And, indeed, there are some who believe this is the best approach. The difficulty, again, is with "externalities." The pervasive and widespread effects of weather modification are such that they might well reach outside the areas of responsibility of the particular mission agencies, thus creating effects reaching beyond the capacity and responsibility of the agency to manage. Not only will there be members of the public directly affected, there may also be other federal agencies or state or local agencies engaged in weather modification which would pose conflicts. It may therefore be essential at some point to create an independent regulatory body to manage this activity.

If and when such an independent regulatory body is created it might well have most of the responsibilities provided in the Weather Modification Association proposal referred to above—in other words, it might have responsibility for comprehensive planning, coordination, project review, data gathering, monitoring, regulating, and licensing. Research would be in the mission agencies, and NSF and operations would be in the mission agencies. Indemnification might be provided for in any one of a variety of ways, including those suggested in S. 2916 or S. 2875.

However, such a major organization rearrangement seems premature at this time. Thus the question is, what should be done now? For the present, while further research and development is proceeding and while some operational weather modification is being undertaken, a number of options for governmental organization seems sufficiently attractive for serious consideration. These might best be approached by considering how the various functions can be handled and then considering how the overall arrangement might appear.

Research

First it seems clear that research should be continued by about the same agencies that have carried this responsibility in the past. Each mission agency has performed research in the weather-modification activity that was related to carrying forward its mission. Such research should continue to assure a maximum feedback between operations—research—operation. NSF should continue its support of basic research in the Colleges and Universities as it is now doing. It may however be

160

time to create one or more new research laboratories, similar to NCAR to carry out more extensive research into the physical makeup of the atmosphere; such matters are beyond the competence of this paper and may best be commented on by the scientists. There is, at present, a view among some respected scientists that weather modification might move along more rapidly if the various federal research enterprises were brought together and were funded far more extensively than at present. If the total research effort is to be substantially increased then serious consideration should be given to placing a major share of the responsibility for that increased effort in one place, one agency. That place could be the Department of the Interior and Bureau of Reclamation, where the largest expenditures of funds have been made to date and probably will continue to be made in the future in precipitation augmentation. However the important lessons to be learned at present probably concern the physical makeup of the atmosphere and the weather and will apply across the board to all weather-modification activities and to all agencies working in the field. Thus it might be better to locate such an increased research effort in the Department of Commerce, somewhat further removed from the other mission agencies and with somewhat more of a detached perspective.

This raises a question about the Department of Commerce as a "mission" agency. That it is such an agency there can be no doubt, and that ESSA and the Weather Bureau are mission oriented is also clear. However, the nature of the missions of these organizations may make them more appropriate for certain weather-modification functions than some of the other mission agencies. The mission of the Weather Bureau is to gather data on and predict the weather and inform the public on its predictions. Much of its current effort is in the fields of research, monitoring, and data gathering. Its mission has to do with the weather, generally—not with making it rain, preventing hail, lightning, or eliminating fog. It is therefore possibly less inclined as an institution to become overly enthusiastic about modifying the weather as a means of accomplishing its mission. Its mission does not really benefit by weather modification. On the other hand this lack of mission orientation may also have contributed to the coolness of the Weather Bureau (along with the well-known views of its top personnel during the 1950's) toward weather modification when it first had an opportunity to move ahead in the field during the 1950's. Recent actions and statements of Department of Commerce representatives, however, indicate a more affirmative attitude and a desire to move ahead in the field.

161

Operations

Operational weather modification should be carried forward by the federal-mission agencies as well as by state and local governments and private business. This new technology should be added to those already available to these entities in carrying out their various roles.

There seems to be no valid reason for concentrating all weather modification operational activities in a single department of the federal government or denying this technology to either the federal, state, or local governments, or to private industry. It is a new technology that can bring many potential benefits to man and should be considered in that light. The special problems it poses, primarily concerning externalities, can best be controlled by regulation rather than by usurpation of the field by one or more existing or new federal departments.

Data Collection

Data collection is a vital function that must necessarily be performed by a federal agency if it is to be performed effectively at all. It would, of course, be possible to create a new, independent regulatory body at the federal level that would include this function among its responsibilities. The decision on this question depends in part on how rapidly it is predicted that weather modification will move ahead in the nation. The slowness of the development of this technology over the past 20 years, combined with the continuing shortcomings in relevant scientific knowledge suggest that the growth over the next few years will continue to be slow. Until there is a significant breakthrough concerning the knowledge of the physical properties of the atmosphere and how modification attempts affect those properties, we can expect continuing reluctance by Congress and private industry to spend large sums on operational weather modification.[64] The evidence is still too uncertain that dollars spent here will result in as certain or as large benefits as dollars spent elsewhere. At the same time it would appear that the potentials for extremely favorable benefit-cost ratios in the future are high and that considerably more money and time might justifiably be spent on research and development than are expended at present.

These factors suggest that it may not be time yet to create a full-blown regulatory agency and that the best approach may be to add the data-collection function, as well as certain others discussed below, to the responsibilities of one or more of the existing mission agencies. The most appropriate agency for this function would seem to be the

162

Department of Commerce, whose ESSA and Weather Bureau are already engaged in similar activities and could add this function with relative ease and efficiency.

There would seem to be little reason to worry here that the data collected would be used or organized in such a manner as to give disproportionate support to the mission orientation of the agency. Neither ESSA's nor the Weather Bureau's various missions would bring such pressure to bear on those who collected the data.

Nor is NSF the proper entity for data collection. Its role is to support research in the Colleges and Universities, and it is neither staffed nor appropriately expert in data collection, in spite of its brief experience in this field. Data collection was and would continue to be an unfortunate diversion of the energies of this organization.

To be effective the data-collection function must be mandatory and the data collected must be put into standardized form from all sources throughout the nation; the data must be comprehensive, and the requirement for submission of data must apply to all persons or entities, both public and private, who purport to modify the weather anywhere in the nation.

It is unrealistic to expect the data collection function to apply to inadvertent weather modification, at least at this time. For one thing we suffer from an enormous lack of knowledge as to weather and to what extent the weather is being inadvertently modified by man. As we gain that knowledge however it would be appropriate to begin to collect data from those identifiable sources of inadvertent modification that are capable of providing it, and to provide authority to an appropriate governmental agency to begin gathering data as it becomes available.

Monitoring

The monitoring function should be located in the same federal agency as the data-collection function. Both activities are clearly interrelated. Data collection is the submission of reports in intentional (and possibly inadvertent) weather modification. Monitoring encompasses at least two activities: (1) checking periodically to assure that intentional modifiers are reporting accurately, and (2) monitoring the atmosphere generally to have a continuing record of its composition and the changes that are occurring over time.

For the information to be optimally useful it should be standardized and integrated with the data obtained from reports of intentional weather modifiers. This can best be done by having the same entity perform both functions.

The Weather Bureau is already in the data-gathering business with weather stations located throughout the nation. One of the most appropriate and efficient ways of handling this function would be to add it to the responsibility of the Weather Bureau or place it somewhere in ESSA so that it could be run in close cooperation with Weather Bureau activities.

Comprehensive Planning

Comprehensive planning can be handled in any one of several ways. It can be left to the composite efforts of the existing governmental agencies. For example, in the water field such plans are the product of the composite efforts of the various water-resource agencies and the "overview" efforts of the Water Resources Council. The Forest Service prepares comprehensive plans for use of the nations forests. These various entities prepare and operate under comprehensive plans designed to further the accomplishment of their various missions. Thus weather modification would be considered merely an additional technique to be used in achieving those goals. On the other hand, weather modification might be considered sufficiently unique and important that planning for it should be done separately, especially during the current research and developmental stage. Without such specific planning this activity may inch along in a far less effective and uncoordinated manner than if an overall plan is designed for its future.

If special comprehensive planning is to be accomplished for weather modification then the responsibility for preparing those plans might be assigned to OST, where it would either be assigned to or receive advice from ICAS. It could also be given to one of the mission agencies, such as Commerce or Interior. It would seem, however, that the most effective assignment would be OST, where it could be assigned to ICAS or some similarly composed group. A particular problem is posed by the fact that OST is not a creature of Congress. It would be possible, however, to assign the responsibility to the Office of the President with the understanding that the planning would actually be done by OST.

As for the methodology of creating a comprehensive plan it will be essential to have a direct input of the views and plans of the mission agencies. Planning that is accomplished without such direct participation by these agencies is likely to be unrealistic and is sometimes ignored. At the same time, experience in the water field has demon-

164

strated that planning carried out by a group composed only of representatives of mission agencies too often turns out not to be planning but merely trading of information and projects. One method of alleviating this tendency is to appoint a chairman from some entity other than a mission agency; in this case the chairman might be appointed from OST. He would thus carry a piece of the authority of the Office of the President as well as his own authority as a scientist and as chairman.

Comprehensive planning may also be materially assisted in areas where new science and technology are involved by the efforts of such nongovernmental bodies as the National Academy of Sciences, the National Academy of Engineering, and various ad hoc Commissions.

Coordination

Coordination applies to two different aspects of the problem: coordination to assure that there is no costly and wasteful duplication among various programs and coordination to assure that different weather-modification activities do not interfere with each other. Coordination can be approached informally through the meetings of representatives of different agencies—which may or may not result in effective coordination, depending on the voluntary efforts of the agencies involved. Or, at the other end of the spectrum, coordination could be accomplished by a regulatory body with full legal authority to tell all the agencies involved exactly what they could or could not do. Probably the most desirable approach is one that falls somewhere in between.

The problem with the first alternative is that too often the mission agencies will use a voluntary coordination mechanism for tradeoffs rather than for real coordination, and the public suffers a new loss from the effort. The second alternative—a fully empowered regulatory body—is premature at this time and in any event is politically unrealistic. This suggests that some in-between approach may be best suited to the situation. That approach might be through ICAS or some similarly constituted body with representatives from the different mission agencies and with a chairman either from OST or directly responsible to the chairman of OST. Although such a body would not have direct legal authority to control the activities of the agencies, it would, through the active participation of the chairman and through the authority he wields from the Office of the President, be able to strongly encourage the necessary coordination.

Needless to say, other organizational patterns might be designed to achieve a greater or lesser degree of coordination, and it is likely that at this early stage of development a fairly flexible and informal structure will suffice. However as the technology progresses more intensive coordination will become essential.

Project Review

The arguments favoring a project-review function in the water field apply equally, if not more strongly, with weather modification. If such a function is to be designed for weather modification, now is the time to consider it, while the technology is still developing and before too many vested interests exist.

To be effective this function must be the responsibility of some entity different than the mission agencies that are designing and carrying out the projects. Someone needs to be specifically concerned with the potential externalities of each weather-modification project to assure that the total benefit to the nation is greater than the total cost and to review the potential effect of the activity on the environment and other unmeasurables, such as recreation and quality of life. We need also to be assured that the particular weather-modification project is, in fact, the most effective means of arriving at the goal sought and not merely the most effective means by which the particular agency can achieve that goal.

If such a function is established it might become the responsibility of one of several entities. It might, for example, become the function of a new weather-modification agency, created specifically for the purpose of managing this new technology; such an agency might also have regulatory powers as indicated earlier. However, such a major organizational effort still seems premature at this stage.

Two of the more plausible alternative possibilities, but both of which have drawbacks, are (a) the Office of the Federal Coordinator in the Department of Commerce and (b) the ICAS, or some similarly constituted body in OTS.

The difficulty with assigning a project-review function to the Federal Coordinator is that this office lacks the institutional independence desired for accomplishing it. The Coordinator is too closely woven into the fabric of the Department of Commerce to be entirely independent of the pressures that a large department always carries within it. Nor does it seem reasonable to believe that, for this purpose alone, the Department of Commerce is likely to grant the Federal Coordinator the independence that might be necessary. Conceivably if this office were somehow sorted out from the Department and provided greater independence in staff and responsibility, it would be a more-likely contender for the project-review function.

The other principal possibility is the ICAS or some similarly constituted body. However, one of the problems posed by this notion is that the ICAS is a creature of OTS and thus of the President's office, and not of Congress, and Congress feels constrained not to assign responsibilities directly to it. It would, however, be possible for Congress to spell out its intent that the project-review function be performed by some independent entity within the Office of the President and possibly obtain an informal understanding that the function would, in fact, be performed by ICAS, or otherwise through OTS (OTS, through its chairman, might assign it to NAS-NAE).

In any event there are too many variables involved to say definitively at this writing how the project-review function might best be handled. The points to be made here are that the function does merit most serious consideration; that it can almost certainly be established at this stage of development of weather modification easier than at any later state; that there are several existing federal entities that might be considered for its location; and that institutional independence is essential to the effective performance of the function.

Regulation

A comprehensive regulatory regime for weather modification may be premature at this time. The timing for its creation depends upon how rapidly Congress and the various departments decide to move ahead in the field. However one fact should be borne in mind: that is that considerable lead time is essential for the drafting and actual promulgation of regulations in such a new field. Extensive interagency discussions must occur, hearings must be held to receive industry and public views, and drafts must be prepared, circulated and redone. All these actions take time, and it is not unusual to find a lapse of three or four years between the intention to create such regulations and their actual promulgation. Thus if a significant increase in weather modification is likely in the next four or five years, serious consideration should be given now to starting the machinery toward creation of regulation.

Whether regulation will be necessary at some time may be arguable, but it is the view of this author that the pervasive effect of weather-modification activities and the difficulty of predicting exactly the effect of a given modification attempt are such that at some point soon regulation will become necessary. One possible approach to this function was suggested in S. 2916, which provided that the Department of Commerce should promulgate regulations to prohibit interference by private modifiers of federal programs. This approach has much to be said for it in getting a modest regulatory system going. It does, however, pose the problem of placing in a mission agency the power of regulation that is best effected by an independent entity. With all of their apparent drawbacks, the experience of the FCC, ICC, EPC, and other independent regulatory agencies has proven that such regulation is better accomplished by an independent entity.[65] Recent attempts by the AEC to sort out and give greater independence to its regulatory functions further attest to this fact. Nor is independence important only in connection with the regulation of other federal agencies. If a mission agency is charged with regulating private operators, it may find itself in a position of conflict of interest in regulating activities that are either in conflict or competition with its own programs.

Within the existing federal structure it is difficult to see where the regulatory function would most ideally rest. Again the Federal Co-ordinator in the Department of Commerce comes to mind, and it is possible that if that office were given the regulatory power at this time it could be moved when the function grew larger. The Federal Coordinator is, however, in the Department of Commerce and as noted above suffers the constraints imposed by such an institutional association.

The ICAS is not designed as a regulatory body and would hardly seem the appropriate entity for that function. Similarly the NSF is not properly constituted for handling this function.

This leaves the problem of either identifying some different agency, or of creating a new one. Both of these avenues offer advantages and disadvantages. One of the drawbacks of creating a new agency for this purpose is that such an agency would be so small at this time that setting it up with separate staff and facilities would seem unduly wasteful—at least until weather modification takes on greater proportions than at present. One alternative approach is temporarily to attach this function to one of the smaller existing regulatory agencies, with the understanding that it would attain separate identity when the size of the role justified it.

Licensing

The licensing power over weather modifiers is an effective way to assure competence to operate in the field. To the extent that the competence of operators is now controlled at all, it is controlled in the private sector by a variety of diverse state licensing laws and in the federal government by the judgment of various departmental administrators. At this early stage of development such an informal approach to licensing is probably appropriate; however, as more operators enter the field, it may be necessary to establish more specific standards of competence. In view of the highly diverse methods that can be used to modify the weather, including seeding from aircraft, ground generators, rockets, and artillery, considerable sophistication will be required to work out rational and meaningful standards.

For the time being this function might well be left to the states and to the federal agencies as is now done. As weather-modification efforts grow, however, and as the impact of this activity becomes more widespread, it seems likely that the interstate implications may require federal control of operators' qualifications.

Indemnification

This function should not be allocated until more study of the issues occurs. There seems to be adequate, albeit, imperfect insurance coverage available in the private sector at the present time, and the federal departments are working out their indemnity needs on a case-by-case basis. It would seem that before major changes are made in this informal system we need to have a serious and comprehensive study of the question. Such a study has not yet been forthcoming.

A Comparison with the Federal Pollution Control Program

Some important lessons can be learned about the management of weather modification by a comparison with the federal-state cooperative program for the management of water pollution. This is not to suggest that the two problems are entirely analogous, for they are not. However, enough similarities exist that a comparison, even though occasionally dwelling on differences rather than similarities, will identify some useful approaches to difficult management questions. The following discussion refers to inadvertent weather modification as well

169

as intentional weather modification; in the long run both are part of the same problem.

A brief sketch of the federal water-pollution control program is an appropriate starting place. Until the 1956 amendments to the 1948 Water Pollution Control Act, the federal government did not much concern itself with problems of water pollution. Prior to this water pollution had been managed by three sources: (1) the market system, (2) the common law system (through the law of riparian rights and nuisance), and (3) state and local governments. The market system didn't work because those who used the rivers for depositing wastes, and who made a profit from that use, were not the same ones who bore the costs. There was no way within the market system to permit those who suffered the costs to charge them back against the polluters. The common law system worked for a time many years ago, when the problems were limited, and when only a few people were involved, but the system gradually failed as the problems became more complex and as some kind of sustained management became necessary. Lastly the state and local governments had, prior to 1956 accomplished much. Some had reasonably good pollution control systems; however, they were entirely lacking in adequate controls. In general the states were, however, limited by finances and overly responsive to the pressures of industries and cities which found it difficult and expensive to change their methods of waste disposal. The result was that in 1956 Congress substantially strengthened the 1948 WPC Act. The 1956 amendments did several things: (1) reaffirmed the federal government's prior policy of recognizing the primary responsibility for pollution control in the state and local governments, (2) authorized increased technical assistance to states and broadened and intensified research, (3) directed the surgeon general to encourage interstate compacts and uniform state laws, (4) authorized grants to states and interstate agencies for water-pollution control activities and municipalities for construction of waste treatment plants, (5) simplified procedures for federal abatement actions against interstate pollution, (6) authorized appointment of a Water Pollution Control Advisory Board, and (7) set up a program to control pollution from federal installations. Further amendments in 1961 extended and strengthened the federal abatement procedures, increased the federal financial assistance to municipalities for construction of waste treatment works, and intensified research. They also continued to affirm primary responsibility in the states for this function.

170

The next major change was in the 1965 Water Quality Act which required all 50 states to submit to the Department of the Interior proposed water-quality criteria or standards for interstate or navigable waters. These state proposals were submitted in June, 1967, including plans for enforcement, and by now have been approved and put into effect in virtually all states.

There are, of course, some marked differences between the problems of water-pollution control and of management of weather modification. At the time the federal government moved into water-pollution control the pollution of the nations rivers and lakes was a well-established fact and was growing steadily worse as the industrial and technological revolutions advanced. A vast and complex system of local and state laws and institutions had been built up to deal with the problem. Solutions could come about only through the expenditure of billions of dollars and through a vast public educational program and through major changes in existing state laws and institutions.

As for intentional weather modification the problem is quite different. Relatively few industries and cities have vested interests in the activity to date, and relatively few local and state laws and institutions have been designed to control it. This is not so, however, of inadvertent weather modification. To begin with we are not at all certain how much inadvertent weather modification is occurring, from industrial waste, automobile exhausts, and the like, although the likelihood of significant changes in the weather from these sources seems great. To the extent that such changes are occurring the problems would seem to have many of the same characteristics as those in the water-pollution field. Industries, cities, and individuals who are discharging wastes into the atmosphere causing the inadvertent modification are causing a loss to others, and neither the market system nor the common law are competent to manage the problem.

One particular aspect of the federal water-pollution control system that seems especially relevant to weather modification concerns the function of use of a federal agency as a watchdog over state. One of these factors is the creation of federal-designed standards of operation. At the present stage of development of weather modification the federal government may wish to leave as much management as possible in the hands of state officials, both regarding intentional and inadvertent modification. At the same time Congress may feel that the welfare of the nation calls for the creation of at least minimum federal standards which state and local governments must meet in managing this activity. These standards might have to do with the qualification of weather modifers, with the testing system used to determine when the weather should be modified and to determine the effect of a given attempt, or with the atmospheric conditions under which a weather modification will be permitted. On this last item, it may well be that cloud seeding in certain areas should not be permitted under any conditions or that it should be permitted only under certain conditions and denied under others. It might, ultimately be necessary to establish zones throughout the United States where only certain types of weather modification could occur or where none at all would be permitted. As the technology progresses there will be a growing need for such mixtures of technology, public awareness, and community decision making. In such event the experience of the FWPCA in requiring establishment of satisfactory standards at the state level might be quite useful.

Both the standards of operation and the methods of enforcement could be reviewed by an appropriate federal agency, at the same time, however, leaving the actual creation of the standards and the enforcement procedures to the state and local governments involved. A second experience of the water-pollution control field that seems especially relevant to weather modification is the Conference technique. It will be recalled that under the 1956 and 1961 Federal Pollution Control Act Amendments the Governors of states affected by the pollution of an interstate river can call a Conference to examine into the problem. The Conference is not an adversary, courtroom type proceeding, and no strict rules of evidence are followed. Rather it is a public hearing at which all views are invited and presented on the nature and solution of the problem. The purpose is both to educate the public and to work toward a voluntary agreement on a program of corrective action. This type of conference has made impressive progress through consensus recommendations and conclusions. One of the chief reasons is the presence and participation, through personal appearance and through the news media, of the public. Similar public awareness and participation will surely be necessary in the area of weather modification as the technology continues to move ahead. For example, at least two questions might need substantial airing: (1) how much inadvertent weather modification will be permitted in the future, and (2) what intentional weather modification will be permitted. The second question is not so readily perceived as a problem requiring public attention so long as the modification is to occur over a remote mountain area, providing the effect does not extend far downwind. However as the knowledge of this technology increases, there will be increasing pressure to modify the weather over more heavily populated areas. The experience with the Tri-state Natural Weather Association in Maryland, Virginia, West Virginia, and Pennsylvania is illustrative of the type of problem that can arise from the lack of understanding of the nature of the technology or of the consequences of its use. Certainly public education will be an important ingredient in the future of this field. At the same time, it is quite possible that some part of the public will be benefited and others harmed by a given weather-modification program and that all of those to be affected should be fully informed on the possible consequences, and on relevance of the activity to their own lives, and be able to participate in the decision process about what weather should be modified and what left alone.

One other experience of the federal water pollution control program is relevant to the weather-modification problem. That is the mandate in the 1956 Act directing the Surgeon General to encourage interstate compacts and uniform state laws. It would be appropriate for Congress to direct an appropriate federal agency to encourage interstate compacts and uniform state laws in the weather-modification field also. These things often do not occur spontaneously, even when they are beneficial to the citizens of states involved. One reason is the very considerable staff and background work that must be done and for which the states are often either politically or financially unsuited to accomplish. Thus the direct interest, encouragement, and support of an appropriate federal official can be a critical factor.

If Congress decides to leave as much authority and as much management responsibility as possible at the state level then there will undoubtedly be other aspects of the federal pollution-control program that should be examined for relevant analogies. This program has proven to be a good model for responsible federal-state cooperation in an important natural-resources field.

Conclusion

In the above analysis I have attempted to explore some of the more plausible institutional arrangements that could be designed for federal management of weather modification. The approach has been to break down the activity into its different functions and consider the optimum ways that each function might be handled, keeping in mind the overall goals to be served by this new technology.

Much, of course, depends upon the pace of development of this new activity. Aside from this, however, there are a few basic notions that should be kept in mind about the relevant governmental organization. First, it must be remembered that weather modification is not an end in itself. It is merely a new technique for achieving certain of man's already identified goals—such as the growth of food from irrigated agriculture, the protections of forests from fire, and the safety of aircraft in landing and takeoffs—and that in nearly every case there are alternative ways of achieving these same goals. Because these goals are already being served by various existing government agencies, it seems appropriate to place most of the operational activity in this field in these agencies. Although they may not meet every man's ideal for governmental organization, they have generally been effective in accomplishing their missions and are about as efficient as practical politics will permit for achieving the nation's most current and pressing needs.

The above analysis also recommends that governmental organization for the management of weather modification, especially in the areas of comprehensive planning, project review, and coordination, should be designed so as to permit consideration of the broadest possible range of alternatives in the achievement of the desired goals. Increasingly, as government grows bigger, it is essential to keep in focus these basic human goals to be served and to design institutions to allow achievement of those goals by as many alternative routes as possible.

Lastly, although some specific suggestions about governmental organization are made in the paper, the intent is not to argue that these are the only possible answers. Rather the intent is to illustrate the nature of the technological and organizational problems and suggest some of the most plausible approaches to solving them.

Notes

1. S. 2916 appeared in various forms during the 1966 session. One form, dated October 17, 1966 contained the above definition in Sec. 102(a). This definition did not appear in the earlier copies of the bill (May 12, 1966), and it is significant to notice its inclusion in the later editions.

2. For example, Sec. 102 of draft bill proposed by the Weather Modification Association. The same definition was also used in a draft considered by the Interdepartmental Committee for Atmospheric Sciences.

3. S. 1182, 91st Cong., 1st sess., Sec. 8 (February 28, 1969). This

definition seems uncertain concerning inadvertent modification, although if taken literally would seem to be broad enough to include such modification. Certainly inadvertent modification is "artifically produced."

4. See testimony of Dr. Walter O. Roberts, Director, National Center for Atmospheric Research in Hearings on S. 2875 before the Subcommittee on Water and Power Resources of the Senate Committee on Interior and Insular Affairs, 89th Cong., 2nd sess. at 363 (April 14, 1966). "On the other hand, it may be that through the release of this rainfall in the atmosphere at the right time, at the right place, by perhaps cloud seeding over the Gulf of Mexico, we may have a bigger effect ultimately on the water resources available to the Great Plains, even though not one drop from the seeded clouds falls from the process of seeding and the effect of this occurrence is an indirect effect."

5. Such monitoring was recommended in the "Newell" report, H. Newell, A Recommended National Program in Weather Modification, 10a Interdepartmental Committee for Atmospheric Sciences, at 21 and 25 (November 1966).

6. Ibid., p. 21, for a comment on the ESSA Benchmark Program.

7. For a description of this coordination see Senate Report No. 1139, 89th Cong., 2nd sess., at 65-70 (April 27, 1966).

8. Ibid.

9. See Task Force on Natural Resources, Report [Appendix L], prepared for the Commission on Organization of the Executive Branch of the Government, at 6-7 (January 1949).

10. See 1, Task Force on Water Resources and Power, Report Prepared for the Commission Organization of the Executive Branch of the Government, at 77 (June 1955).

11. 1 The President's Water Resources Policy Commission, A Water Policy for the American People, at 49 (1950).

12. See Communications Act, 47 USCA Section 151 (1934); Interstate Commerce Act, 49 USCA Section 1 (1887); and Civil Aeronautics Act, 49 USCA Supp. Section 425 (1938).

13. This Commission was created by the Act of August 13, 1953, Public Law No. 85-256, ch. 426, 67 Statutes 559.

14. Dr. A.B. Chamberlain, Colorado State University, Chairman of this Commission reported on its mandate and recommendation in Hearings

on S. 2875 before the Subcommittee on Water and Power Resources of the Senate Committee on Interior and Insular Affairs, 89th Cong., 2nd sess., at 94-107 (March 21-23, 1966).

15. Under a broad interpretation of section 202 of S. 2875, 89th Cong., 2nd sess. (1966), one might argue that virtually all weather modification could come under the control of the Secretary of the Interior. Such interpretation is discussed more fully later.

16. Section 201, S. 2875, 89th Cong., 2nd sess. (1966).

17. Section 304(a).

18. A multiagency approach was recommended in Senate Report No. 1725, 89th Cong., 2nd sess., at 8 (October 13, 1966).

19. J. Fesler, "National Water Resources Administration", in *Economics and Public Policy in Water Resource Development*, at 368; ed. S. Smith and E. Castle (Iowa: Iowa State University Press, 1966).

20. See 1 *President's Water Resources Policy Commission Report* (1950).

21. Committee on Water Division of Earth Sciences of the National Academy of Sciences—National Research Council, Alternatives in Water Management, Publication 1408, at 9 (1966). This report contains an excellent analysis of the problems of water management, much of it highly relevant to an analysis of weather modification management.

22. Ibid.

23. Act of August 13, 1953, Public Law No. 83-256, ch. 426, 67 Statutes 559.

24. Act of July 11, 1958, Public Law No. 85-510, 72 Statutes 353.

25. See the discussion in Senate Report 1725, 89th Cong., 2nd sess., at 4 (October 13, 1966).

26. Senate Report No. 1725, 89th Cong., 2nd sess., at 5 (October 13, 1966).

27. Interdepartmental Committee for Atmospheric Sciences of the Federal Council for Science and Technology, *National Atmospheric Science Program—Fiscal Year 1970*, 13 Interdepartmental Committee for Atmospheric Sciences, at 8 (January 1969).

28. Information obtained in interview with Mr. Myron Tribus, As-

sistant Secretary of Commerce and Chairman of Interdepartmental Committee for Atmospheric Sciences.

29. See also note 30. The Bill cited is identical with S. 23, 89th Cong., 1st sess. (1966).

30. Hearings on S. 23 and S. 2916 before the Senate Committee on Commerce, 89th Cong., 2nd sess., Serial No. 89-59, part 2, at 320 (April 1, 1966).

31. An opinion from the Office of the Solicitor, Department of the Interior of July 13, 1966 (G-66-1042.3) advised the Commissioner of Reclamation that there was authority under existing law to authorize the Secretary of the Interior to carry out an engineering and scientific research program in atmospheric water resources wherever necessary and advantageous throughout the United States. Reprinted in Hearings on Progress in Weather Modification, before the Subcommittee on Water and Power Resources of the Senate Committee on Interior and Insular Affairs, 90th Cong., 1st sess., at 4 (April 4, 1967).

32. See page 10-11 Hearings on S. 2875 before the Subcommittee on Water and Power Resources of the Senate Committee on Interior and Insular Affairs, 89th Cong., 2nd sess., at 10-11 (March 21-23, 1966).

33. Thus, in formulating and conducting a comprehensive program of research, experiments, test and operations to increase atmospheric water yield, the Secretary is authorized to sponsor, among other things, scientific analyses of cloud systems and general continental or hemispheric circulation; economic, legal and other research; and the training of scientists and engineers. Other federal agencies are directed to participate in the comprehensive program; any activities by these other agencies that might affect the program can be carried on only pursuant to license issued by the Secretary.

34. Further criticism was voiced by Dr. J. Herbert Hollomon, Assistant Secretary for Science and Technology, Department of Commerce, to the effect that Section 202 of S. 2875 might be construed as giving the Secretary of the Interior control over virtually all weather modification activity in the nation whether or not directly concerned with precipitation augmentation. See Hearings on S. 2875 before the Subcommittee on Water and Power Resources of the Senate Committee on Interior and Insular Affairs, 89th Cong., 2nd sess., at 69 (March 21-23, 1966).

35. See statement of John A. Carver, Jr., Under Secretary of the Interior in Hearings on S. 23 and S. 2916 before the Senate Committee on Commerce, 89th Cong., 2nd sess., Serial No. 89-59, part 2, at 319-321 (March 31 and April 1, 1966).

36. See discussion between Senator Clinton P. Anderson, New Mexico and Dr. J. Herbert Hollomon, Assistant Secretary for Science and Technology, Department of Commerce in Hearings on S. 2875 before the Subcommittee on Water and Power Resources of the Senate Committee on Interior and Insular Affairs, 89th Cong., 2nd sess., at 73 (March 21-23, 1966).

37. See letter of Stewart L. Udall, Secretary of the Interior in Senate Report No. 1725, 89th Cong., 2nd sess., at 16-20 (October 13, 1966).

38. Letter of Leland J. Haworth, Director, National Science Foundation in Senate Report No. 1725, 89th Cong., 2nd sess., at 24 (October 13, 1966).

39. The authority to gather data might also be derived from Sec. 101, an objective of the act being the "development of the necessary scientific basis," from Section 201(a)(1) authorizing the Secretary of Commerce to "carry out a comprehensive program in the field of weather modification," from Section 202(1) authorizing the Secretary to issue regulations, pursuant thereto, and Section 205(a) authorizing the Secretary to regulate private weather modifiers whose operations conflict with or impede federal agency programs.

40. See comments on proposed coordination in Senate Report No. 1725, 89th Cong., 2nd sess., at 9 (October 13, 1966).

41. See this criticism voiced in Hearings on S. 2875 before the Subcommittee on Water and Power Resources of the Senate Committee on Interior and Insular Affairs, 89th Cong., 2nd sess., at 11, 7, and 96 (March 21-23, 1966).

42. Section 301(5).

43. Section 302.

44. This approach was critized on the ground that the indemnification issue was both important and complex and should be studied further before enactment of such comprehensive legislation. See Hearings on S. 2875 before the Subcommittee on Water and Power Resources of the Senate Committee on Interior and Insular Affairs, 89th Cong., 2nd sess., at 11 (March 21-23, 1966).

45. Section 304(a).

46. Section 202.

47. This legislation apparently resulted from pressure from the Tri-State Natural Weather Association with membership or support claimed

from a few people in Pennsylvania, West Virginia, Virginia, and Maryland. The recent drought in this region has been attributed by the Association to weather modification, although both official and unofficial investigations reveal no weather modification in the area. Some of the people of the region are, however, convinced otherwise, as indicated by statements reported in the 1969 annual meeting of the Tri-State Association: ". . . since 1 Sept. 1968 there has been no federal law regulating or even recording cloud-seeding activities. . . .current seeding is the work of a vicious underground. . . . no rain has ever been 'made' by seeding—it has been moved around from here to there, and the results are floods here, drought there. . . . the record shows that 18 lbs. of (Portland Cement) will entirely dissipate a large storm in eight minutes. The average time varies from one to 12 minutes and rain was stopped in all cases. Note that this data cannot be got from the USA experiments—here it is all kept secret." Mr. Hoke then referred to the 9th Annual Report, NSF which states that ESSA is engaged in making cirrus clouds; jet aircraft produce contrails that spread into cirrus clouds which cover the sky. This action of jet planes can keep cumulus clouds from forming when they are not needed. "I . . . have seen this done over Baltimore day after day, 12 months of the year, for three years." "Four motor jets are used for this, and no one but the federal government would own a sufficient supply. Thus this is another example of a lie told by Wyckoff, when he says that the federal government is not seeding. Lies are a big problem in the capital. . ." Minutes of 3rd annual meeting of the Tri-State Natural Weather Association, Inc., held at the Ranch, Lincoln Way East, Chambersburg, Pennsylvania, March 22, 1969.

48. Section 5(5).

49. Section 201.

50. Section 203.

51. Section 204(e).

52. Section 301.

53. Section 301(b).

54. The failure to include the Defense Department may result from the fact that the proposal purports to give very comprehensive control over all weather modification to the new Commission. Presumably the Defense Department would reject such comprehensive control and the enactment of the bill would be politically difficult if not impossible if they were opposed to it.

55. Section 401, Weather Modification Association draft.

56. Section 403.

57. Section 201.

58. Section 301.

59. Section 301(b).

60. Section 301(c).

61. Section 401.

62. Section 501.

63. See Davis *Administrative Law Text*, at 14, Hornbook Series, West Publishing Co. (1959 edition).

64. At the same time, without major federal funding a technological breakthrough will be difficult to achieve, thus tending to make a closed circle.

65. See Davis *Administrative Law Text*, Chapter 13 "Separation of Function," at 225-244, Hornbook Series, West Publishing Co. (1959 edition).

6   Strategies for State Regulation of Weather Modification

Ray J. Davis

For two decades scientists have been modifying the "composition, behavior and dynamics" of the atmosphere by introducing substances such as silver iodide, dry ice, water, and salt into clouds.[1] Through laboratory studies and cloud seeding in field tests and operations weathermen have increased their understanding of cloud physics and have developed weather-modification techniques, equipment, and materials.[2] In the near future weather scientists will be able, under proper circumstances, to alter the intensity and duration of precipitation and to effect a spatial and temporal redistribution of it.[3] Moreover, meteorologists are seeking practical means to reduce hail and lightning losses and to moderate severe storms. Cold-fog dissipation is operational in some parts of the country, and there are promising tests of warm fog dispersal techniques.[4]

Although reshaping our atmospheric environment will in some ways benefit us, there will also be undesirable consequences. Precipitation changes could bring unwanted rainfall, droughts, or floods. Even moderate shifts in weather can trigger ecological and biological consequences, some of which may be important.[5] Altering the weather will have social, economic, and psychological results as well.[6] Not all of the changes will be beneficial.

Operation of a weather-modification project is justifiable only if society derives a net gain from it. Should the economic, social, biological, and ecological losses outweigh the benefits of a cloud-seeding operation, it should be altered so losses will be minimized or benefits increased. If a beneficial balance cannot be struck, the project should be curtailed. Should a beneficial weather-changing project give rise to losses that can be measured in monetary terms, those persons whose interests have been injured have a strong argument for receiving financial compensation. Both control over projects and award of compensation call for governmental intervention. Some states have assumed this regulatory role and have adopted legal controls over weather modification.

States' strategies for regulation of weather modification might involve use of their courts, legislatures, and administrative agencies. Legal norms designed to control weather modification might be developed by the judiciary, legislative, or an administrative agency with judicial or administrative enforcement of those norms. These control methods might be employed alone or in conjunction with each other.

Judicial Control

The common law has been built through judicial adherence to prior precedents, a process known as stare decisis. There are three main strengths that may be found in relying upon this doctrine: (1) impartiality, (2) stability, and (3) efficiency.

In any civilized system of government, the law should attempt to achieve impartiality. Law that is applied to one set of circumstances usually should also be applied to similar situations. When courts do not adhere to prior rulings, the new norms applied by them may change what otherwise would have been the outcome of a lawsuit. In that event the losing litigant has not been afforded the same treatment as litigants who in similar prior cases prevailed because the older legal norm was applied. The shift from prior precedent denies an impartial result.

Following the past may, however, lead to an undesirable sort of uniformity. "From the standpoint of justice little can be said in favor of equality in error."[7] Even though like cases are not treated in like fashion, it is necessary to discard mistakes from the past and to keep the law in tune with the times. The sacrifice of impartiality to the extent involved in keeping the law of weather modification free from the complexities and misunderstandings of the past is a small price to pay if it leads to results which are justifiable on their own merits.

Moreover, complete impartiality is unsatisfactory, unless it can be safely assumed that the claims among which selection is to be made are equal. Casting dice or using a lottery to reach a decision is normally an

182

inadequate means of making a choice even though it is an impartial one. Chance takes no account of the relative merits of the possible decisions. Mechanical application of prior precedents may also neglect weighing the claims involved.

Stability in the law is a worthy aim, for it promotes in society the necessary security of acquisitions and security of transactions. Frequently it is more important that the law be settled than that it be settled right. When the law is settled, the lawyer has a basis for giving his client professional advice concerning the legal consequences of a given course of conduct, and the layman has a basis for reasoned reliance. Uncertainty about the legal implications of weather modification can hinder both development and operation of weather-modification techniques.

Stare decisis tends to break down with wide and rapid change in society. The law must have more than mere stability; it must have flexibility. Security should not be obtained at the expense of rigidity. The law must change. Old norms that have outlived their utility should be sloughed off, and other rules should be adapted to prevailing conditions.

Effective administration of justice requires at least an examination of proper precedents when presented with new problems. Constant redetermination of legal norms would be a tremendous waste of time and energy. Drawing from the learning of the past complements the necessarily limited experience of the judge. It guides him as to the social standards of justice and the moral concepts of the community.

The inefficiency inherent in creating new rules, however, may in the long run serve the needs of society more effectively than repetition of past solutions to new problems. The painful process of re-analysis of legal issues raised by application of new technology, such as that employed in weather alteration, is certainly slower than the use of earlier case law. But the result may be superior. This is particularly true when the potentially applicable precedents do not really fit the present problems.

Protection of Investment

The major groups seeking to obtain the benefits from weather-modification activities will be modifiers (and their clients) and landowners. In storm modification the benefits generated from modifier activities will more or less automatically accrue to their clients and to other landowners. Thus the owner of a neighboring tract of forested land will benefit from suppression of lightning strikes over the area subject to weather modification. Diminution of the forest-fire threat next door benefits the neighbor. The person paying for the weather-modification activity does not lose because of the fact that it collaterally benefits his neighbor. The same is true where there is direct application of incremental precipitation to the ground. But where there is an increase in upstream or upwind precipitation for purposes of downstream use, the modifier and his client have a problem of protection of their investment. If other persons were permitted to use the additional waters, the modifier would be benefiting them and at the same time losing such benefits for himself. This then is an area where the interests of the modifier and of the other landowners may collide.

Modifier Rights. Weather modifiers may claim the benefits of their upwind or upstream modification using arguments like those employed by other resource developers. "We were there first; we expended our capital and developed this additional water source. Through us the community benefits. We are entitled to protection, for without it there is inadequate incentive to develop the resource." Similar logic has been persuasive in states following the doctrines of prior appropriation of ground and surface waters.[8] These arguments underlie the law concerning developed and salvaged waters.[9] They also have an important bearing upon oil and gas law and mining law.[10]

Judicial reliance upon precedents which recognize the interest of developers of ground and surface waters and of oil, gas, and mineral deposits would have to take into accout the physical differences between these resources and atmospheric water resources. Winds shift more readily than do stream courses; the atmosphere is a more immediate part of the environment of the community than are subsurface minerals or subterranean waters; and measurement of the extent of any rights recognized in the clouds involves more difficult technical problems than determining the quantity of other resources which may legally be extracted.

The caselaw which protects ownership rights in water and minerals is a product of an earlier time. Development of natural resources held a high priority until well into this century, and the law placed the developers' rights in a favored position in order to give effect to that priority. Today, however, sound management and conservation of natural resources is a more important national goal than their exploitation. Use of arguments which protected the rights of nineteenth century resource developers in order to protect today's weather modifiers may not further our need to manage atmospheric water resources in the public interest.

Thus far there have been no cases in court concerning weather modifiers' claims to water alledgedly reaped by them. Litigation has been about liability for cloud seeding. When modifiers and landowners do become involved in lawsuits about atmospheric water rights, there will be formidable problems of proof by the claimant to establish that his efforts caused the waters in controversy to be available. Laying claim to specific amounts of water harvested by past cloud seeding will, however, be easier than protecting the cloud seeder in court from future interference with new waters that he will produce. There is no guarantee that atmospheric conditions will repeat themselves so that future cloud seeding will bring about results similar to past weather-modification efforts.

No state statute thus far enacted provides guidelines which judges may follow in allocating atmospheric waters. It would seem, though, that inherent in all of the legislation concerning weather changing is the implied assumption that the modifier will receive the benefits of what he has brought about. This unstated policy might well be relied upon by the judiciary in recognizing in modifiers legal right to waters developed by them. The courts would still have to determine when a modifier would become entitled to a water right, duration of the interest, and quantity of water included within the right.

Landowner Rights. The principal theory of water law employed in the common-law world today is that of riparian rights—rights to waters on and under the surface of the owner's land.[11] The logic of riparian rights could be invoked by landowners to claim the benefits of weather-modification activities performed by or paid for by other persons. The landowner might assert that the clouds over his land and their water content are his property. Other persons seeking to harvest the atmospheric water would be meddlers who would not derive any property right from their activities.

In three instances of weather-modification litigation judges have spoken on the matter of landowner rights in the atmosphere. In Jeff Davis County, Texas, ranchmen sought to enjoin cloud seeding by weather modifiers who were employed by a large number of farmers to conduct a hail-suppression program. The ranchers claimed and the trial judge found that the seeding retarded rainfall upon the plaintiffs'

185

properties. Temporary injunctive relief was granted and upheld by the Court of Civil Appeals in *Southwest Weather Research, Inc. v. Rounsaville* and *Southwest Weather Research, Inc. v. Duncan,* in which the opinions said the landowner has a right to "such precipitation as Nature designs to bestow . . . to such rainfall as may come from clouds over his own property that Nature, in her caprice, may provide."[12]

In tune with the Southwest Weather Research cases is the view expressed by a Pennsylvania judge in *Pennsylvania Natural Weather Association v. Blue Ridge Weather Modification Association,* where he noted that "every landowner has a property right in the clouds and the water in them."[13] The judge further indicated that this right was subject to "weather modification activities undertaken under . . . governmental authority" while the private modifier has no right "to determine for himself what his needs are and produce those needs by artificial means to the prejudice and detriment of his neighbors."[14]

During the infancy of scientific weather modification, New York City employed a meteorologist to seed clouds in order to increment rainfall over watersheds where city water works reservoirs were located. The owners of a Catskill resort brought an action to secure an order barring the seeding. The trial judge in *Slutsky v. City of New York* stated flatly that property owners "clearly have no vested property rights in the clouds or the moisture therein"—at least, as against the water needs of New York City.[15]

The precedent value of the pronouncements from these opinions is diminished not only by the fact of their contradiction with each other, but also because the cases in which they were uttered involved only the narrow issue of the right of landowners to obtain an injunction against seeding. Both the Pennsylvania and New York judges denied injunctive relief, because the plaintiffs did not produce evidence that they had in fact been harmed. In the Texas case evidence of injury and causation was found to be sufficient, but the trial court relied heavily upon lay testimony of the ranchers.

Further lawsuits on landowner rights could well consider the distinction between surface waters in watercourses and underground waters in aquifers and the variant paths taken by atmospheric waters in "flowing" through the skies. The riparian doctrine does not well fit the different physical setting. Also judges should develop reasons why landowners should (or should not) be entitled to unmodified weather or to water produced by the efforts of other persons.

Apart from their arguments to ownership of atmospheric water resources, landowners where rain or snow falls or where water flows have a strong practical position with regard to such waters. If the landowner uses the water, the burden is then on the modifier to prove that the use was improper because the waters were derived from weather-modification activity. The modifier may have a great deal of difficulty in proving his case.

Redistribution of Losses

State courts have been dealing with the law of liability since the founding of the country. Their expertise is born of this long experience. Payment for losses through the mechanism of the state court system is a strategy for state regulation of weather modification that has a great deal to commend itself. Judges are experienced in the matter of redistributing losses resulting from the interaction of persons and groups in our society.

Development of the law of liability has, however, been very slowly accomplished. In the hundreds of years prior to the industrial revolution, only glimmerings of the law of negligence had evolved; but in the nineteenth century the pace did not pick up with the coming of modern technological advances.[16] In spite of that, judicial building of the law of liability takes time. The time lag may inhibit modification efforts by persons who do not know what legal norms may be applied to their cloud-seeding activities.

The use of the jury for fact-finding provided a means of obtaining a community evaluation of what had taken place. So long as the problems involved were within the normal experience of the average juror, employment of twelve men good and true provided a sound method for giving the community a voice in redistribution of losses. However, when jurors are called upon to cope with problems of a scientific and technological nature, they are dealing with matters beyond the range of experience of society in general. It is therefore not surprising that in *Adams v. California,* a case involving claims by flood victims against a public utility and its weather modifier asserting that the defendants had added to the magnitude of the flood, counsel for both plaintiffs and defendants agreed to waive a jury.[17]

Even when the matter is being determined by a judge, as has been the case in most weather-modification lawsuits, the problem of lack of continuity of experience remains.[18] Judges can educate themselves to understand the issues involved in storm and precipitation modification-liability problems, but an individual judge will likely handle only a few lawsuits of this nature during his career. Instead, they will be passed around among judges at large; there will be no continuity in experience in dealing with the problems at hand. The very thin number of lawsuits to date manifests something of this problem. No judge has yet been called upon to cope with more than one round of weather-modification litigation.

Thus far there have been very few lawsuits involving weather-alteration activities. The sporadic nature of legal activities here almost inevitably leads to overemphasis upon the few cases decided. Consequently, the mistakes in these cases can carry unusual weight in shaping future development of the law. In many other areas of liability litigation, the volume of cases is great enough that there can be a balancing of erroneous decisions by those determinations which seem to be more legally defensible. Such is not necessarily the case in the area of weather modification.

Before going further to examine judicial application of liability theories and defenses, it should be determined whether there will in fact be such losses. In the area of storm modification it is clear that some types of activity will involve economic losses to certain persons. Changing the track of a hurricane could lead to devastation of an area.[19] Hail suppression improperly performed may lead to loss of precipitation. In the *Southwest Weather Research* cases this was alleged.[20] There was lay testimony to this effect, although scientific evidence seems to support the proposition that hail modification properly performed does not diminish precipitation.[21] Lightning suppression conceivably could cause redistribution of precipitation, and this could result in economic losses to persons who would have had more or less precipitation over specific areas.[22] Even with fog dissipation there could be losers, although normally the effects are so localized that it takes quite a stretch of the imagination to find anyone really being hurt.[23]

In the field of precipitation modification there is also loss potential. There can be shifts in the amount, timing, and intensity of precipitation.[24] This can have not only direct effects, but can also affect runoff patterns.[25] It can also affect access to areas.[26]

Assuming that there will be losses, the next problem is proof in court of such losses. So far no claimant seeking damages has satisfactorily explained in court that weather-modification activities proximately caused losses for which he has sought compensation. In the *Southwest Weather* cases a temporary injunction was granted, but there was no proof of losses made on which compensation could be based.[27] In the *Pennsylvania Natural Weather Association* case, injunctive relief was denied. There was no proof that loss had been caused.[28] *Slutsky v. City of New York* was another case in which relief was denied because the plaintiff had not proven his case.[29] In *Adams v. California* the plaintiffs did not establish any causal relationship between cloud seeding in the Sierras and the flood damages suffered by the downstream claimants.[30] It is this difficulty of proving loss, as well as the likelihood that there have been very few individual losses of an economic nature caused by weather modification, that has limited the number of cases brought to court.

It is ironical that as weather modifiers improve their techniques, they will be opening themselves to the potential of a greater number of lawsuits and more success on the part of claimants. Plaintiffs will be able to utilize records from the modifiers to prove causation.[31] So as the science improves and its instrumentation is perfected, losses will become easier to prove and the number of lawsuits is likely to increase.

Assuming that there are losses and that these can be established by evidence acceptable in court, the next issue is the extent to which the losses should be compensated. Suggestions have been made that at least some of the losses from weather modification are the inevitable price of technological development.[32] We may not care for the raucous sounds of modern life, the uglification of the world in which we live, or the spoilation of our environment; but the law seldom compensates us for these undeniable losses. Perhaps some of the inconvenience and even economic loss resulting from weather modification should also be considered damnum absque injuria. This is not to say that all persons suffering loss from weather-modification undertakings should be satisfied with an explanation that they are paying part of the cost of living in a technological society. Those persons who have been flooded, who have suffered drought, or who have undergone the rigors of a storm that has artificially been made more damaging should be permitted to recover.

If we decide that those persons with provable losses (or at least some of them) should be compensated, we are left to determine the means by which compensation may be forthcoming. The law of liability furnishes us with a number of different theories which could be employed. These are subject to various defenses, and such losses can be shifted by insurance and indemnification.

Liability Law. The difficulty with employing present liability theories as a means for judicial control over weather modification is that anyone's theory is about as good or as bad as the next person's. In the legal periodical literature in this area, there is no agreement as to what theory or theories the courts should impose here.[33] Litigation generally has followed a shotgun approach. Counsel for claimants have asserted every possible theory they could think of.[34] The problem is that there are too many theories in the lawyer's bag of tricks.

From the point of view of the claimant, perhaps the most popular approach would be to employ some "no-fault" theory—absolute liability, liability without fault, ultrahazardous activity or abnormally dangerous activity.[35] This approach minimizes problems of proof. The claimant does not need to establish that the modifier intended to do any harm or that he fell below any standard of care. However, liability is not automatic under a no-fault theory. It is necessary to establish that the modifier acted, that the claimant was injured, and that there was a causal relationship between the activity and the injury. Moreover, it must be proven that the weather-modification activity involved was the sort that gives rise to liability without fault.

Pennsylvania and West Virginia have legislated that cloud seeding which causes storms or droughts is the kind of activity which gives rise to no-fault liability.[36] On the other hand, Texas has enacted the rule that no type of weather-modification activity, if it is properly licensed, would give rise to absolute liability.[37] Perhaps the courts will treat different types of modification differently. They might rule that severe storm modification involves such high potential risk as to give rise to absolute liability. They might decide that rainfall augmentation is not so dangerous an activity as to be deemed ultrahazardous. No one can tell at this time what course the courts will chart. They ought not to prejudge the issues and lump all types of weather modification and all kinds of activities into one category or the other.

Theories of fault as a basis for weather-modifier liability would all require proof of the activity, proof of loss, demonstration of a causal relationship, and proof of fault.[38] A negligence approach would require the plaintiff to establish that the defendant did not live up to the standard of care required of him. The standard expected of modifiers is a matter with which the courts have not yet dealt; but following general tort principles, it would seem that a modifier would be free from any responsibility if he acted as carefully as would a reasonable, prudent modifier. In other words, the standard would be that of the industry.[39]

190

Proof of violation of this professional standard could be a very difficult undertaking for claimants. This in turn could lead to adoption of a no-fault system.

In most cases trespass would not be a sound approach. Neither the intrusion of the delivery vehicle into the airspace, of the seeding material, or of the resultant precipitation should normally justify a lawsuit; there usually would be no substantial interference with the use and enjoyment of the land below.[40] Of course, if a modifier intrudes upon the land of another in setting up equipment, he could quite likely be held responsible for such a trespass.

Nuisance is a catchall in the law of torts which may provide an avenue for determining weather-modifier liabilities. Its attractiveness results from the fact that the courts sitting on nuisance cases are called upon to balance the various interests involved as part of the determination of whether liability should follow.[41] This type of balancing act led the New York court in the *Slutsky* case to rule in favor of the city and its weather modifier.[42] It led the Pennsylvania court in the *Natural Weather Association* case to rule in favor of the claimant. That court, however, noted that should a governmental entity undertake the activity there, it might rule differently because of the public interest involved.[43]

Defenses. Under present liability law, a defendant will prevail if the plaintiff fails to prove his case; additionally, he may win even where the plaintiff does prove his case, if the defendant can prove a defense. Where a governmental entity is the modifier, the defense of governmental immunity might be employed. There has been considerable erosion in this defense, and it is not necessarily available to modifiers acting under contract with governmental entities.[44] Moreover, governments are limited by constitutional requirements so that there must be compensation for their activities which are deemed to constitute a taking of private property.[45]

Consent by the claimant is likely to be an important defense.[46] Although it would be impossible for a modifier to obtain consent from all persons who might in some way be affected by his undertaking, advance consent may be obtained from those persons most likely to be directly affected. Thus an airport authority involved in fog modification could secure advance consent to its fog seeding from neighboring property owners if the authority feels they will be sufficiently affected to give the agency legal troubles. Private or governmental property owners in high mountain country where additional snows would be deposited from cap cloud seeding could be asked in advance to give their consent. Frequently consent would involve financial compensation. But this may be cheaper than waiting until after the losses to make adjustment for them.

Conceivably in an emergency situation the defense of privilege of necessity might be employed.[47] Where fire danger is great, suppression of lightning through weather modification, even though it may result in some losses to neighbors, may be privileged. The same approach could be applied to hail modification or emergency increases in precipitation to meet problems like that faced by the City of New York when it undertook the cloud-seeding program that led to the *Slutsky* case.

Insurance and Indemnification. A recent questionnaire sponsored by the Weather Modification Association indicates that thus far weather modifiers have experienced a minimal amount of difficulty with liability suits.[48] Based on these findings, private insurance should be available at comparatively low rates. Some persons and organizations, however, have experienced difficulty in obtaining the kind of insurance coverage they want and feel they need; and many modifiers feel that rates are higher than they ought to be. This has led to agitation from some quarters for a governmentally created insurance program.[49]

Should the present system of private insurance be continued, it would likely be administered by the state-court systems. They would, as they do generally in the field of liability insurance, interpret the clauses in the insurance contracts and oversee their enforcement. Liability-insurance contracts used in weather-modification cases read substantially like the regular automobile-liability policy; consequently, the courts have amassed a good deal of experience with the provisions of these contracts.

Any change from the present state of the law would have an impact upon present insurance practices. Should the law be clarified and should it become clearer to insurance companies that their losses will not be great, rates ought to decrease. On the other hand, should causation become easier to establish with resultant recoveries by plaintiffs, insurance rates will reflect the situation.

Weather modifiers through indemnification agreements with their sponsors have provided for shifting losses. Both governmental and private sponsors frequently require the modifiers to indemnify them for any losses suffered.[50] These indemnification contracts are subject to judicial scrutiny both as to their validity and interpretation.

Judicial Enforcement of Legislative Enactments

There is a need for legislation to clarify the law of weather modification. Legislation of one sort or another has been enacted in 29 states.[51] This includes those states in which the primary weather-modification experimentation and operations have taken place. But these laws for the most part have very little to say about the major issues arising from weather-modification activities. In some states they amount to nothing more than an official pronouncement that weather modification is a subject concerning which there is legislative interest.[52] Some jurisdictions have provided for weather-modification regulation through licensing, requirements concerning operational permits, and reporting.[53] Yet no state has enacted laws stating anything concerning ownership rights, and only three have had specific legislation regarding liability.[54] Should the current interest in weather modification continue, it is quite possible that further legislation on the state level might be forthcoming. Future statutes should be more all-encompassing than are the present enactments. Such legislation could set forth the basic principles of weather-modification law and leave the courts the power to interpret these rules and enforce them.

Two major areas in which legislative guidelines would assist the courts are redistribution of losses and allocation of benefits. Statutory provision concerning liability could range from immunization of cloud seeders from suit for losses caused by them to imposition of liability upon them without regard to any fault on their part. The first course has been followed in the Australian state of Victoria. The law there provides that no "person carrying out rain-making operations authorized by the Minister under this Act shall in any way be liable in respect of any loss or damage caused by or arising out of the precipitation . . . in consequences of the rain-making operations so carried out."[55] This immunity for licensed rain-making activities would tend to encourage such cloud seeding. No threat of liability, ruinous or slight, would hang over the head of the meteorologist. There should, however, be some sort of remedy available to persons suffering from rainshadow, unwanted precipitation and floods where such phenomena have been caused by weather changes. Citizens deprived of compensation for losses likely would seek anticloud seeding laws.

Rather than exempting certain types of modification activities from liability, state laws could stipulate that persons adversely affected by cloud seeding could recover only if they establish that their injuries were caused intentionally or through negligent conduct on the part of the meteorologist. The Texas provision concerning exemption of all licensed activities from the category of ultrahazardous activities is a possibility here.[56] Legislation of this sort is neither self-interpreting nor self-enforcing. The judiciary would be called upon to perform these functions.

The Pennsylvania and West Virginia weather-modification statutes state that "any licensee who causes a drought . . . shall compensate farmers for damages."[57] On its face this provision would appear to require only that the claimant establish that the modifier conducted activities, that there was a drought which injured him, and that there was a causal connection. The law's apparent meaning would seem to rule out any need on the part of the claimant to establish that the modifier fell below the standard of care of a reasonable, prudent man or that he intended any harm to the plaintiff. Although these laws delegate the judicial power to an administrative agency, the same power of interpretation could be given to a court. The judge might not read the statute to grant absolute liability. Other legislative enactments could leave similar problems of interpretation.

When courts administer statutory enactments, they have the advantage of having before them a set of authoritative guidelines. Assume that the legislature has determined the rules for ownership of runoff from snowmaking. It is merely up to the courts to interpret the legislation, find the facts involved, and apply those facts to the interpreted legal norms. Courts have long experience in legislative interpretation, and state judges could doubtless do this in a satisfactory fashion. Also, state courts are competent in applying facts to the law at hand. The basic difficulty is fact-finding. Whether this chore is accomplished by judges or by juries, they are dealing in an area requiring scientific understanding—a kind of understanding which they may not in fact possess. Even legislative guidelines would probably not have saved the Texas court from reaching an erroneous conclusion of fact in the *Southwest Weather Research* cases.[58] Also, they probably would not have prevented the Pennsylvania court from being carried away with notions of the potential danger of weather modification in the *Pennsylvania Natural Weather Association* case.[59] Indeed, in the Pennsylvania case there was a background of legislative enactment which tended to color the proceedings.

By and large, judicial enforcement of legislative enactment would be effective only as a matter of post-activity regulation. Private parties or governmental officials, if they were so empowered, would need to institute legal proceedings by presenting to the courts claims concerning activities that had already taken place. Even in seeking injunctive relief, they would have to satisfy requirements concerning "case or controversy."[60] None of this would help much as a means of pre-activity regulation. This would be much better handled by administrative control. In fact, it is much more likely that states would leave this area of regulation for administrative control. The bureaucracy would flesh out the legislative enactments rather than the judiciary.

Administrative Control

There are obvious advantages to delegating authority from the legislature to an administrative agency to carry out a weather-modification regulatory program. Among these are (1) administrative expertise, (2) continuity of the administrative regulatory program, (3) flexibility, and (4) completeness of control.

In theory at least, administrative agencies are headed and staffed by experts. Thus a weather-modification regulatory agency would have as its head or heads persons who have expert knowledge about cloud seeding and its consequences. Appropriations for the operations of such an agency would be large enough to permit it to employ meteorologists, hydrologists, engineers, and other technical staff members who could carry out its regulatory program with the highest degree of professional excellence.

The difficulty is that not always are experts appointed or elected as agency heads. Frequently, and this is particularly true on the state level, selection is a matter of politics in which qualifications of the commissioner or other bureaucrat is a secondary consideration. Moreover, typically these agencies have not been provided with sufficient funds to employ enough high-grade professionals to carry out their program in an effective fashion. Nevertheless, an administrative staff usually provides more technical expertise than can be found in a courtroom.

When judges are called upon to determine matters of liability caused by weather-modification activities, they deal with such cases on a very intermittent basis. Thus they do not have an opportunity to provide for continuity of a regulatory program. An administrative agency is a continuing and ongoing entity which has constant contact with the fields involved. It can promote and react to any developments, for example, in storm modification or in the area of streamflow augmentation. This possibility of making and following long-term plans makes administrative control by state-regulatory agencies a very attractive possibility. Even though such agencies are subject to occasional changes

195

of direction and political upheaval, their programs basically have a type of continuous supervision not found in judicial regulation.[61]

Administrative agencies may become afflicted with ossification and hardening of the arteries. They can become rigid and set in their ways.[62] But usually they are a flexible means of providing public control over areas of human activity. This is particularly true when legislative guidelines are sufficiently broad to permit an agency to adopt shifts in position. Thus, where technological advancement in cloud seeding dictates the need for change in agency policy, most state weather-modification agencies would be in a position to provide flexible legal response.

As has been indicated above, judicial control over weather modification is incomplete. Administrative control can be very broad. Agencies can be delegated rule-making powers. They can obtain quasi-judicial power enabling them to adjudicate disputes, and they can be and have been given licensing and other supervisory powers. Questions have been raised concerning the advisability of putting into the hands of a group of governmental employees such complete control. In an effort to alleviate this problem, our legislators have circumscribed administrative control by limiting the powers delegated and otherwise exercising legislative oversight and by making possible judicial review of administrative activity. Also, executive control over administrative agencies has been utilized.[63]

Professional Regulation

Administrative control may take the form of professional regulation; in other words, state law may provide for licensing of personnel involved in cloud-seeding operations. Licensing prior to performance of operations by the licensee is an effective strategy for regulation of weather modification; but who should perform the licensing function? Should this power be delegated to an existing state agency, a specialized weather-modification agency created by the state, or to a special weather-modification division within an existing agency? All three approaches have been utilized by states.[64] Also, there may be participation by private organizations in certifying competency. Such groups as the American Meteorological Society or the Weather Modification Association could play a role here.[65]

Licensing criteria differ from state to state. Generally, though, there are three types of qualifications: licensees should have technical competency.[66] They should be persons of professional integrity.[67]

They should also have the financial resources to carry out projects successfully.[68] Unfortunately, irrelevancies have a tendency to creep in as unnecessary criteria. A classic illustration in the field of weather modification is the Wyoming requirement that a weather-modification license applicant be previously licensed by the State of Wyoming as a "registered professional engineer."[69]

Professional licensing is most effective when the appropriate agency is empowered to determine whether applicants in fact possess the requisite qualifications set forth by the statute or by administrative regulation. Some existing provisions concerning licensing do not, however, delegate such power. Applicants merely list their alleged qualifications; but no one passes on whether they are competent, honest, and solvent.[70] Laws of this sort are essentially mere registration provisions and have only limited usefulness.

If administrators do possess the power to pass on professional qualifications, there should be some guidance given them concerning the means by which they will determine whether applicants measure up to the criteria. Judging competence is ticklish business. Not all meteorologists are qualified to perform all kinds of weather-modification operations. Consequently the receipt of a college degree in the field of meteorology does not assure competence. Neither does long experience in one field of weather modification—say snowmaking from cap clouds—guarantee that the modifier would also be competent to seed hurricanes. Examination of applicants may be no more effective than looking to college credentials or practical experience.

Licensing should take into account differences among types of weather modification. Perhaps licenses could be limited to specific types of activities and issued only upon demonstration of competence in those areas. Also, there are differences between states and areas in the country; hence, snowmaking in the Upper Colorado River Basin is not the same kind of operation as warm fog dispersal in California or snowmaking in New England. There might be some justification for requiring licensing in each of the states where a modifier operates. Of course, the basic principles of cloud physics do not change with political boundaries.

In any weather-alteration operation many people will be involved who need not be licensed. The truck driver, the pilot, the radar operator, the stenographer—none of these people need to have professional licenses as weather modifiers. However, where more than one person is actually involved in the modification activity, more than one person ought to be licensed. It is not enough to have one licensee fronting for the entire operation. The issue is whether the individual is involved directly enough in modification to be required to be licensed.

Operational Regulation

In several states operational permits are required in addition to or in lieu of professional licensing.[71] The Arizona law has a section reading:

> Any individual or corporation who proposes to operate weather control or cloud modification projects or attempts to artificially induce rainfall shall, before engaging in any such operation, make application to the State Land Department for a license to engage in the particular weather control or cloud modification operation contemplated.[72]

This provision does not, however, undertake to define what constitutes a "weather control" project. Air conditioning the mall of a large shopping center is one species of weather control with which the law may not be concerned. But what of fog dissipation and smudging citrus groves? The legislature likely did not even consider the possibility of fog in Arizona, and it specifically exempted from the law use of weather-modification equipment "owned by the owner, lessee or licensee of real property used for agricultural purposes on the property for his exclusive benefit."[73] The problem nevertheless remains: demanding operational permits without adequate definition of what constitutes "weather modification" leaves areas of uncertainty. Statutes should spell out whether they embrace unintentional modification or not, and what types of intended efforts to change the weather are covered.

Operational-permit requirements pose many issues similar to those raised in matters of professional licensing. Are projects merely registered, or do agencies have the power to pass on whether they will or will not be undertaken? What should be the criteria for issuance of such permits? What procedure should be followed to determine whether applicants meet the requirements for receipt of a permit? Should all types of weather-modification activities be handled in the same fashion, or should seeding for some purposes be treated differently? Some laws allow for shortcut procedures in emergencies.[74] Fog-modification permits might well be handled by an agency other than the body dispensing rainmaking authorization.

One of the reasons for requiring an operational permit is to give the general public notice of impending modification activities and to provide persons affected an opportunity to present their views before a decision is made concerning whether an operation conforms to legal requirements. Notice requirements in most states speak in terms of notice by publication.[75] This is not always an effective means for informing the public. Some states have statutory provisions calling for hearings at which the public can present their views.[76] Full-scale hearings on cloud-seeding permit applications could become onerous both to the applicants and the agencies. Nevertheless there should be procedures through which the positions of persons other than permit applicants can be received and considered.

Some of the state agencies require reporting weather-modification activities.[77] Reporting is one means of ascertaining compliance with permit and professional licensing requirements. It also provides for acquisition of information which might be helpful in development of the field of weather modification. States vary as to what information must be reported and as to whether the modifier must evaluate his project. A line should be drawn between seeking too little and burdening modifiers by requiring reporting of unnecessary information.

In the absence of a requirement for centralized reporting on a federal level, state reporting requirements are filling a void in the field of weather-modification regulation.[78] Reporting to state as well as federal officials could become burdensome; but even if the federal requirement is reimposed, state-regulatory agencies have a legitimate interest in receiving reports of activities. Information obtained through reporting helps them keep advised about compliance with state law.

Contractual Control

Administrative regulation of weather modification can be accomplished through the power of the purse. A state, acting through appropriate agencies, can become the proprietor of weather-modification operations. State proprietorship could be organized to use government employees to operate projects or to hire contractors to run them. Should weather-modification activities be performed by government personnel, the state (or its subdivisions) as proprietor would control such in-house efforts. To the extent that state and local governments would finance weather-modification activities performed by outside groups, they would be able to have extensive power over the activities of such organizations. Within certain constitutional bounds, they could set the conditions of employment of their contractors, and they could

199

use their very considerable powers of financial persuasion to see that the conditions were met.[79]

The laws of some jurisdictions provide specifically for participation of state agencies in weather-modification activities. For example, the Nevada Department of Conservation and Natural Resources "may conduct weather modification research programs."[80] And in New Hampshire any "agency of the state may, with the approval of the Governor and Council . . . engage in . . . weather modification . . . ."[81] In other states interpretation of powers given to state departments may permit them to employ weather modifiers to help them perform their statutory duties. Thus an aeronautics commission may have power to hire meteorologists to clear airport fogs if it possesses authority to establish means of reducing hazards to airport operations.[82]

State regulation of weather modification by contract has certain advantages: (1) it is comparatively easy to administer; (2) it provides a means for raising funds which permits acquisition of the benefits which can be derived from employment of weather-modification techniques; and (3) it makes possible means of enforcing payment for weather-modification benefits.

When a governmental entity as a proprietor undertakes weather-modification activities, only a limited number of persons from the bureaucracy are required to fill overtly regulatory roles. The regulation will be more-or-less automatic on a sort of a "you do business with us our way" basis. Men who do business with the government will usually "turn square corners."[83]

Payment for state-supported weather modification can come from the general state treasury or from special funds. The states can delegate their taxing power and borrowing power to agencies or subdivisions. As illustrations of this, there are the provisions in the Dakotas for mill levies by counties.[84] There are also provisions by the portions of the Nebraska statute giving bonding power and taxing power to weather modification districts.[85] Existing state and local entities may also have access to such governmental powers. This makes it possible for them to accumulate larger sums of money to expend for weather-modification activities than may be possible through private means. However, it should be kept in mind that private organizations can and have raised adequate funds for some projects. Public utilities have financed snow-making.[86] Airlines have been responsible for work in supercooled fog dispersal and warm-fog dissipation.[87]

At some stage the beneficiaries of weather-modification activities

200

will bear at least part of the cost of state programs. Hail-suppression work in South Dakota has been paid for by mill levy upon the property owners in the area benefited.[88] Funds for payment of fog modifiers by airport authorities can be raised through use of the normal landing fees or fuel-tax exactions. Customers of irrigation districts can be required to pay for incremental water produced by snowmaking.

There is the problem of the freeloaders. Persons outside the counties raising funds for hail modification might also benefit from their expenditure. Moreover, even those who pay might be receiving a partial subsidy. Weather modification has been heavily subsidized through governmental payments for experimentation and development. Of course, in response to this, it might be noted that the community as a whole ought to bear part of the cost, because the public at large has benefited.

Allocation of Benefits and Redistribution of Losses

The operational permit system brings about some allocation of benefits from weather-modification activities. Exercise of administrative discretion in issuing or denying permits acts as a device for granting or withholding the potential benefits from storm modification. The problem is more complicated in connection with precipitation management. This is particularly true of weather modification designed to increase runoff. The mere grant of a permit to seed clouds does not necessarily guarantee a downstream water user on whose behalf the weather modification is undertaken that he will receive any benefits at all. He may have to contend with upstream riparians for the right to use the water.

Many states, including all of those in the West, have adopted a permit system for distribution of ground and surface water resources.[89] These existing water resources administrative agencies may well be authorized under their present legislative charters to allocate runoff from weather-modification undertakings. A serious problem in fair distribution of such waters would be measurement. When the water-allocation agency is not the same state board as the weather-modification agency, there exists a potential for conflict between the two groups. In some jurisdictions, however, weather-modification administrative power is lodged in the state agency already empowered to allocate other water resources.[90] This solution is quite sensible in the area of precipitation management. However, water resources agencies may not be the proper place for administrative power to grant permits for storm modification.

201

Administrative agencies working on the state level could be given power to determine losses caused by weather-modification operations and to order payment of damages or suspension of operations. Legislation could provide a framework on which they would judge whether losses are compensable. They could consider whether the modifier fell below the standard of professional care, whether the cloud seeding caused the losses complained of, and the extent of damages brought about by the modification activities. Expert administrators well-versed in the technology could render justice in an effective manner.

Pennsylvania's most recent weather modification statute (which has been copied by West Virginia) provides for administrative control over damage compensation. It stipulates that:

> Any licensee who causes a drought as determined by the board shall compensate farmers for damages. Any licensee who by causing heavy downpours or storms which shall cause damage to lands as determined by the board shall compensate farmers and property owners for such damages.[91]

Although this statute is ambiguous, it has the germ of a good idea. Weather-modification boards could be authorized to hear cases between private individuals or between the government and private claimants. A multitude of existing state boards in other areas of economic regulation possess similar powers and perform their functions effectively.

Advantages and Disadvantages of State Regulation

Regulation of weather modification may be the kind of undertaking which the federal government can perform more effectively than can state governments. The federal government acting either as proprietor or regulator of weather modification possesses many advantages the states do not. In spite of this, we now find ourselves in a situation where the federal government has talked a lot about weather modification but has done little by way of regulation. The states, on the other hand, have enacted regulatory measures. There are some advantages as well as disadvantages in state weather-modification control.

Several states now have almost 20 years of experience in regulating weather modification.[92] Others, while their regulatory programs are comparatively new, have entered the field and are gaining useful insight into regulatory problems. Thus, one of the principal advantages now found in state regulation is that the states in which modification activities are being carried out have regulatory programs.

One of the benefits of our federalized system of government is that the experience of each of the states is available for use as a model by the other states. An experiment in regulation in one state which succeeds can be copied in other states; a failure will warn other states against attempting to reach the same goals by the same means. States can undertake a variety of programs differing from state to state; and from all this mix, the best can be selected.[93]

There are parts of the country in which there is no present need for regulation of weather modification quite simply because no weather modification is taking place. States in such areas have not enacted legislation. On the other hand, it is in those jurisdictions where modifiers are the most active that we find the most active regulators.

State-regulatory agencies have at least the potential of being closer to those persons subjected to regulation than do federal agencies. Also, they are more susceptible to influence from the public at large. Thus the voice of those affected by regulation may be more readily felt when regulation is undertaken on the state level.

The principal disadvantages of state weather-modification regulation are those imposed by nature. Cloud systems recognize no state boundaries. Storms skip willy-nilly from state to state. Precipitation and runoff ignore political boundaries. The consequence is that regulation by individual jurisdictions can only begin to cope with problems which are interstate in character.

There are also political disadvantages in state regulation. State legislatures are susceptible to lobbying. Unfortunately, in at least three states the legislatures have responded to pressure with enactment of laws designed to end weather modification. Maryland for several years has had on its books an outright prohibition of weather modification within its boundaries.[94] Pennsylvania and West Virginia have statutes which are obviously hostile to weather modification. Indeed, they flatly prohibit lightning suppression.[95] Moreover, they establish high financial-responsibility requirements and authorize the imposition of very severe penalties.[96]

Options

Control of weather modification need not necessarily be accomplished in any particular manner. The various options available each have their strengths and weaknesses. Selection of one over the others might result in greater advances in the field or might hinder development; but no matter which option comes into being, it is quite likely that scientific, rather than legal, considerations will dictate advancement.

Federal Pre-emption

It is possible that the federal government may completely pre-empt the field of weather modification legal control. This would, of course, minimize the problems of state boundaries, of coordination with states, and of conflicts among the states. It is, however, the kind of solution which may have little political appeal. Some role is likely to be reserved for the states.

Federal-State Coordination and Cooperation

Most regulatory programs primarily carried out by the federal government have not been the sort that have pre-empted the field; rather, the states have been left a role sometimes large, sometimes small. Thus in regulation of transportation, labor relations, and communications, the states have important regulatory powers even though there is federal primacy.

Should a federal weather-modification agency be created, professional licensing and granting of permits could very well be entrusted to it. However, matters such as liability and property rights might be left to state determination. The federal program, in other words, need not necessarily occupy the entire field.

In many federal programs there is provision for cooperation with the states in carrying out regulation. Thus the states are called upon to submit water pollution control standards for federal approval.[97] Also, state highway departments expend federal funds in construction of roads but must measure up to federal standards.[98] This kind of cooperation in regulation or operation of weather-modification projects is quite possible. Currently the state of Washington is acting as a contractor with the federal government in a snowmaking project.[99] Future federal-state cooperation could follow a similar pattern.

Reciprocal Legislation

The problem of political boundaries which ignore meteorological and hydrological realities can be alleviated by states enacting reciprocal and cooperative legislation. Pennsylvania and West Virginia have a provision which takes into account the law of their neighbors. It provides that nothing in their statute ". . .shall authorize any person to carry out a cloud seeding operation from Pennsylvania [and West Virginia] to seed in another state where such cloud seeding is prohibited."[100] This obviously was enacted with the Maryland prohibition in mind.

Colorado law stipulates that persons may not carry on weather-modification operations within Colorado "for the purpose of affecting weather in any other state which prohibits such operations to be carried on in that state for the benefit of Colorado or its inhabitants."[101] New Mexico, whose statute followed that of Colorado, has a similar provision which obviously is a response to the Colorado enactment.[102] The New Mexico and Colorado laws are a type of negative-reciprocal legislation.

States could stipulate that they would recognize licenses granted by other states, that they would permit persons authorized to seed in other states to bring about effects in their jurisdiction, or they might recognize ownership of runoff in their states as vested in persons who seeded clouds in other states.

Interstate Compacts

Multistate agreements might relate to cloud seeding. Public officials of neighboring states could enter into informal agreements concerning weather-modification activities that have an impact in two or more states. Regional planning agencies have been established in this fashion.[103] Such organizations are born with a minimum of red tape but possess little power to make decisions that are binding upon all parties concerned.

The interstate compact is a mechanism through which real regulatory powers can be given to an agency whose authority crosses over state lines. During an earlier period in the nation's history compacts usually related to boundary disputes. Now, however, there has been a shift to use of the interstate compact as a device to cope with problems which single states cannot and Congress will not control. Numerous interstate authorities have been created by compacts. They have come into being as the result of the irrelevancy of state boundaries to the problems arising in the area which they cross.[104]

Thus far no efforts have been made to create interstate authorities for weather-alteration regulation. But there are existing compacts which may have a bearing upon the legal ramifications of weather modification. Arguments have been advanced contending that some compacts which allocate waters of interstate streams may be interpreted to include division of water produced by cloud seeding.[105] Also it might be asserted that an agency like the Port of New York Authority may have power to engage in fog dissipation, or that other interstate agencies can undertake rainmaking operations.[106]

In both the fields of water-resources management and air-pollution control states have entered into compacts which could serve as models for agreements creating weather-modification interstate authorities.[107] Thus, acting under the authority of The Clean Air Act of 1963 gave congressional consent to compacts for prevention and control of air pollution and establishment of enforcement agencies.[108] Acting under the authority of this Act Indiana and Illinois entered into a compact setting up an interstate pollution-control agency with enforcement powers.[109] Its provisions could be a source of information for draftsmen of a weather-modification control compact.

The process of creation of a compact is one in which the interests of the states involved and the nation can be considered. The legislature of each state possesses a veto power. Compacts are frequently compromises between the state officials of the jurisdictions negotiating them. But should the elected legislators of a state feel that the agreement does not adequately protect the interests of their constituents, they can reject the compact. Congress, however, can assert considerable influence upon the states through its power to approve or disapprove a compact.[110] And federal administrative officials have at times asserted that federal benefits urgently needed for projects desired by the states involved will be contingent upon their reaching a proper compromise by compact. By such means was the agreement of Arizona to the Colorado River Compact acquired.[111]

Although not all interstate compacts make provision for an administrative structure for their operation, it is now common for compacts to create or establish the means for setting up such an interstate body.[112] In the field of weather modification, an interstate agency could be given not only operational authority but also could be delegated regulatory and supervisory power. Such an operating authority could become unresponsive to the states which authored it, but probably could be controlled by the federal government.[113]

A drawback to use of the compact device is the possibility of inflexibility. Unless a compact so provides, a state may not be able to withdraw from the arrangement. Congress may not be competent to revoke its approval, but Congress can enact legislation conflicting with compact provisions if the agreement involves a subject about which that body can legislate.[114] That is the case with weather modification. Also the states and Congress could negotiate a new compact with provisions differing from those of the old one.

State Primacy

Except for federal proprietorship of weather-modification activities,

206

there is today state primacy of weather-modification regulation. There is no doubt that this system has its defects, but the fact that we have used this as our legal framework for weather modification testifies to its advantages. It is fair to say that this system in general has not unduly hampered the growth of weather modification. Unfortunately, neither has it fostered the field; and that is what is needed.

Notes

1. "Weather modification" has been variously defined. The phrase "composition, behavior and dynamics" of the atmosphere comes from proposed federal legislation. H.R. 9212 and S. 373, 90th Cong., 1st sess. § 202(a) (1967). The regulations of the NSF requesting reports concerning modification of weather refer to (1) intentional efforts, (2) designed to modify the atmosphere and (3) through use of artificial means. The NSF rules list various substances as illustrations of materials that are dispersed to accomplish this purpose. 45 C.F.R. § 635.2 (1968), *as amended,* 33 Fed. Reg. 12654 (1968).

2. Development of practical techniques, equipment, and materials for seeding has been the subject of several conferences of Bureau of Reclamation weather-modification contractors. Office of Atmospheric Water Resources, *Proceedings: Skywater Conferences I-IV (1967-1969).* Improvement in the skills of weather changers can be traced through examination of the series of reports of the NSF on weather modification. National Science Foundation, *Weather Modification, First-Ninth Ann. Rep. (1960-1969).*

3. A. Chamberlain and L. Grant, *Weather Modification and Its Relationship to Environment,* Western Resources Conference Proceedings 69 (1967) pp. 74-75.

4. For reports on efforts to improve various aspects of our atmospheric environment, see D. Fuquay, *Weather Modification and Forest Fires,* in Ground Level Climatology 309 (1967) (lightning suppression); L.R. Schleusener, *Project Hailswath: Final Report* (1966) (hail suppression); Dep't of the Navy and Essa, *Project Stormfury,* Annual Report (for years 1965 through 1967) (hurricane modification); B. Beckwith, *Impacts of Weather on the Airline Industry: The Value of Fog Dispersal Programs* in Human Dimensions of Weather Modification 195, ed. W. Sewell (1966) (cold fog dispersal); Air Transport Assoc. of America, *Airline Warm Fog Dispersal Test Program at Sacramento,* California (1968) (warm fog dispersal).

5. C. Cooper and W. Jolly, Ecological Effects of Weather Modification: A Problem Analysis, Rep. to Bureau of Reclamation (May 1969); Ecological Soc'y of America, Ad Hoc Weather Working Group, *Biological Aspects of Weather Modification,* 47 Bull. Ecol. Soc'y Am. 39 (1966).

207

6. See Human Dimensions of the Atmosphere, ed. W. Sewell (1968); Human Dimensions of Weather Modification, ed. W. Sewell (1966).

7. A. Goodhart, *Precedent in English and Continental Law,* 50 L.Q. Rev. 40, 56 (1934).

8. See W. Hutchins, *Background and Modern Developments,* in 1 Waters and Water Rights § 18, ed. R. Clark (1967).

9. One authority has stated that:

> If one by his own efforts adds to the supply of water in a stream, he is entitled to the water which he has developed, even though an appropriator with a more senior priority might be without water. The reason for this rule is the obvious one that a priority relates only to the natural supply of the stream as of the time of appropriation.

J. Sax, Water Law: Cases and Commentary 225 (1965); see also R. Clark, *Background and Trends in Water Salvage Law,* in *Fifteenth Ann. Rocky Mountain Mineral Law Institute Proceedings* 421 (1969).

10. See Westmoreland and Cambria Natural Gas Co. v. DeWitt, 130 Pa. 235, 18 A. 724 (1889).

11. 4 Restatement of Torts, Scope Note 339-350 (1939).

12. 320 S.W.2d 211, 216 and 319 S.W.2d 940, 945 (Tex. Civ. App. 1958), *both aff'd sub nom.* Southwest Weather Research, Inc. v. Jones, 160 Tex. 104, 327 S.W.2d 417 (1959).

13. 44 Pa. D.&C.2d 749, 759-60 (C.P. Fulton County 1968).

14. Ibid. at 760.

15. 197 Misc. 730, 731, 97 N.Y.S.2d 238, 239 (Sup. Ct. 1950).

16. For a short history of the law of negligence, see W. Prosser, Handbook of the Law of Torts § 28 (3d ed. 1964).

17. No. 10112 (Super. Ct. Sutter County, Cal., April 6, 1954).

18. The jury was waived in the *Adams* case. In other instances judges were also called upon to make the factual determinations. See Slutsky v. City of New York, 197 Misc. 730, 97 N.Y.S.2d 238 (Sup. Ct. 1950); Pennsylvania *ex rel.* Township of Ayr v. Fulk, No. 53 (C.P. Fulton County, Pa., February 28, 1968); Pennsylvania Natural Weather Ass'n v. Blue Ridge Weather Modification Ass'n, 44 Pa. D.&C.2d 749 (C.P.

Fulton County 1968); and Southwest Weather Research, Inc. v. Rounsaville, 320 S.W.2d 211, and Southwest Weather Research, Inc. v. Duncan, 319 S.W.2d 940 (Tex. Civ. App. 1958), *both aff'd sub nom.* Southwest Weather Research, Inc. v. Jones, 160 Tex. 104, 327 S.W.2d 417 (1959).

19. See E. Morris, *The Law and Weather Modification*, 46 Bull. Am. Meteor. Soc'y 618 (1965), for a discussion of the legal ramifications of changing the track of a hurricane.

20. Southwest Weather Research, Inc. v. Rounsaville, 320 S.W.2d 211, and Southwest Weather Research, Inc. v. Duncan, 319 S.W.2d 940 (Tex. Civ. App. 1958), *both aff'd sub nom.* Southwest Weather Research, Inc. v. Jones, 160 Tex. 104, 327 S.W.2d 417 (1959).

21. National Science Foundation, Weather Modification 31 (Ninth Ann. Rep. 1968).

22. Lightning suppression efforts of the Forest Service involve seeding clouds with silver iodide. J. Barrows, "Weather Modification and the Prevention of Lightning-Caused Fires" in *Human Dimensions of Weather Modification* 169, 177, ed. W. Sewell (1966).

23. In discussing a warm fog-suppression operation, one meteorologist noted that "[a]t the present time, salt is being used for this purpose, but it is believed that the corrosion problems associated with sodium chloride are not acceptable and substitute materials will have to be used in the near future." Report by L. Davis to Weather Modification Ass'n Annual Meeting (February 17, 1969).

24. The Bureau of Reclamation planning document for atmospheric water-resources development contemplates achievement of operational-precipitation control on a regional basis. It projected the target date of 1980 for "a general capability for . . . enhancing, under favorable conditions, precipitation for direct use on lands and crops in most regions." Office of Atmospheric Water Resources, *Plan to Develop Technology for Increasing Water Yield from Atmospheric Sources* 50 (1966).

25. The only reported case concerning flooding alleged to have been induced by cloud seeding is Adams v. California, No. 10112 (Super. Ct. Sutter County, Cal., April 6, 1954). The case is discussed in E. Morris, *Preparation and Trial of Weather Modification Litigation*, in Weather Modification and the Law 163, ed. H. Taubenfeld (1968).

26. Plaintiffs have experienced difficulty in proving causation in cases outside the weather-modification field where they have claimed disruption of access. See Annot., 120 A.L.R. 896 (1939). The problems of

proof certainly would not be easier in an action against a weather modifier.

27. Southwest Weather Research, Inc. v. Rounsaville, 320 S.W.2d 211, and Southwest Weather Research, Inc. v. Duncan, 319 S.W.2d 940 (Tex. Civ. App. 1958), *both aff'd sub nom.* Southwest Weather Research, Inc. v. Jones, 160 Tex. 104, 327 S.W.2d 417 (1959).

28. Pennsylvania Natural Weather Ass'n v. Blue Ridge Weather Modification Ass'n, 44 Pa. D. and C. 749 (C.P. Fulton County 1968).

29. 197 Misc. 730, 97 N.Y.S.2d 238 (Sup. Ct. 1950).

30. No. 10112 (Super. Ct. Sutter County, Cal., April 6, 1954).

31. Rule 34 of the Federal Rules of Civil Procedure permits inspection and copying of an opposing party's nonprivileged records upon motion and a showing of good cause. Records required to be kept by statute are not usually privileged. L K. Davis, *Administrative Law Treatise* § *3.09 (1958).* A number of states already require record keeping. See discussion at note 77, infra. Seeking to obtain material which provides an evidentiary basis to establish the litigant's case constitutes good cause. See cases cited in 2A W. Barron and A. Hotlzoff, *Federal Practice and Procedure* § *796, n.62 (C. Wright Rev. Supp. 1967).* Most states have adopted rules of discovery parallel to Rule 34.

32. See, for example, P. King, *Comments as to Legal Aspects of Weather Modification* at ASCE meetings at Phoenix, Ariz. (November 14, 1968).

33. For a bibliography of publications concerning the legal implications of weather modification, see R. Davis, *The Legal Implications of Atmospheric Water Resources Development and Management 133-37 (Rep. to Bureau of Reclamation, Oct. 1968).*

34. For example, Adams v. California, No. 10112 (Super. Ct. Sutter County, Cal., April 6, 1954), in which there were counts charging negligence and seeking recovery for an alleged ultra-hazardous activity. D. Mann, *The Yuba City Flood: A Case Study of Weather Modification Litigation,* 49 Bull. Am. Meteor. Soc'y 690, 695 (1968).

35. See Restatement (Second) of Torts § § 519, 520 (Tent. Draft No. 10, 1954).

36. Pa. Stat. Ann. tit. 3, § 1114 (Supp. 1969); W. Va. Code § 29-2B-13 (Supp. 1969).

37. Tex. Rev. Civ. Stat. Ann. art. 8280-12 § 18 (Supp. 1969).

38. Restatement (Second) of Torts §§ 158, 281 (1965).

39. Ibid., § 299A.

40. The "substantial interference" doctrine is now adopted by the Restatement of Torts with relation to air commerce. Ibid., at § 159.

41. Restatement of Torts §§ 822, 826-828 (1939).

42. Slutsky v. City of New York, 197 Misc. 730, 97 N.Y.S.2d 238 (Sup. Ct. 1950).

43. Pennsylvania Natural Weather Ass'n v. Blue Ridge Weather Modification Ass'n, 44 Pa. D. and C. 749, 760 (C.P. Fulton County 1968).

44. For discussion of governmental immunity, see L F. Harper and F. James, *The Law of Torts* §§ 29.1 to .6, 29.8 to .15 (1956).

45. For an analysis of the concept of "inverse condemnation" that is involved in such "takings," see J. Sax, *Takings and the Police Power*, 74 Yale L.J. 36 (1964).

46. See C. Morris, Torts § 2 (1953).

47. Restatement (Second) of Torts § 196 (1965).

48. R. Davis, *Weather Modifiers' Liability Insurance Experience* (Prepared for Presentation to Weather Modification Ass'n Meeting, February 1969).

49. For example, Special Comm'n on Weather Modification, Weather and Climate Modification 111 (1965).

50. Bureau of Reclamation weather modification contracts, for instance, provide that:

> [T]he Contractor agrees to indemnify and to hold harmless the Bureau against and from any and all liability . . . for claims on account of property damage, personal injuries, or death resulting from the acts or negligence of any and all employees and other personnel working under the direction of the Contractor or any of its subcontractors in connection with the performance of its obligations under this contract.

51. See the appendix for a list of the state weather modification laws and their citations.

52. For example, Conn. Gen. Stat. Ann. §§ 24-5 to -8 (1960), *as*

amended, (Supp. 1969); Hawaii Rev. Stat. § 174-5(8) (1968); Kan. Stat. Ann. § 82a-927(4) (Supp. 1968); N.H. Rev. Stat. Ann. § 432.1 (1968); Okla. Stat. Ann. tit. 82, § 1078, n.§§ 2(I), 2(V) (Supp. 1969).

53. For charts depicting state licensing, permit issuance, and reporting requirements, see R. Davis, Legal Guidelines for Atmospheric Water Resources Management 16-19, 20-25, 58-61 (1968).

54. Pa. Stat. Ann. tit. 3, § 1114 (Supp. 1969); Tex. Rev. Civ. Stat. Ann. art. 8280-12 § 18 (Supp. 1969); W. Va. Code §§ 29-2B-1 to −15 (Supp. 1969).

55. Rainmaking Control Act of 1967 § 12(1), Act. No. 7637, 1968 Victoria Gov't Gaz. 709.

56. Tex. Rev. Civ. Stat. Ann. art. 8280-12 § 18 (Supp. 1969).

57. Pa. Stat. Ann. tit. 3, § 1114 (Supp. 1969); W. Va. Code § 29-2B-13 (Supp. 1969).

58. Southwest Weather Research, Inc. v. Rounsaville, 320 S.W.2d 211, and Southwest Weather Research, Inc. v. Duncan, 319 S.W.2d 940 (Tex. Civ. App. 1958), *both aff'd sub nom.* Southwest Weather Research, Inc. v. Jones, 160 Tex. 104, 327 S.W.2d 417 (1959).

59. Pennsylvania Natural Weather Ass'n v. Blue Ridge Weather Modification Ass'n, 44 Pa. D. and C.2d 749, 760-62 (C.P. Fulton County 1968).

60. The "case or controversy" requirement is examined in C. Wright, Handbook of the Law of Federal Courts § 12 (1963).

61. W. Gellhorn and C. Byse, Administrative Law Cases and Comments 1-7 (1960).

62. John Galbraith, in something of an overstatement, has commented upon this tendency of administrative agencies:

> Regulatory bodies, like the people who comprise them, have a marked life cycle. In youth they are vigorous, aggressive, evangelistic, and even intolerant. Later they mellow, and in old age—after a matter of ten or fifteen years—they become, with some exceptions, either an arm of the industry they are regulating or senile.

J. Galbraith, *The Great Crash* 171 (1955).

63. See L. Jaffe, *Judicial Control of Administrative Action* (1965); L.

Jaffe and N. Nathanson, *Administrative Law Cases and Materials* 173-180 (1961).

64. See R. Davis, supra note 53, at 16-19 for chart on licensing requirements.

65. See M. Williams, *Professional Standards in Weather Modification*, 1 WMA 33 (1969).

66. For example, Mont. Rev. Codes Ann. § 89-315 (Supp. 1969); Nev. Rev. Stat. § 544.140 (1967); Tex. Rev. Civ. Stat. Ann. art. 8280-12, § 9 (Supp. 1969); Wash. Rev. Code Ann. § 43.37.100 (1965).

67. Existing state laws do not spell out this requirement. However, in some states agencies are delegated authority to set licensing rules, and, acting under such power, could provide that licenses will not be issued to persons with proven lack of professional integrity. La. Rev. Stat. Ann. § 37-2207 (1964); S.D. Comp. Laws § 38-9-13 (1967).

68. For example, Colo. Rev. Stat. Ann. § 151-1-6(b) (1963); Fla. Stat. Ann. § 373.301 (1960); Ore. Rev. Stat. § 558.050 (1967).
Pennsylvania goes so far as to require bonding. Pa. Stat. Ann. tit. 3, § 6(5) (Supp. 1969).

69. Wyo. Stat. Ann. § 9-271 (Supp. 1969).
Weather modification is not the only field of professional licensing into which irrelevancies as qualifications have intruded. W. Gellhorn, Individual Freedom and Governmental Restraint 125-40 (1956).

70. For example, Cal. Water Code § 404(b) (West 1956).
The rainmaking statute of Idaho purports on its face only to require registration of "producers of artificial rainfall." Idaho Code Ann. § 22-3201 (1968).

71. See R. Davis, supra note 53, at 20-25 for chart on permit requirements.

72. Ariz. Rev. Stat. Ann. § 45-2402 (1956).

73. Ariz. Rev. Stat. Ann. § 45-2406 (1956).

74. For example, Cal. Water Code §§ 413, 413.5 (West 1956); Mont. Rev. Codes Ann. § 89-314 (Supp. 1969) (exemption only from fees); Pa. Stat. Ann. tit. 3, § 9 (Supp. 1969) (exemption only from publication requirement).

75. For example, Cal. Water Code §§ 407-10 (Supp. 1968); Fla. Stat. Ann. §§ 373.331 to .371 (1960); Nev. Rev. Stat. §§ 244.160 to .180

(1967); Wash. Rev. Code Ann. §§ 43.37.120 to .140 (1965).

76. For example, Mass. Ann. Laws ch. 6, § 72 (1966); Mont. Rev. Codes Ann. § 89-318(6) (Supp. 1969).

77. See R. Davis, supra note 53, at 58-61 for chart on reporting requirements.

78. Formerly the NSF required reporting. 45 C.F.R. §§ 635.1-.7 (1968), *issuance authorized by,* 42 U.S.C. § 1862 (1964). But by virtue of the Act of July 18, 1968, Pub. L. No. 90-407, § 11, 82 Stat. 360, the Foundation's authority to require reporting was repealed. For the new regulations, see 33 Fed. Reg. 12654 (1968).

79. Federal procurement law is filled with statutory and administrative provisions which set forth contract provisions placing limits on contractors. See, for example, such "boilerplate" provisions as the disputes clause, 31 C.F.R. § 1-7.101-12; termination clause, 41 C.F.R. § 1-8.704-1(a); contingent upon appropriations clause, 41 U.S.C. §§ 11, 12; renegotiation clause, 50 App. U.S.C. §§ 1191-1233 (Supp. 1967); and equal opportunity clause, 41 C.F.R. § 1-12.803-2.

80. Nev. Rev. Stat. Ann. § 544.030 (1967).

81. N.H. Rev. Stat. Ann. § 432.1 (1968).

82. Note the parallel reasoning in 25 Calif. Attn'y Gen. Rep. 164 (1955).

83. Rock Island, A. and L.R.R. v. United States, 254 U.S. 141, 143 (1920).

84. N.D. Cent. Code §§ 2-07-06 to −07 (Supp. 1969); S.D. Comp. Laws § 10-12-18 (Supp. 1969).

85. Neb. Rev. Stat. § 2-2444 (Supp. 1967).

86. See, for example, D. Eberly, *Weather Modification and the Operations of an Electric Power Utility: The Pacific Gas and Electric Company's Test Program* in Human Dimensions of Weather Modification 209, ed. W. Sewell (1966).

87. See B. Beckwith, supra note 4.

88. E. Boyd, *Summary of Cloud Seeding Operations in South Dakota During 1968,* 10, 11, 13 (1969); see also *The Farmer,* 28, 37 (August 3, 1968).

89. See W. Hutchins, supra note 8, §§ 20-25.

90. For example, Arizona, California, Montana, Texas and Washington.

91. Pa. Stat. Ann. tit. 3, § 14 (Supp. 1969); W. Va. Code § 29-2B-13 (Supp. 1969).

92. For example, California and Colorado.

93. Elements of the California law appear in the Texas and Montana statutes. West Virginia unfortunately copied the Pennsylvania law.

94. One Maryland provision expired by its terms on September 1, 1967. It became effective on March 30, 1965. Md. Ann. Code art. 66C, § 110A (1967). A subsequent prohibition was effective from July 1, 1968 to September 1, 1969. Md. Ann. Code art. 66C, § 110A (Supp. 1968). The present prohibition extends to September 1, 1971. Md. Ann. Code art. 66C, § 110A (Supp. 1969).

95. Pa. Stat. Ann. tit. 3, § 15(b) (Supp. 1969); W. Va. Code § 29-2B-14(b) (Supp. 1969).

96. Pa. Stat. Ann. tit. 3, § 6(5) (Supp. 1969); W. Va. Code § 29-2B-5(5) (Supp. 1969).

97. 33 U.S.C. § 466 (Supp. 1965).

98. 23 U.S.C. §§ 101 et. seq. (1966).

99. S. Shumway, Cascades Atmospheric Water Resources Program (1966).

100. Pa. Stat. Ann. tit. 3, § 15(a) (Supp. 1969); W. Va. Code § 29-2B-13(2) (Supp. 1969).

101. Colo. Rev. Stat. Ann. § 151-1-11 (1963).

102. N.M. Stat. Ann. § 75-37-12 (1968).

103. See discussion in Tobin, *The Interstate Metropolitan District and Cooperative Federalism*, 36 Tul. L. Rev. 67 (1961).

104. Leach, *Interstate Authorities in the United States*, 26 L. and Contemp. Prob. 666-668 (1961).

105. Pierce, *Legal Aspects of Weather Modification Snowpack Augmentation in Wyoming*, 2 Land and Water L. Rev. 273 (1967).

106. Compare N.J. Stat. Ann. § 32:107 (1963).

107. See Documents on the Use and Control of the Waters of

Interstate and International Streams, ed. T. Witmer (1956).

108. 42 U.S.C.A. § 1857a(c) (1964).

109. Ill. Rev. Stat. ch. 111 1/2, § 240.31 (1965); Ind. Ann. Stat. § 55-4621 (1965). For discussion of this compact, see *A Model Interstate Compact for the Control of Air Pollution*, 4 Harv. J. Legisl. 369 (1967).

110. Congressional power rests upon U.S. Const. art. I, § 10, cl. 3.

111. C. Meyers, *The Colorado River*, 19 Stan. L. Rev. 1, 48 (1966).

112. C. Corker, *Water Rights in Interstate Streams*, in 2 Waters and Water Rights § 133.2, ed. R. Clark (1967).

113. *Congressional Supervision of Interstate Compacts*, 75 Yale L.J. 1416 (1966).

114. C. Corker, supra note 112 at § 133.4.

Appendix

State Weather Modification Statutes

Arizona: Ariz. Rev. Stat. Ann. §§ 45-2401 to −2407 (1956).

California: Cal. Water Code §§ 400-415 (West 1956), *as amended*, (Supp. 1969); Cal. Water Code—App. § 48-9(13) (West 1968) [authorizes weather-modification activity by Riverside County Flood Control and Water Conservation District] ; Cal. Gov't Code § 53063 (West 1966) [authorizes weather modification by political subdivisions] .

Colorado: Colo. Rev. Stat. Ann. §§ 151-1-1 to −12 (1963).

Connecticut: Conn. Gen. Stat. Ann. § 24-5 to −8 (1960), *as amended*, (Supp. 1969).

Florida: Fla. Stat. Ann. §§ 373.261-.391 (1960), *as amended*, (Supp. 1969).

Hawaii: Hawaii Rev. Stat. § 174-5(8) (1968) [only authorizes investigation of weather-modification feasibility] .

Idaho: Idaho Code Ann. §§ 22-3201 to –3202 (1968).

Kansas: Kan. Stat. Ann. § 82a-927(4) (Supp. 1968) [merely mentions atmospheric water].

Louisiana: La. Rev. Stat. Ann. §§ 37:2201-2208 (1964).

Maryland: Md. Ann. Code art. 66C, § 110A (Supp. 1969) [this statute expires by its terms September 1, 1971].

Massachusetts: Mass. Ann. Laws ch. 6, §§ 17, 72 (1966), *as amended*, (Supp. 1969).

Minnesota: Minn. Laws 1969, ch. 771.

Montana: Mont. Rev. Codes Ann. §§ 89-310 to –331 (Supp. 1969).

Nebraska: Neb. Rev. Stat. §§ 2-2401 to –2449 (1962), *as amended*, (Supp. 1967).

Nevada: Nev. Rev. Stat. §§ 244.190, 544.010-.240 (1967).

New Hampshire: N.H. Rev. Stat. Ann. § 432.1 (1968).

New Mexico: N.M. Stat. Ann. §§ 75-37-1 to –15 (1968).

New York: N.Y. Gen. Munic. Law § 119-p (McKinney Supp. 1969).

North Dakota: N.D. Cent. Code §§ 2-07-01 to –13 (Supp. 1969); N.D. Cent. Code § 58-03-07(19) (1960), *as added*, (Supp. 1969) [township expenditure].

Oklahoma: Okla. Stat. Ann. tit. 82, § 1078, n. §§ 2(I), 2(V) (Supp. 1969) [notes atmospheric water as a natural resource].

Oregon: Ore. Rev. Stat. §§ 558.010-.990 (1967).

Pennsylvania: Pa. Stat. Ann. tit. 3, §§ 1101-18 (Supp. 1969).

South Dakota: S.D. Comp. Laws §§ 38-9-1 to –24 (1967); S.D. Comp. Laws § 10-12-18 (Supp. 1969) [county tax levy].

Texas: Tex. Rev. Civ. Stat. Ann. art. 8280-12, §§ 1-19 (Supp. 1969).

Utah: Utah Code Ann. §§ 73-15-1 to −2 (1968).

Washington: Wash. Rev. Code Ann. §§ 43.37.010-.200 (1965), *as amended,* §§ 43.27A.080(6), .180(1) (Supp. 1969).

West Virginia: W. Va. Code §§ 29-2B-1 to −15 (Supp. 1969).

Wisconsin: Wis. Stat. Ann. § 195.40 (1957), *as amended,* (Supp. 1969).

Wyoming: Wyo. Stat. Ann. §§ 9-267 to −276 (1957), *as amended,* (Supp. 1969).

Weather Modification Cases

Substantive Cases

Samples v. Irving P. Krick, Inc., Civil Nos. 6212, 6223, and 6224 (W.D. Okla. 1954).

Adams v. California, No. 10112 (Super. Ct. Sutter County, Cal., April 6, 1954).

Summerville v. North Platte Valley Weather Control Dist., 170 Neb. 46, 101 N.W.2d 748 (1960).

Slutsky v. City of New York, 197 Misc. 730, 97 N.Y.S.2d 238 (Sup. Ct. 1950).

Pennsylvania *ex rel.* Township of Ayr v. Fulk, No. 53 (C.P. Fulton County, Pa., February 28, 1968).

Pennsylvania Natural Weather Ass'n v. Blue Ridge Weather Modification Ass'n, 44 Pa. D. and C.2d 749 (C.P. Fulton County 1968).

Southwest Weather Research, Inc. v. Rounsaville, 320 S.W.2d 211, and Southwest Weather Research, Inc. v. Duncan, 319 S.W.2d 940 (Tex. Civ. App. 1958), both aff'd sub nom. Southwest Weather Research, Inc. v. Jones, 160 Tex. 104, 327 S.W.2d 417 (1959).

Auvil Orchard Co. v. Weather Modification, Inc., No. 19268 (Super. Ct. Chelan County, Wash., 1956).

Procedural Cases

Summerville v. North Platte Valley Weather Control Dist., 171 Neb. 695, 107 N.W.2d 425 (1961) [proceeding for allowance of attorney's fees and expenses].

Avery v. O'Dwyer, 305 N.Y. 658, 112 N.E.2d 428 (1953) [considers propriety of denial of motion to amend title of summons and complaint].

Reeve v. O'Dwyer, 199 Misc. 123, 98 N.Y.S.2d 452 (Sup. Ct. 1950) [ruling upon motion for change of venue].

7   The Role of Local Governmental Units in Weather Modification: California

Sho Sato

Because the science of weather modification is in an embryonic stage, one cannot predict with assurance what, where, when, and how the changes in our weather will ultimately be wrought. One can be fairly certain, however, that the consequences of successful alteration will be of such order of magnitude, including the possibilities of effecting an irreversible harm to the ecology, that it behooves us to think seriously about the problems which have already arisen and those which might be anticipated. Moreover, where successful alteration promises immense benefit and power, it is unlikely that extralegal political, economic, social, or moral forces alone will exert sufficient direction and restraint to optimize the benefits flowing from atmospheric resources or to provide protection to existing interests adversely affected. In short, it would seem that ultimately stringent control will have to be exercised through the legal order and institutions.

The dimensions to the legal problems become, however, virtually limitless when one projects atmospheric control to the point of ordering the daily weather regime to meet a community's need or changing the climate in a global region. In addition, the unintended changes which are the by-products of other activities cannot be ignored. Interacting with the above problems are the various levels of government—nations, states, local governmental units—each operating within its established parameters. The complexity and the magnitude of the task of a comprehensive legal analysis of these forces suggest a modest, segmental approach.

221

This report then examines the role of local governmental units in weather modification, concentrating, however, upon local governments in California in order that a cohesive analysis of the problem may be presented. We focus on intrastate problems, leaving to others an analysis of interstate problems. We also concern ourselves here primarily with precipitation-augmentation activities inasmuch as most of the weather-modification operations in California appear to be restricted to this purpose. With this limited perspective, the areas of inquiry may be broadly identified as follows: first, the general allocation of power between the state and local governments in terms of whether (a) local governmental units can engage in weather-modification activities in the absence of statutory authority, (b) they can regulate modification activities within the private or public sector, and (c) they should have the power to do one or both, and if so, to what extent; and, second, the restraints which operate, or should operate, upon local governmental units engaging in weather-modification activities.

Basic Allocation of Power Between the State and Local Governmental Units

A short summary of the type of local governmental units existing in California, their relationship to the state and to each other, and the sources of their authority is presented as a background to the later discussion directly related to weather modification.[1]

There are three types of local governmental units in California which can be concerned with weather modification: a county, a city, and a special district. A fourth, a city and county (San Francisco is the only entity in this category) generally has all the powers and duties of a city and a county and, thus, a separate discussion concerning a combined city and county entity is unnecessary.

County

A county is a legal subdivision of the state and has only those powers which have been expressly or impliedly granted by the state. Some powers are conferred directly by the state constitution, but the bulk of them has been delegated by the state legislature which has plenary control over a county except as constrained by constitutional provisions. The source of county power is important. Where the power is granted by the constitution, the state legislative supervisory power over the county is circumscribed to that extent, and conversely, the county has a measure of either local initiative or protection from legislative interference.

The counties may be classified into chartered counties and those which are unchartered. Of the 58 counties in California, approximately 10 are chartered.[2] The constitution permits a county to adopt a charter, subject to state legislative approval.[3] The adoption of a charter permits a county to formulate its internal organization instead of complying with the legislatively prescribed scheme. For example, although the statute may require a given office to be elective, the county may make it appointive.[4] The county may create, consolidate, or eliminate offices contrary to statutory requirements.[5] Whether a county by the adoption of a charter can engage in any enterprise activity or impose taxes without statutory authorization cannot be answered definitively, although the conclusion that a county does not have such broad authority appears more reasonable.[6] Because of this conclusion, it becomes unnecessary to classify the counties in the ensuing discussion; the considerations applicable to county involvement in weather modification are equally applicable to chartered and non-chartered counties.

The constitution grants to every county the power to regulate the conduct of those within its territorial jurisdiction.[7] Several qualifications to the above statement, however, are necessary. First, the constitution, although granting this regulatory power, expressly limits the exercise of the power to such regulations as do not conflict with state statutes.[8] Second, although the county can enforce its regulatory measure with a criminal sanction and possibly by injunctive relief, it seems very doubtful that the county can create civil liabilities in favor of one private party against another.[9] But the courts, in adjudicating a tort suit, may adopt the county regulatory measure as providing the requisite standard of care.[10] Third, the regulations, which are otherwise valid, do not operate within the territorial limits of a city, since a city is deemed to be a coordinate rather than a subservient unit of local government with regulatory power equal to that of a county.[11] In other words, a county regulation is valid only within the unincorporated areas. It must be made clear that the immediate discussion is concerned with regulatory power only, for a county is required to provide certain services even to those residing within a city and does impose taxes, such as the ad valorem property tax, within incorporated areas. Fourth, a county regulation might not be applicable to other public entities acting within the county territorial limits.[12] This may be either on the ground that other public entities are deemed to be state agencies or that, because the state legislation defining the powers of such public entities has occupied the field, the local regulation would be in conflict therewith.[13]

Relating the above to weather modification, a county does not have the authority to engage in weather-modification activities unless a statute has conferred such authority, but it does have the constitutional power to regulate those activities, subject to the qualifications mentioned above.

City

A city differs from a county in one fundamental respect: A county is established by the state primarily as a subadministrative area for many state functions, although a county may be authorized to provide locally determined services. On the other hand, a city owes its existence to local initiative—that is, a city is formed only upon the vote of the affected electorate.

Like a county, a city has only those powers conferred by the state, since the theory of "inherent right of self-government," although asserted during the last quarter of the nineteenth century, is probably a discredited concept.[14] This is not to say that cities to not have a right of self-government.

The constitution provides that a city with a population of more than 3,500 inhabitants may adopt a charter subject to approval by the legislature.[15] The charter may provide that the city governed thereunder "may make and enforce all laws and regulations in respect to municipal affairs, subject only to the restrictions and limitations provided in their several charters and in respect to other matters they shall be subject to general law."[16] Upon acceptance of this broad constitutional delegation (1) the charter becomes an instrument of limitation of powers rather than one of enumeration of specific authority,[17] (2) the constitution has granted local initiative with respect to "municipal affairs,"[18] and (3) the constitution has carved out the area of "municipal affairs" in which the city is free from state interference.[19] Although the constitution refers to "municipal affairs" for the grant of power as well as the protection from state legislative interference, the scope of the term is greater in the case of grant of power than in the other.[20] Moreover, unlike the limited "home rule" given to the chartered counties, the local initiative under the "municipal affairs" concept is far greater in that a chartered city does not need statutory authority to provide services or levy taxes.[21]

In contrast, a general law city, that is, a city established under the general laws of the state, does not have the broad constitutional grant of local initiative over "municipal affairs" and is generally restricted to those powers which have been expressly granted by the legislature and those which are implied therefrom, subject to significant exceptions noted below.[22]

A city, whether chartered or general law, however, is granted the authority to adopt police-power regulations as long as they are not in conflict with the general laws.[23] Because this grant is found in the same constitutional provision conferring similar power to a county, the regulatory power possessed by a city within its territorial jurisdiction is subject to the same limitations as are applicable to a county.[24]

A city, whether chartered or general law, is given the authority under the constitution to "establish and operate public works for supplying its inhabitants with . . . water . . ."[25] and pursuant to the doctrine of implied power, this constitutional authority may support its entry into precipitation-augmentation acitivity without further authority from the legislature.[26]

In summary, the two types of cities can have regulatory power over weather-modification operations, subject, however, to many significant limitations. A chartered city has the constitutional authority to provide various types of services to its inhabitants, including various types of weather-modification services, but a general-law city needs statutory authority to engage in weather-modification activities except with respect to precipitation augmentation which might be granted by the constitution.

It should be noted at this point that there are approximately 398 cities in California, about 74 of which are chartered cities.[27]

Special District

While there is a degree of homogeneity among the counties and cities despite variations in their organization and functions, "special district" as a local governmental unit defies a single description. A special district may be created by the vote of the electors under a special law (a law which by its terms is applicable only to a specified geographic area).[28] It may be created under a general law.[29] It may also be created by the legislature.[30] It may be governed by officers who are elected for that purpose.[31] It may also be governed by existing county officials as ex officio governing body of the special district.[32] Sometimes it is governed by officers selected by other elected officials.[33] Its purpose may be very limited, being restricted to providing a single service to its

225

inhabitants; or its purpose may be multiple. Its revenue may be restricted to tolls or fees from its services; it may levy an assessment on land only, or in addition, on improvement; or it may levy an ad valorem property tax.

Despite these differences, it may be generalized that a special district is a creation of the legislature and it has only expressly granted powers and those implied therefrom.[34] Unlike a county or a city, the constitution grants no authority to a special district to adopt police-power regulations; on the contrary, the constitution has been construed to forbid the legislature from delegating to special districts the power to affix penal sanctions.[35] The legislature may, however, delegate the power to make regulations to special districts if the legislature provides the penal sanctions and standards within which to adopt regulations.[36]

With this background, a discussion is now in order to determine the role of local governmental units in weather modification.

Existing Authority of Local Governmental Units to Engage in Weather Modification

Authority Under California Government Code Sec. 53063

A statute enacted in 1955 provides:

> Any county, city, city and county, district, authority or other public corporation or agency which has the power to produce, conserve, control or supply water for beneficial purposes shall have the power to engage in practices designed to produce, induce, increase or control rainfall or other precipitation for the general benefit of the territory within it.[37]

It is to be noted that section 53063, quoted above, has a dual function: first, it specifies the kind of weather-modification activity which is authorized; and, second, it identifies the governmental units to which the authority is granted. But the above section is not without its constructional difficulties. First, what is the scope of authority granted under the phrase "practices designed to produce, induce, increase or control rainfall or other precipitation?" That phrase conceivably can refer to any related activity, including basic research in the laboratory, or it may be more restrictively read as referring to a field activity which has as its purpose the inducement, augmentation, or control of precipitation and which has a reasonable probability of success.

A plausible argument can be advanced for a restrictive interpretation. The argument runs as follows: the local governmental units are organized for the benefit of their inhabitants; the revenues derived by the entity from the inhabitants should advance their interests; indeed, the constitutional prohibition against the lending of credit or making gifts of public funds by a public entity is a manifestation of this policy; basic research in atmospheric science, while of benefit to the local public entity conducting the research, has a substantial external benefit as well; because of these considerations, it is improbable that section 53063 was intended to confer the authority to the local entities to engage in basic research; and at most, the implied power to conduct research and experiments should be restricted to a study of local conditions.[38]

A contrary argument would stress the fact that there is no violation of any express constitutional prohibition in making public expenditures for these purposes inasmuch as the public entity engaged in research will realize a benefit, although it might not be able to capture all the benefits for itself.[39] And even if the word "practices" may connote operational activities, the authority to engage in basic research may be implied from the expressly conferred power since research may be a condition precedent to efficient operational activities. Thus, whether the public entity should engage in research is simply a matter of local discretion.

There is no need to resolve this issue here. The above discussion, and those which follow, are intended to show existing ambiguities, to identify policy considerations in resolving these ambiguities, and to emphasize the need for a more precise draftsmanship.

A second issue centers upon the purpose for which weather-modification activity may be conducted under section 53063—that is, whether for fog dispersal, precipitation augmentation, lightning control, etc. The statutory phrase is "designed to produce, induce, increase, or control rainfall or other precipitation for the general benefit of the territory within it." If this term were read in isolation, it would confer a broad power, since many different purposes of weather modification involve the control of precipitation, either an increase or even change in the nature of the precipitation. But perhaps the phrase in question should be read in conjunction with the preceding phrase which identifies the entities to which the power is granted; namely, entities which have the power "to produce, conserve, control or supply water for beneficial purposes." If this latter phrase casts a restrictive gloss, it

227

becomes necessary to determine the meaning of producing, etc., water for beneficial purposes. In other words, if an entity's power is restricted to the acquisition and distribution of water for beneficial uses, it does not make sense to attribute to such entity the power to engage in fog dispersal or hail suppression.[40] It would seem more reasonable to construe section 53063 as a clarification of the implied power doctrine in order to make certain that the entities would have the power to engage in such atmospheric activities as are related to its other powers.

If this conclusion is correct, the critical phrase becomes "beneficial purposes" since the statute confers the power in question upon an entity having the power to produce, etc. water for "beneficial purposes." Is "beneficial purposes" synonymous with "beneficial use?" If it is, a district such as the American River Flood Control District, which is empowered to engage in activities to further its purpose of "control and disposition of the storm and flood waters of said district," or the Knight's Landing Ridge Drainage District, the power of which appears to be restricted to providing drainage within the district, would not have the power to engage in precipitation augmentation for increased water supply.[41] At the minimum the term "beneficial uses" connotes use of the water rather than disposal of the water.[42] On the other hand, if "beneficial purposes" is broader in meaning than "beneficial use," one can plausibly argue that the aforementioned districts with flood control and drainage powers would have the power under section 53063 to nucleate the clouds artificially to produce precipitation, since that would be an activity designed to control precipitation and would be done by an entity which has the power to control water for "beneficial purposes," i.e., to avert drainage problems and flood damages.[43]

While no definitive conclusion can be offered, one can fairly be certain that the legislature had precipitation augmentation principally in mind and probably was unaware of the problems created by its imprecise language.[44]

Authority Under a General Power
or as Implied

To the extent that the power to engage in certain activities has been expressly conferred on an entity by section 53063, it is unnecessary to resort to the implied power doctrine to determine the existence of authority, but if the power has not been expressly granted, the implied power doctrine may fill the lacuna. In other words, even though an

228

entity does not have the authority under section 53063 to reduce precipitation as a flood control practice, the power might be implied from its general power to reduce flood hazards or to prevent flood damage.

The Attorney General of California has published an opinion which referred, among others, to the power of the irrigation district to "do any act necessary to furnish sufficient water in the district for any beneficial use" as impliedly authorizing the district to engage in precipitation-augmentation activities.[45] The word "necessary" was said to mean that which was "convenient, useful, appropriate, or suitable, and not indispensable." And the opinion continued, "What is convenient, useful or appropriate to accomplish the purposes of a district or a municipal corporation is within the sound discretion of its governing authority."[46] Given this broad implication, a district such as the Los Angeles Flood Control District, which has, as one of its purposes, protection from damage from flood or storm waters, would have the authority to engage in precipitation control.[47]

Express Authority to Specific Agencies

The general authority to engage in atmospheric-alteration activities has been discussed above. The legislature has, in addition, conferred express authority to at least one agency. The Riverside County Flood Control District is authorized to "carry on a program of artificial nucleation for the purposes of increasing and controlling rainfall within, or in the immediate vicinity of, any watershed located wholly or partially within the district."[48] It should be noted that the authority of this District encompasses a "program" in contrast to "practices" under section 53063 of the Government Code, which may connote a broader delegation. In addition, the power granted to Riverside Flood Control District expressly authorizes activities outside the district.[49] It is difficult to determine how many more districts have been given express power under a special act without going through each special act with utmost care.[50]

Local Units Having Authority to Engage
in Weather Modification

Our attention is now directed to local governmental units which are authorized to engage in some aspect of weather modification activity.

County. A county has the power to "acquire, develop, distribute, and sell water to the county and its inhabitants for domestic, irrigation, agricultural, and other beneficial uses."[51] Thus, a county has the authority under section 53063 of the Government Code to engage in the type of activities authorized therein.

In addition, a county has the power to construct "works, improvements, levees, or check dams to prevent the overflow and flooding of streams and rivers in the county."[52] The authority extends to "works" outside the county if the watercourse flows through more than one county.[53] Perhaps the power to reduce precipitation or otherwise control storm clouds can be implied from the above authority.

Consider also the power to protect forest, brush and grass lands against fire, which might imply the authority to conduct lightning-suppression activity.[54] And the authority to maintain a public airport might carry with it the power to engage in fog dispersal.[55]

City. A city, whether chartered or not, has been authorized by the constitution to "establish and operate public works for supplying its inhabitants with ... water...."[56] Section 38730 of the Government Code authorizes a city to acquire water and to supply water for the use of the city and its inhabitants. Thus, every city has the power to conduct activities mentioned in section 53063 of the Government Code.

A city may perhaps have additional powers by implication. For example, a city has the authority to protect itself from water overflow, and the works for such purposes may be located outside the city limits.[57] This may imply a power to control precipitation. A chartered city, pursuant to its powers over "municipal affairs," would be able to engage in fog dispersal at its airports and in other activities relating to atmospheric alteration.[58]

Special District. To determine which special districts have the power to engage in weather-modification activities, it is necessary to examine every general-enabling law and every special act. It suffices for the purposes of discussion to identify the principal general-enabling laws to demonstrate the order of magnitude with respect to special districts having the power.

The irrigation districts, of which there were about 110 in existence at the end of 1967, have section 53063 powers.[59] This is because of their general power to "do any act necessary to furnish sufficient water in the district for any beneficial use."[60] In addition, it may be surprising to learn that an irrigation district, under restricted conditions, may operate an airport, and hence by implication might be authorized to conduct fog dispersal at its airport.[61] It may provide flood control service and thus may be able to engage in other related activities in addition to precipitation control.[62]

The county water districts, of which there were 207 at the end of the 1966/67 fiscal year, have section 53063 powers.[63] This is because their general power to furnish water is similar to that of the irrigation districts.[64]

The California water districts, which form another substantial group, numbering 150, have broad powers to produce and distribute water for beneficial uses.[65] They thus have section 53063 powers.[66]

Other general law districts which have section 53063 powers are:[67]

1. Community services districts[68]—about 155 existing districts.[69]
2. Municipal water districts[70]—about 51 existing districts.[71]
3. California water storage districts[72]—about eight existing districts.[73]
4. General law reclamation districts[74]—the number existing under general laws not known.
5. County waterworks districts[75]—about 93 existing districts.[76]
6. Public utility districts[77]—about 66 existing districts.[78]
7. Probably the following fire protection districts: fire protection districts;[79] and local fire districts.[80]

In addition to the entities formed under the general laws, there are many districts which exist by virtue of special laws, and many of these have section 53063 powers. It is unnecessary to examine each special act; it suffices to indicate that there are a substantial number of these.

Beyond the powers granted by section 53063, each enabling general law and special act must be examined to determine the implied powers if a complete picture of local entity power to engage in weather modification is desired.

The Extent of Weather Modification Activities in California

The reports of the State Department of Water Resources indicate that the number of entities engaging in weather-modification activities is relatively very small in comparison to the number of local governmental units having the power to engage in such activities. The reports of the Department available to this writer covered the periods 1947-1952 and 1961-1967.[81] During the eleven years covered by the reports, nine

231

local governmental units engaged in weather-modification activities, either through their own personnel or independent contractors, and invariably the purpose of the activity was to increase precipitation, although in some instances research was also a stated objective. There was no other activity or purpose mentioned. During the period 1961-1967, five public entities (viz., Kern County, Kings River Conservation District, San Bernardino Valley Municipal Water District, Santa Clara Valley Water Conservation District, and Los Angeles County Flood Control District) conducted precipitation-augmentation activity annually. Two entities (viz., Tulare County and Vista Irrigation District) have five-year records. The County of San Benito had engaged in the activity for two years.

During the same period, weather modification to increase precipitation was carried on by three private groups, of which two were public utility companies and the other was a farm-labor cooperative. The two utility companies were engaged in the activity annually and the cooperative for two years.

Fresno State College Foundation conducted applied research on orographic cumulus clouds during 1965-1967. Several projects of public entities had a research orientation. The report does not indicate the extent to which laboratory research is being conducted in California.

Local Governmental Research

Because the licensing requirements for weather modification do not include laboratory research, the reports of the Department of Water Resources do not mention these activities. Whether the local governmental units are engaged in such research, either through their own personnel or independent contractors or by making grants, is not known.

Certainly, as a matter of financial feasibility, most local governmental units can hardly afford the type of basic research which would cost millions of dollars.[82] Of the special districts engaged in weather-modification activities, the district with the greatest revenue for the fiscal year 1966/67 was the Los Angeles County Flood Control District (approximately $30 million).[83] The one with the least for the same period was the Kings River Conservation District (approximately $61,500).[84] The revenue of the two counties involved in this activity was much greater, but it is questionable whether even counties can support basic research on the order of millions of dollars.

More important, as a matter of policy, basic research in weather modification, if conducted by a local governmental unit, would produce a great deal of benefits external to that unit. Under these conditions the research is apt to be undersupported or, if adequately supported, may result in fiscal inequity.[85] It is arguable that the appropriate unit or units for financing the costs of research should be that unit which encompasses all beneficiaries, and this would suggest that much of the basic research ought to be financed at least by the state and more probably by the federal government. This does not mean that the local governmental units should be absolved of all financial responsibility, since it would not be unreasonable to require the local governmental units to bear a burden to the extent that the research relates to local conditions and there is insubstantial spillover of benefits.

Local Governmental Field Experiments and Operational Activities

If the community of interests represented by a local government were identical and if the weather-modification activity could be conducted with precision within its territorial boundaries, little or no conflict would arise. But such ideal conditions are probably fanciful. There are bound to be heterogeneous interests existing in the target area, and conflicts from weather-modification activities are apt to occur. For example, precipitation augmentation may be conducted at a time when the increased precipitation is beneficial to one type of crop but harmful to another. The augmentation may require redesigning of drainage facilities to accommodate the increase. Even if augmentation activities are carried on in remote mountain areas during the winter, the increased run-off might injure those at lower elevations. And if cloud seeding does in fact create a rain shadow, thereby depriving others in the downwind area of needed moisture, their crops may be lost or made less productive due to insufficient water or they may be required to rely upon higher cost water. An endless variety of these conflicts can happen, but one consequence is apparent. The local governmental unit engaging in precipitation augmentation has presumably undertaken the enterprise because of the benefit to be derived by all or some segment of its constituency, but in doing so, it has imposed a cost on those adversely affected.[86] The issue of whether those who have suffered the costs should be compensated becomes relevant to the questions whether there is to be an equitable redistribution of resources among those who are benefited and burdened and whether sound decisions will be

233

made at the local level if the operating entity need not pay for the cost.

It is to this issue of loss distribution that we now turn our attention, and in doing so, the problems attendant upon precipitation-augmentation activities will be taken as a model to explore the issues. But even with respect to precipitation augmentation, it is convenient to distinguish the causes which impose the cost, that is, the loss which arises from abundance of precipitation and those which stem from deprivation, simply because the nature of the legal interests is much more certain in one case than in the other.[87]

Existing Law on Redistribution of Losses

The common law has established, within the private sector, an involuntary loss redistribution scheme under tort law where one party injures the person or the property of another. The conceptual tools employed to effect loss redistribution have been negligence, strict liability, nuisance, and the like. Funding schemes, such as compulsory automobile liability insurance and workmen's compensation, which have been legislatively established, are common. Whether the standard of negligence or strict liability is applied to any given activity has been the result of judicious balancing of a variety of factors, such as the utility of the conduct which causes the injury, the substantiality of harm, the admonitory function to be served by imposing liability, the availability of a mechanism for a wide distribution of loss (insurability of the loss or distribution to the consumers generally), the degree of risk of injury to others created by a given activity, and others. In contrast to the above legally compelled loss redistribution schemes, many forms of insurance are available as a voluntary redistribution device.

While the involuntary redistribution schemes existed in the private sector, public entities had been virtually immune from liability for their loss-inflicting conduct because of the doctrine of sovereign immunity, except as compelled by the constitution to compensate for losses when the public entity took or damaged private property for a public use and except as modified by judicial doctrines and statutory waiver of immunity.[88] This was the pattern existing in California until 1961 when the state supreme court rejected the doctrine of sovereign immunity.[89] In response to this decision, a comprehensive statute on governmental tort liability was adopted by the state legislature in 1963.[90] This act governs the liability of public entities, even chartered cities whose "municipal affairs" home rule has never extended to its responsibility for tortious conduct.[91] Thus, the following discussion on the extent of loss redistribution effected by the new statute is applicable to every public entity in California.

Generally, a public entity is made vicariously liable for the acts of its employees acting within the scope of their employment.[92] And a public employee is generally liable for injury proximately caused by his act or omission to the same extent as a private person, except as otherwise provided by statute.[93] One of the more important exceptions to the general rule of liability is the immunity from liability for harm resulting from the exercise of discretion.[94] It becomes especially critical to define the limits of this pervasive immunity since it would be fruitless to examine the basis of liability or the standard of care required in weather-modification activity without overcoming the hurdle posed by this immunity.

In a very recent case, *Johnson v. California,* the California Supreme Court had the occasion to explore this immunity.[95] Plaintiff's complaint alleged that a youth, who was a ward of the California Youth Authority, was placed in her home for foster care; that the youth attacked her and inflicted personal injuries; and that the Youth Authority's failure to warn plaintiff of the youth's homicidal tendencies, known to the Authority, was the proximate cause of the injuries. The principal issue was whether the discretionary immunity shielded the state from liability, the state contending that the conditions under which a person should be paroled was within the discretion of the public official. The Supreme Court rejected this argument because the rationale usually offered for the discretionary immunity—that is, if liability is imposed upon official acts, it will dampen the ardor of the officer in performing his duty zealously—no longer obtains in California inasmuch as the officer is entitled to be defended in action against him and to payment of the judgment against him by the public entity.[96] The basis for the discretionary immunity was rested upon the separation of powers doctrine in that the judicial branch should not exercise supervisory responsibility over decisions which have been entrusted to a coordinate branch of the government. But the judicial restraint was deemed to extend only to basic policy decisions, for any broader definition of discretion would swallow completely the areas of liability, since any act involves some discretion. The court recognized that the decision to parole would be a discretionary act, but the decision concerning what information should be divulged is a "determination of the lowest, ministerial rung of official action" and, thus, not within the purview of discretionary immunity.

A lower court, in *Sava v. Fuller,* analyzed discretionary immunity in the following manner:

> The rationale of the *Costley* rule is that government may in its sole and uninhibited discretion, reasonably or arbitrarily (even maliciously) exercise, extend or withhold services to its citizens, but once the determination has been made that a service will be furnished and the service is undertaken, then public policy demands (except when the Legislature specifically decrees otherwise) that government be held to the same standard of care the law requires of its private citizens in the performance of duties imposed by law or assumed. To us that seems a sounder policy than the "dampen the ardor" theory of governmental immunity. It also applies a test much more susceptible of ascertainability than the "policy-making-level versus operational-level" rule.[97]

If one were to paraphrase the above opinions, discretionary immunity is designed to place nonreviewable loss—redistribution decisions within the political process when such process, rather than the judicial, is more efficient and adaptable to the decision-making function and leads to greater stability of governmental operations. And relevant to this determination are factors, such as responsiveness of the decision maker to the people affected, the multitude of disparate but relevant factors which should and can be considered in the decision-making process, and the expertise of the decision makers.

If the above analysis is applied to our immediate inquiry, the conclusion that the government is not liable for its decision to engage in weather-modification activities seems unassailable. This much is easy. But does the discretionary immunity protect the government for its decisions as to where, when, and how the activities should be performed. This cannot be answered categorically. The intrusion of the judicial branch into these decisions will probably depend upon the state of technology, the care with which the decision makers have weighed the relevant factors, and the range of options with varying known consequences available to the decision makers.[98]

The above discussion has assumed that the government will be liable only for negligent operation if discretionary immunity does not apply. Another difficult question is whether the existence of the discretionary immunity will necessarily preclude the imposition of liability on the basis of strict liability—that is, liability without negligence. The argument for an affirmative answer would be that strict liability is inconsistent with discretionary immunity, since a decision without its

236

execution is generally meaningless; and if liability were to be imposed without regard to negligence, that is, where no option is available to perform the act in different ways, one of which may meet the standard of due care and another might not, it would mean that the government is being made liable in effect for having made a decision to act. This argument, however, is not compelling. Tort liability based on strict liability does not impinge upon basic decision making much more than negligence liability. The law would require public responsibility only if injury ensues from the execution of the decision. The financial consequences flowing from the act cannot be made the measure of discretionary immunity, for most acts carry the possibility of, at least, negligence liability. It is the political balance between the legislative and the judicial branches that must define the limits of this immunity, and the basis of liability, strict or negligence, should be immaterial to that issue.[99]

Another possible basis of liability for governmental entities is provided by California Constitution article I, section 14, which provides, "Private property shall not be taken or damaged for public use without just compensation. . . ." The constitutional mandate concerns only property damage caused under certain conditions; consequently, the previous discussion on tort liability is by no means made moot by the inverse condemnation principles. The most significant case elaborating upon inverse condemnation liability is *Albers v. County of Los Angeles,* in which a county was held liable for triggering a landslide during road construction and damaging private property, even though the slide condition was not foreseeable.[100] A public entity, according to the court, is liable for actual physical damage to property, proximately caused by the construction of a public work as deliberately planned and carried out by the entity, without regard to whether the damage was intentionally or negligently caused. In other words, strict liability is imposed by the constitution when injury to property ensues from a public project as deliberately planned and performed.[101] However, even prior to the Albers case, it had been held that a public entity is liable for damage caused by the escape of water from a natural watercourse where the probable consequence of the improvement as planned was such diversion, even though there might not be any negligence in making the improvement.[102] The conclusion is compelling that a public entity would be liable for property damage caused by increased precipitation due to augmentation activities conducted as planned, especially since the purpose of the activity is to increase precipitation.

237

This conclusion is urged as the correct one even as a matter of policy. First, to make the public entity bear the cost inflicted upon others will compel the entity to make rational decisions. Otherwise, there will be the inevitable tendency for the entity to be myopic and overlook the total costs involved in the undertaking. Second, if reparation for the loss is not made, sacrifices are exacted from a random segment of the community without a guiding principle in order that others may reap a benefit. Third, there may be a dampening of economic activity within the community unless compensation is awarded under these circumstances. While one may make investments subject to risks imposed by natural conditions, he may not do so when exposed to majoritarian arbitrariness.

One may legitimately question, however, why public entities should be made responsible for damages for which private parties under similar circumstances might not be. The answer might be threefold: first, the Albers case has clearly stated that public responsibility under the inverse condemnation doctrine is not limited by private tort principles; second, the public entity has a risk-sharing mechanism at hand, that is, through its taxing power; and third, perhaps the standard of liability within the private sector, to the extent that it is less demanding, should be re-examined.

If the public entity should be made liable on the above basis, what will be its impact upon local governmental units? There is apparently neither experience nor study upon which to predicate an answer at the present time. It would appear advisable that a study be undertaken immediately, not only for the purposes of establishing a proper loss-redistribution scheme but also to provide data upon which to make rational decisions concerning weather-modification activities. A total accounting may possibly indicate that precipitation augmentation at a given time at a given place or for a given duration may not be as profitable to society as one might prophesize. Not only the economic cost but physical and psychological adjustment and changes in ecology must be taken into this accounting. At any rate, if experience or study should indicate that the financial burden upon a local public entity which is required to compensate for these losses is fairly heavy, since it might not be able to recapture all of the benefits stemming from its activities, one might conclude that (1) a financially irresponsible entity ought not to be permitted to engage in augmentation activities, (2) an insurance scheme, public or private, ought to be devised, if not already available, for the operating entity, or (3) the entity should be excused from liability for those risks which are commonly insured against by private parties.[103] It should be noted, however, that California presently provides a mechanism to fund large losses by permitting a public entity to pay a tort judgment by installments over a period of ten years.[104] It may also reissue bonds to borrow funds.[105]

Difficulty of Applying Existing
Loss Redistribution Principles

In the above discussion, the ability of the injured party to prove causation has been assumed. With the advance in technology, proof of causation should be possible. In the meantime, when the state of the art is such that the complainant faces a virtually impossible task of carrying his burden of proving the amount of augmentation at a given place at a given time, a complainant is effectively denied relief. One answer to this dilemma is that a complainant has not been injured by precipitation-augmentation activities so long as he cannot legally prove the fact. But this conclusion, which flows from our adversary nature of litigation, does not necessarily refute that the complainant was in fact injured. Should there be a scheme of risk-pooling in order to minimize the hardship arising from an unanticipated loss? What alternatives are there?

Alternative Methods of Loss
Distribution or Risk-Pooling

A scheme for loss distribution or risk-pooling which is dependent upon proof of causation of damage from a precipitation-augmentation activity would be self-defeating at the present time, and, thus, some type of loss-insurance scheme might be considered. To the extent that there is commercial or federal insurance available at a reasonable premium to protect against damage to property from certain risks which might be increased by augmentation activities, such a risk-pooling institution can be utilized. For example, commercial water damage insurance might be available to cover certain kinds of losses from precipitation.[106] Federal crop and flood insurance might also be available.[107] However, local governmental units might consider participation, either singly or jointly, in filling a hiatus in existing loss insurance by (1) establishing a loss insurance administered and funded by the local unit or with reinsurance with the state or federal government, (2) acting as reinsurers to commercial insurers, (3) guaranteeing loans to make available cheaper loans from commercial sources or providing cheap loans directly, or (4) providing tax relief.[108] The cost of any of these schemes might be financed partially by an increased assessment or water toll, depending upon the extent to which the burden should be cast upon direct and indirect beneficiaries of the precipitation-augmentation project. In determining the financial feasibility of a direct-insurance program, one should consider the various means by which the cost might be reduced, such as minimum loss deductibility, compensation for out-of-pocket losses only, or exclusion of high-risk crops in target areas. It might well be that any of these schemes will be beyond the financial or administrative capability of a local unit or even of several entities acting jointly under the Joint Powers Act. It is not the purpose here to recommend any or all of these above schemes, for they will require study beyond the competence of this writer.

Responsibility of the Operating Unit
for Precipitation Reduction

The responsibility of a local governmental unit for physical damage inflicted by its precipitation-augmentation activity and the possible alternative responses have been discussed above. There remains the situation where its augmentation activity causes precipitation reduction in the downwind area.[109] The private rights to weather resources have been researched elsewhere, and one can safely conclude that a legal allocative scheme for atmospheric resources based on private rights is far from settled.[110]

This very uncertainty, however, may provide propitious conditions for establishing an allocative scheme which minimizes internal conflicts that might otherwise arise from assertion of private property rights to atmospheric resources. The following examples illustrate the institutional solutions which have been devised to meet a community resource problem.

Many areas of California face serious groundwater overdraft with its many attendant problems. An insistence upon allocation of percolating groundwater based upon individual water rights would mean a long and expensive lawsuit to determine a quantitative allocation, and after such determination, the judicial decree may enforce a proportionate reduction of current withdrawals, leaving the claimants with a water shortage.[111] In many areas, in lieu of such litigation, the water districts have employed the pricing structure to influence the amount of groundwater used by the irrigators. The water district has supplied cheap water to the irrigators to increase their use of district-supplied water, thereby augmenting the groundwater basin by percolation of water used for irrigation.[112] In some cases, the price of district water has been pegged at such a level as to discourage the use of groundwater. In other cases, the price of delivered water has been fixed at an amount equal to the cost of pumping so that those who are beyond the reach of district delivery would pay no more for their groundwater than those who receive what otherwise might be cheaper district-delivered water. To the extent that water tolls are insufficient to meet district obligations, the district must impose an assessment upon real property, but the assessment is generally district-wide and is based on the value of real property rather than upon the amount of water used so that, through a proper adjustment of water toll and assessment, the landowners throughout the district would contribute to the cost of meeting the groundwater problem or the inequitable district-distribution problem. In other words, the advantages of a private-water right within a water district may be diluted in many cases.

Another example of this is found in the Orange County Water District. Because of the long history of groundwater overdraft, the area must contend with sea-water intrusion into the groundwater basin, not to mention the increased pumping costs. In order to alleviate this condition, the District has purchased water from the Metropolitan Water District for artificial recharge into the basin. In order to defray the cost of water purchase, a "pumping" tax has been imposed upon all users of groundwater regardless of whether they have prior rights to the groundwater, and thus all groundwater users are made to contribute to the solution of a community problem.[113] More recently, the legislature has authorized the District to levy a basin equity assessment, levied upon the groundwater users who use more than a given amount of groundwater, for the purpose of compensating those who may be required by the District to reduce their groundwater extraction and thereby rely upon higher cost surface supply.[114]

Relating these experiences to precipitation-augmentation activities conducted by the public entities, the result of which may be a decrease in needed precipitation for some within the district but which may be difficult of proof, a greater reliance upon assessment, as opposed to toll, for district financing will tend to equalize the burden among those who recieve their water supply through increased precipitation upon their land and those who must rely to a greater extent upon water supplied by the district. In a situation where some water users are

241

diverting water, pursuant to their private water rights, from surface supplies or groundwater basins which have been augmented by the district activity, a water user's tax, comparable to the pumping tax, might be imposed upon all water users in order to reduce the price of district delivered water. The tax might offer a rough solution for recapturing benefits and compensating others.

The foregoing discussion has focused on internal conflicts. Where the operations are conducted outside the territorial limits of the operating entity, the resolution of the conflicts becomes far more complex in some respects. The pricing scheme to alleviate the possible loss of natural precipitation from the operations cannot be extended to out-of-district users. One facile answer is to suggest the unification of existing entities to encompass target and shadow areas. But this solution may be politically infeasible, especially if a county is engaged in weather-modification activities. Another suggestion is the establishment of a special weather-control district to include all territory which is beneficially and adversely affected. Within the district, zones of benefit can be established for the imposition of an assessment, albeit on a rough approximation, to be used to reduce the cost of water in zones of disbenefit. The creation of a super district is not an imperative to the operation of this scheme, however. A state agency which is charged with regulating and allocating atmospheric resources might require any public entity who desires to carry on weather modification to assure compensation to extraterritorial interests which are adversely affected.

Regulating Research, Experiments, and Operations

Existing Regulations

There is no known regulation in California of laboratory research in weather modification. The reason may be a simple one. There is no apparent need for such regulation at the present time.

The state has, however, established minimal regulations pertaining to weather-modification operations.[115] Any person, defined to include public agencies as well as private parties, who seeks to engage in precipitation augmentation or reduction activities, must file an application with the Department of Water Resources setting forth certain information and pay a fee. Upon compliance with these conditions, the Department must issue a license to the applicant. The Department has no authority nor duty to review the qualifications of the applicant to determine his fitness to conduct the operations, even though the applicant must give information concerning his education, experience, and qualification.

The licensee, before undertaking the operations, must file a notice of intention to undertake operations with the Department and also publish the notice for three consecutive weeks in a newspaper of general circulation in the county where the operations are to be conducted. The notice must state the name and address of the licensee, the purpose of the operations, and the person on whose behalf the operations are conducted, the area where, and the time during which, the operations will be conducted, and the area which will be affected by the operations. Most significantly, the Department has no authority to regulate where or when the operations may be conducted. The prior notice provisions may be suspended in the event of an emergency to fight fire or to alleviate drought (in the case of drought, the application to suspend the prior notice requirement must come from a local governmental unit). Every licensee is required to keep a record of its operations and submit specified information to the Department after each operation. Although a license revocation proceeding is provided, it would seem that the only reasons for which a license can be suspended or revoked are the making of incorrect statements in the application and the failure to comply with the notice and reporting provisions.

Appraisal of Existing Regulations

The present statute is principally a notification and reporting provision and cannot be characterized as truly regulatory. Perhaps under present circumstances this scheme might be adequate, but it would appear that in the future an appropriate agency should be given the responsibility of regulating the who, how, where and when of the weather-modification activities. The consequences of the operations can be too serious to be left to uncoordinated determination with post facto court supervision. Moreover, unregulated operations can lead to needless waste of time and money if experiments and operations should contaminate other operations.

If the state were to determine intrastate allocation of weather resources, the function should be assigned to the State Water Resources Control Board.[116] Prior to 1967, California had one agency to regulate appropriation of water from watercourses and another to deal with water pollution. Realizing the indivisibility of these functions, since appropriation and pollution involve demands upon the same resource, the legislature assigned both functions to a single agency in 1967.[117] By the same token, precipitation is a part of the same interrelated resource and should be allocated by the same agency which presently regulates water resources for beneficial use or for waste transportation, guided by the standards which require the consideration of the public welfare, demands upon the resource, and the state water plan.[118] It should be noted, however, that regulation of qualification of modifiers is a separable function from weather-resources allocation and need not be assigned to this Board.

Regulation as a State Function

The conclusion that these functions belong to a government at a level higher than the local government appears incontrovertible. The logical agency at the state level to which this responsibility should be assigned is the State Water Resources Control Board, since it already has a statewide supervisorial power over most water resources. The local governmental units as they presently exist, even if they had the power, cannot intelligently allocate the interrelated resource by assuming jurisdiction over only a part of the hydrologic cycle and by having a limited geographic jurisdiction when the water resource is not so limited.[119] Moreover, it is desirable to establish uniform standards regulating the qualifications of the weather modifiers. Local regulations in this regard may lead to confusion and parochialism.[120] One exception to the above generalization may be fog dissipation if the effect is truly local.

There is no impediment to bringing the local governmental units under state control in terms of regulating their weather-modification activities. Even the chartered cities would not be able to seek shelter within "municipal affairs" to escape state regulation concerning qualifications of those undertaking weather modification.[121] Moreover, the case for bringing local governments within the ambit of state allocative administration is fairly clear. Earlier, we noted the number of local governmental units having the power to engage in precipitation augmentation and reduction activities. Many of these units cover overlapping territory. For example, the cities and special districts will necessarily overlap county territory. It does not make sense to have competing activities for precipitation augmentation conducted in the same area if the consequence is to reduce the effectiveness of all activities by overseeding or to effect augmentation in unanticipated amount with resulting damage. It is sheer folly to have an irrigation district nucleating the clouds to induce precipitation while a flood control district is conducting operations in the same formation to prevent precipitation.

Regulation of Intentional Weather
Modification Activities by Local Entities

What if the state fails to take corrective measures to have an effective regulation? Can the local governmental units act to fill the void? In answering this question, one must distinguish the status of the counties and cities, on the one hand, and the special districts, on the other. As mentioned earlier, the state constitution gives to counties and cities the power to enact regulatory measures so long as they do not conflict with the general laws. But in the case of special districts, not only has the constitution failed to give this power to the special districts but the court has held that the legislature cannot delegate to special districts the power to enact police-power measures and to fix the penalties for their violation.[122] However, it would appear that, if the legislature has provided adequate standards and has provided the penalty for violation of regulations promulgated by the district, the district regulation would be upheld.[123] Despite the legal method of vesting a district with the authority to adopt regulatory measures, it is not recommended that the districts be given the authority to regulate the private sector with respect to weather-modification activities. There are several reasons for this. The counties and the cities are the traditional entities for enacting local measures regulating private conduct and more importantly the legislative bodies of counties and cities are frequently representative of more people and interests than would be the legislative bodies of many special districts.[124]

Our attention is now directed to the constitutional authority of the counties and cities to adopt regulatory measures. Because the state has already enacted minimal regulations over precipitation augmentation and reduction activity, local regulatory power will necessarily be somewhat limited, since local regulation cannot conflict with state provisions. A conflict will exist if the local regulation (1) permits that which the state prohibits, or conversely, prohibits that which the state permits, (2) duplicates the state regulation, or (3) enters a field occupied by the state.[125] In light of these constraints, what can the local entities presently do? Can the local entities establish standards of professional competence before a person may engage in precipitation-modification activities and impose a license requirement? The state statute, although making provision for revocation of a permit to engage in weather-modification activity, does not seek to regulate professional competence, and, thus, the state law can be characterized as a registration scheme. A local regulation of professional competence would not be in direct conflict with a registration law. In the recent case of *Galvan v. Superior Court,* the court, by distinguishing registration and licensing requirements, held that a local gun-registration ordinance was not in direct conflict with the state law which stated that "no permit or license" shall be required to keep a weapon at one's place of residence or business.[126] In the court's words, "Any requirement that an item be registered before it can be lawfully used involves, of course, 'permission to do a particular thing,' and to that extent 'registration' is the same as 'licensing.' But the basic and commonly held distinction between licensing and registration is that licensing regulates activity based on a determination of the personal qualifications of the licensee, while registration catalogs all persons with respect to an activity, or all things that fall within certain classifications."[127]

The more difficult question is whether the state has occupied the field of precipitation-modification control so as to preclude further regulation by the local entities. The court has provided the following test for state preemption:

(1) the subject matter has been so fully and completely covered by general law as to clearly indicate that it has become exclusively a matter of state concern; (2) the subject matter has been partially covered by general law couched in such terms as to indicate clearly that a paramount state concern will not tolerate further or additional local action; or (3) the subject matter has been partially covered by general law, and the subject is of such a nature that the adverse effect of a local ordinance on the transient citizens of the state outweighs the possible benefit to the municipality.[128]

The test quoted above provides a broad framework of relevant inquiry, rather than offering litmus certainty.

With respect to regulating the professional competence of modifiers, it can be argued that the state has preempted the field since varying standards fixed by the local units are not conducive to sound control over these activities, nor are there varying local conditions which would call for differing local standards. This argument would be persuasive had the state fixed even minimal standards of competence, but in the absence of any control by the state, even varying standards may be more desirable than none at all. Moreover, the interests of transient citizens are hard to identify in this instance inasmuch as weather-modification activities invite regulations and should place a person engaging in such activity upon notice of probable regulation. The benefits to be derived from preventing incompetent tampering with weather conditions would far outweigh any conceivable interest of the operators. If an unarticulated principle can be distilled from past decisions, it would seem that generally more stringent regulations adopted by local entities to protect the health and safety, as contrasted with regulation of morals, of the local inhabitants will be sustained by the court.[129]

Moreover, because state regulation deals solely with precipitation control, the whole field of lightning suppression, possibly fog dispersal, and other activities are left unregulated.[130] It is difficult to attribute to the legislature an intent that, by regulating precipitation control, other weather-modification activities were to be left unregulated. The greater likelihood is that the legislature failed to regulate other activities, because at the time the current legislation was enacted the extent of other activities was probably minimal at best. This would mean that at the present time local entities are free to regulate modifiers of weather for purposes other than precipitation control.

Another aspect of weather-modification regulation must be analyzed. Do local entities have the power to allocate weather resources? Do local entities have the power to regulate the when, where, and how of the modification activities to avert or minimize physical damage to others? It is extremely dubious that the local entities would be able to set the guidelines for the allocation of resources for the private or the public sector. The formulation of basic property rights has never been within the domain of local public entities, and rightly so, because of the supervening state interest in having a uniform state law as to these matters. It matters little whether this incapacity of the local entities is based on fundamental lack of power to determine civil jural relationships or on the theory that the exercise of such power will necessarily conflict with state laws.

But the exercise of the traditional police power, founded upon a conceptually different theoretical basis, by the local entities may have allocative consequences. For example, basic property rights are defined by state law. But local entities commonly regulate by penal ordinances the use of property in order to minimize the disbenefits which may be thrust upon others. Zoning is a very good example of this interplay between state-determined property rights and local land-use regulations.

In short, although local entities will not be able to determine the basic rights to atmospheric resources, they may regulate the when, where, and how of weather-modification activity in order to prevent harm to persons and to property of others, subject to the qualification that such regulations do not conflict with the state law. Under existing law, local entities might not be able to require different or additional notification requirements upon weather modifiers, but they might be able to impose other restraints upon modification which are designed to protect the health and safety of others.

Now that the power of local entities to regulate has been analyzed, the question remains as to whether they should. The question might be better posed in terms of whether it is worth the effort.

Up to now only two parties in the private sector have engaged in precipitation modification of any significance, and these two have been public utilities. The others have been public entities, generally special districts. If a county or a city should adopt regulatory measures, will it be applicable to these parties? First, as to public utilities, the professional competency standards adopted by the local entities would probably be applicable to the employees and the independent contractors employed by the utilities in conducting the modification activities. The Public Utilities Commission has the authority to regulate the safety standards of public utility operations.[131] This includes possibly the competency of the personnel, if it chose to do so.[132] But it seems that the Commission has not acted in the field of weather modification, and until it does so, it would appear that the public utilities would be subject to local safety regulations as would any other private party.

Second, a city or a county might not be able to regulate the activities of other public entities on the ground that the other entities are state agencies and, thus, immune from local regulation.[133] Further, the state may have preempted the field in prescribing the powers and duties of other entities.[134]

If the above conclusions are correct, it would appear that local regulation of precipitation augmentation in most areas at the present time would be an idle act since the precipitation-modification projects are generally conducted by public entities excepting those conducted by the two public utilities.

Regulation of Unintended
Weather Modification

Another aspect of regulation will be briefly explored. Can local entities be effective in regulating land use and other activities in order to

248

control unintended atmospheric modifications? There are many dimensions to this problem. First, if the concern is over the accumulation of carbon dioxide in the atmosphere which will affect global climate, clearly uneven local efforts to alleviate the problem may be much too insignificant to warrant further examination. Moreover, the problem is complex in terms of availability of substitute fuels, determining the cost of such substitutes, the effect on the economy by making the substitution, etc. In short, the scope of the problem is a national one at the minimum and an international one for truly effective resolution. Second, if pollutants will have significant local effect on weather conditions, the state ought to control the standards of pollutant emission in order that economic costs will not be exported by one area to another. If the cause and effect are local within a given local governmental unit, perhaps the local units should be given concurrent jurisdiction to impose either more stringent standards than the state standards or to regulate those activities unregulated by the state. Local units, however, should not be given the power to control transportation activities and other like activities, since local control may interfere with commerce within the state.

The other type of unintended atmospheric modification comes from land use. The filling of bodies of water may have a profound effect on the climate of adjacent communities. The type of land cover may likewise have an effect. Can we sustain under the police power a regulation of the local entity which prohibits the filling of a bay or which requires the continued maintenance of a green belt in order that existing weather and climatic conditions may continue? Would it make any difference if the changes in the weather which would occur from either the filling or development are mere inconveniences to the welfare of the community, such as higher mean temperature or if they have a profound effect on the economic well being of the community? Land-use control has been traditionally the concern of the local entities, although there is a greater present awareness of a need for regional planning and implementation where artificial local governmental boundaries have placed an impediment to rational control over interrelated areas. Regulation of land use for climatic control by counties and cities must be assessed in light of this limitation.

But aside from territorial-jurisdictional restraints, there is the fundamental problem of whether a government may regulate land use for this purpose without the need to compensate the landowners whose land is to be restricted. The degree to which the landowner may constitutionally be made to suffer a loss through land-use restriction will depend upon the extent to which the use, which is prohibited by regulation, would otherwise have visited disbenefit to others and the degree to which there may be reciprocal benefits flowing from a common restriction. The greater the external costs from the activity, the greater may be the restraints imposed upon the activity. For example, if mining or manufacturing operations near a residential area pose serious problems of health and safety to the residents, the discontinuance of the operations may be compelled even though it will result in a substantial loss to the operator.[135] If a given land use involves diseconomy to neighboring lands but not to the extent of posing a serious health or safety hazard to others, the commencement of the use may be prohibited, but discontinuance of existing uses in nonconforming structures may be compelled only under a reasonable amortization scheme.[136] And generally, where a proposed or existing use does not export costs, the prohibitory power over such use becomes commensurately circumscribed.[137]

From the above principles, one might conclude that a prohibition against converting a greenbelt or a water area to other uses would be sustained, despite due process arguments, if it can be shown that the conversion would significantly and detrimentally alter weather conditions in the community. However, before one readily accepts the validity of such regulation, he should realize that the disbenefit in question arises from the mere fact of changing the natural conditions of land and may be a disbenefit in common with all other land uses, and, therefore, one class of landowners is being required to forego use of its property in order that others may be protected in their uses which are equally contributory to the harm sought to be alleviated by the restriction. For example, would a court uphold a prohibition against development of land against some landowners on the ground that the development would curtail percolation of water into the groundwater basin and that such prohibition is necessary to protect the water supply of other landowners who have already developed their land and extract water from the groundwater basin?[138] While there might be authority for an affirmative answer, a serious question remains.

A Sampling of Enabling Acts for Weather Modification Districts in Other States

Weather Control Districts in Nebraska

Nebraska has enacted a general enabling act for the formation of weather-control districts.[139] A proposal to form a district is commenced by a petition of landowners filed with a state agency after which a noticed hearing must be held by the agency. If the agency determines that the organization of a district "would be desirable and necessary in the interest of the public welfare," it shall approve the petition and fix the boundary.[140] This decision is appealable to a court by any taxpayer within the proposed district.[141] If no appeal is taken, or if appealed upon final determination by the court an election is held at which those who own taxable property, other than intangible property, within the district are entitled to vote. If 55 percent of the votes are in favor of formation, the district is formed, but the statute provides that any precinct in which the votes in favor of the formation are less than 55 percent shall not be made a part of the district.[142] The members of the first board of directors are designated in the petition for the formation of the district, and evidently no opposing candidates are permitted at the first election.

The significant powers of the district in relation to weather control are "(2) gather information concerning weather control; (3) aid or conduct, alone or in conjunction with other districts, any program of weather control; (4) contract with any private individual, association, or corporation, or with any governmental agency, engaged in weather control, for performance of the activities mentioned in subdivision (2) and (3) of this section."[143] The activities are financed by a tax, at a rate not to exceed one mill on the dollar, upon all taxable property except intangible property.[144] It is "unlawful for any aircraft of such district or its contractor to fly outside the boundaries of such district during any seeding operations or to seed any cloud formation situated outside the boundaries of such district."[145]

There are several features of the weather control district law of Nebraska which merit comment. First, the district is a single purpose district—weather control. Thus, if the district engages in precipitation augmentation to the extent of producing a supply which can be stored for later distribution or substantially increases the runoff in a watercourse, the statute is silent as to the disposition of the increased supply. If the operations of the district are confined to hail suppression or precipitation augmentation which is intended to irrigate the land directly by precipitation, the aforementioned problem, of course, would not arise.

A second concern about the Nebraska district law is the option given to each precinct within the district to refuse to join the district. If the district is formed for the purpose of hail suppression and if the suppression activity can be operated with such accuracy as to benefit

251

only those precincts which have joined the district, the local option should not lead to inequity. However, if the operations will benefit the excluded lands, it would seem that such landowners ought to be required to bear a share of the cost.

Third, the activity of the district is financed by an assessment based on the assessed value of taxable tangible property. It seems unfair that exempt property, such as that of the state and its political subdivision and that owned by and used for the purpose of agricultural societies, should escape the burden of the service which is provided to them. Moreover, it is uncertain whether the taxable property as a tax base offers the most equitable means of financing the activities if the objective is to allocate the burden based on the benefit received. Unlike the usual district where its service is fairly predictable, the hail-suppression activity of the district is much like an insurance among the landowners whose risk exposure may differ from year to year and from one parcel to another. The landowners are in effect pooling their resources to finance the cost of suppressing hail wherever and whenever it is likely to occur within the district. Upon further investigation, it might be determined that the risk exposure may differ among the various parts of the district, in which case zones of benefits might be defined to vary the rate of contribution.

Another aspect of the Nebraska law is puzzling. The petition for formation is not required to state the kind of activities which will be conducted by the proposed district. Without a knowledge of proposed functions, the property owners should find it rather difficult to lodge an intelligent protest against inclusion of their land within the district based on lack of benefit or to vote at the election.

Finally, the Nebraska law restricts certain operations to the area within the district. It is clear that aircraft of the district or of its contractor cannot fly outside the district during seeding operations, even though seeding is conducted within the district. This restriction may be necessary to police the more basic restriction that cloud formations outside the district cannot be seeded. It is much easier to determine the paths of aircraft flights than it is to determine when the seeding ingredients are released from the aircraft. But it is to be noted that there is no restriction as to where ground-based generators may be placed. Presumably, ground-based generators may be located outside the district if it can be assured that only clouds within the district will be seeded. Whether such geographical limitations upon operational activities should be imposed is debatable. If the purpose of the restriction is to prohibit weather-modification results outside the district, the statute should be so framed. Otherwise a geographical restriction might mean that lands close to district boundaries will not realize any benefit depending upon the time required for seeding agents to produce results and the speed at which the seeded clouds travel. Perhaps the existing restrictions might be excusable in light of the present experimental state of weather modification.

Weather Modification Authority in North Dakota

North Dakota permits the formation of a weather-modification authority, having a county-wide jurisdiction, upon approval by the board of county commissioners of a petition of 51 percent of the electors.[146] The authority is governed by five commissioners who are nominally appointed by the board of county commissioners but are in fact nominated in the petition by the petitioners.

The authority is empowered to levy a tax upon the "net taxable valuation of the property" in the county and expend funds "only for weather-modification activities within the county, including research and investigation."[147] "Weather modification" is broadly defined as "the control, alteration, amelioration of weather elements" followed by examples which leave no doubt as to its comprehensiveness.[148] The authority has a life of five years unless renewed under the formation procedure.

The scheme for local governmental participation in weather-modification operations in North Dakota appears to be somewhat rigid in several respects. First, the county boundaries might not be the appropriate definition of the area in which the weather-modification activities should be conducted since atmospheric conditions, watershed, streams, community of interests, and other considerations may dictate a different territorial unit for efficient operation. Second, an ad valorem assessment on taxable property might not be the most equitable method of distributing the burden if a particular activity results in disproportionate benefits among the county inhabitants or property owners.

The North Dakota, like the Nebraska, statute makes no mention of the means for distributing an increased water supply. And if the legislature had intended to restrict the intended effects of weather-

253

modification activities to the county in which the authority exists, a restriction on the place where the activities can be conducted might be an improper formulation to accomplish the legislative objective.

It might be noted that North Dakota extends the authority to expend funds for weather-modification activities to townships as well.[149]

An Appraisal of Local Governmental
Responsibility in Weather Modification

In the previous sections, the issues relevant to local governmental responsibility in weather-modification activities have been discussed. Some tentative conclusions, some of which are fairly obvious, are now offered.

1. In determining the role of local governmental units in weather-modification activities, the various kinds of weather-modification activities must be considered separately. Each type of activity, whether it be precipitation augmentation or reduction, fog dispersal, hail suppression, lightning suppression, or wind control, will present its peculiar set of problems.

2. The responsibility for engaging in a given type of weather-modification activity should generally be assigned only to those local entities whose other services would be supplemented by that activity. A corollary to the above is that a new local governmental unit for the sole purpose of engaging in weather-modification activity ought not be established when existing entities can adequately perform that activity or when the creation of a new unit will unnecessarily add to the complexity of atmospheric resource allocation.

The existing water districts with their storage and distribution facilities would be the appropriate units for engaging in precipitation-augmentation activities. This would also be true of cities engaged in their own water development and distribution as it would be of state and federal governments with respect to their water-wholesaling functions. Generally, it seems unwise to superimpose upon the existing public entities a district which has as its sole purpose precipitation augmentation. Such a super district can be justified only if an entity with greater financial resources is necessary or if existing units of government may be geographically inadequate to make precipitation augmentation feasible. But even under those circumstances, a super district is not the only solution. A cooperative organization among the existing local governmental units and with state or federal government

254

participation may offer viable alternatives. A super district may result in another local governmental unit of low political and financial visibility with its concomitant insulation from voter control.

A new special district for lightning or hail suppression may be justified if assignment of these functions to existing units might mean a low order of priority for such activity or if territorial jurisdiction of existing units formed for other purposes might be inappropriate for these activities. Fog dispersal for airport landings can probably be best handled by the entity which owns or operates the airport.

3. Weather-modification activities will inevitably impose conflicting demands upon the atmospheric resources. It is better to have a system of pre-activity allocation under a licensing scheme rather than a post-activity judicial allocation. Local governmental units with their limited territorial jurisdictions, however, should not perform this function. A state agency should be responsible for intrastate allocation.

In California where it appears that weather modification will be directed principally toward precipitation augmentation, at least in the near future, the allocation of cloud resources ought to be handled by the State Water Resources Control Board, which is already charged with water-resources allocative function. With the present state of science, it may be difficult to make any precise allocation of a temporal resource as clouds, but the Board can at the minimum, prevent the contamination of weather-modification operations.

4. It is not essential that the agency that performs the allocative function should also regulate the weather-modification activities—for example, prescribing the professional standards for modifiers, designating the permissible seeding agents, etc.—although consolidation of functions in one agency may simplify administration without loss of other values at the present time. In the formulation of these standards, the responsible agency in question should be required to coordinate with other state agencies which also have a vital interest in weather-modification activities.

In California, if the allocative and regulatory functions are assigned to the State Water Resources Control Board, the Board, in formulating its standards, should be required to consult with the Department of Water Resources, Department of Public Health, Fish and Game Commission, Department of Agriculture, and relevant pollution control boards, or in the alternative, the regulations might be made subject to the approval of these agencies.

5. A state law should provide that a governmental entity should be

financially responsible for any physical damage caused to the person or property of another from its weather-modification activity on the basis of strict liability.

6. The local governmental entity should be given flexible authority to devise loss-distribution schemes.

Notes

1. The reader is cautioned that each state must be examined independently to determine the precise allocation of power between the state and the local governmental units; it is hoped that a discussion of California institutions will give the reader a framework of inquiry which might be utilized in other states and offer relevant considerations in making a determination of the proper role of local governmental units.

2. Crouch, Bollens, Scott and McHenry, California Government and Politics 234 (4th ed. 1967).

3. Cal. Const. art. XI, § 7-1/2.

4. Ibid.

5. Ibid.

6. Cal. Const. art. XI, § 7-1/2. subd. 4, requires a charter to provide:

> For the powers and duties of board supervisors and all other county officers, for their removal and for the consolidation and segregation of county officers, and for the manner of filling all vacancies occurring therein; provided, that the provisions of such charters relating to the powers and duties of boards of supervisors and all other county officers shall be subject to and controlled by general laws.

The legislative history of the above provision is less than illuminating. See Sato, Municipal Occupation Taxes in California: The Authority to Levy Taxes and the Burden on Instrastate Commerce, 53 Calif. L. Rev. 801, 802 (1965). The other provisions in section 7-1/2 deal wholly with internal administration and organization, and, if the charter was intended as an independent source of entity power, the draftsman surely could have used such terms as "county affairs" as opposed to powers and duties of the officers, especially since the model of "municipal affairs" for chartered cities was in existence at this time.

Cal. Const. art. XI, § 11, which provides, "Any county, city . . . may make and enforce within its limits all such local, police, sanitary and other regulations as are not in conflict with general laws," might be urged as a constitutional authority for a county to engage in weather-modification activities. However, the Supreme Court of California has held that the authority under this provision extends only to regulating the conduct of the inhabitants and not to authorize services. Von Schmidt v. Widber, 105 Cal. 151, 38 Pac. 682 (1894). Although there have been contrary lower court decisions, for example, De Aryan v. Butler, 119 Cal. App. 2d 674, 260 P.2d 98 (1953), *cert. denied,* 347 U.S. 1012 (1954), it seems unlikely that section 11 was intended to confer a broad power equivalent to a charter.

7. Cal. Const. art. XI, § 11.

8. Ibid.

9. 6 McQuillin, Municipal Corporations § 22.01 (3rd ed. 1949).

10. Prosser, Law of Torts 191-192, 202-203 (3rd ed. 1964).

11. Ex parte Roach, 104 Cal. 272 (1894).

12. Hall v. City of Taft, 47 Cal. 2d 177, 302 P.2d 574 (1956); County of Los Angeles v. City of Los Angeles, 212 Cal. App. 2d 160, 28 Cal. Rptr. 32 (1963).

13. Hall v. City of Taft, supra note 12; Baldwin Park County Water Dist. v. County of Los Angeles, 208 Cal. App. 2d 87, 25 Cal. Rptr. 167 (1962).

14. Rhyne, Municipal Law 57 (1957).

15. Cal. Const. art. XI, § 8.

16. Cal. Const. art. XI, § 8(j); Cal. Const. art. XI, § 6.

17. West Coast Advertising Co. v. City and County of San Francisco, 14 Cal. 2d 516, 95 P.2d 138 (1939).

18. Ibid.

19. Raisch v. Myers, 27 Cal. 2d 773, 167 P.2d 198 (1946).

20. See, for example, Professional Fire Fighters, Inc. v. City of Los Angeles, 60 Cal. 2d 276, 32 Cal. Rptr. 830, 384 P.2d 158 (1963), in which the court held that the state statute regulating fire fighters' labor relationship with a public entity applied to a chartered city because of a predominant state concern. But in the absence of a state statute, a chartered city would unquestionably have the authority to resolve problems of labor relations between it and its employees. See, for example, City of Pasadena v. Charleville, 215 Cal. 384, 10 P.2d 745 (1932).

21. For example, West Coast Advertising Co. v. City and County of San Francisco, 14 Cal. 2d 516, 95 P.2d 138 (1939).

22. City of San Mateo v. Railroad Commission, 9 Cal. 2d 1, 68 P.2d 713 (1937).

23. Cal. Const. art. XI, § 11.

24. See text to footnotes 7 and 13, supra.

25. Cal. Const. art. XI, § 19; see In re Orosi Public Utility Dist., 196 Cal. 43, 235 Pac. 1004 (1925) (dictum).

26. See text to footnotes 45 and 46, infra.

27. Crouch, supra n. 2 at 249.

28. For example, Palo Verde Irrigation District Act, Cal. Water Code App. §§ 33-1, 33-3.

29. For example, Irrigation District Law, Cal. Water Code §§ 20500, 20720, 20960.

30. For example, Los Angeles County Flood Control Act, Cal. Water Code App. § 28-1.

31. Cal. Water Code § 21551 (election of directors of irrigation districts formed under a general enabling act).

32. For example, Cal. Water Code App. § 51-7 (board of Supervisors of Santa Barbara County to act as ex officio directors of Santa Barbara County Water Agency).

33. For example, Cal. Water Code App. § 35-6 (board of directors of Metropolitan Water District to consist of at least one representative from each municipality within the district; presumably the governing body of the municipality makes the appointment); Cal. Pub. Util. Code § 28733 (certain number of directors of San Francisco Bay Area Rapid Transit District chosen by board of supervisors of each county and by city selection committees of each county within the district; city selection committee to consist of the mayor or chairman of city council of each city in the county).

34. Crawford v. Imperial Irrigation Dist., 200 Cal. 318, 253 Pac. 726 (1927) ("An irrigation district, like any other public or private corporation, derives its powers from the statute under which it is created. . . .").

35. Gilgert v. Stockton Port Dist., 7 Cal. 2d 384, 60 P.2d 847 (1936).

36. Moore v. Municipal Court, 170 Cal. App. 2d 548, 339 P.2d 196 (1959).

37. Cal. Govt. Code § 53063.

38. Cal. Const. art. XIII, § 25; see Mallon v. City of Long Beach, 44 Cal. 2d 199, 292 P.481 (1955).

39. Cf. City of Oakland v. Garrison, 194 Cal. 298, 228 Pac. 433 (1924).

40. If this conclusion were adopted, an irrigation district, although admittedly formed to help the farmers, would not be able to engage in hail suppression merely because it has the power to acquire and distribute water to the farmers.

41. Cal. Water Code App. § 27-2.

42. Cal. Water Code App. § 21-5.

43. For the sake of discussion, it has been assumed that modification activity can reduce precipitation on an operational basis.

44. It is difficult to believe that the legislature would not have added the term "reduction" to the list, if the legislature had reduction operations in mind, when it has employed the term "increase" in addition to "control."

45. 25 Ops. Cal. Atty. Gen. 164 (1955).

46. Ibid. at 166.

47. Cal. Water Code App. § 28-2. Indeed, the Los Angeles County Flood Control District has engaged in precipitation augmentation programs, Dept. of Water Resources, Cal., Bull. No. 16-67, Weather-Modification Operations in California 8 (1968), but the authority to engage in such activity would be derived from Cal. Govt. Code § 53063 which empowers a district with the authority to conserve water for beneficial purposes to conduct precipitation-augmentation practices. The Los Angeles County Flood Control District is organized for the purpose of "control and conservation of the flood, storm and other waste waters of said district," Cal. Water Code App. § 28-2, and thus, literally meets the terms of § 53063, although it is questionable whether a district having the power to conserve flood and storm waters was intended to have the power to increase precipitation. Perhaps the

District is engaged in weather modification to alter the geographical and time distribution of precipitation in order to conserve water which otherwise would have been wasted if allowed to precipitate and create flood conditions.

48. Cal. Water Code App. § 48-9 (13).

49. The statute granting this authority to the District was enacted in 1951, 1951 Cal. Stat. 3289, four years prior to the adoption of the general provision in Cal. Govt. Code § 53063, 1955 Cal. Stat. 3365.

50. For the purposes of this discussion, such information is not necessary.

51. Cal. Govt. Code § 25690.

52. Cal. Govt. Code § 25680.

53. Ibid.

54. Cal. Govt. Code § 25642.

55. Cal. Govt. Code § 26020.

56. Cal. Const. art. XI, § 19.

57. Cal. Govt. Code §§ 8010, 8011.

58. See discussion in text to footnotes 16-21, supra; the reader is cautioned that the authority granted by the constitution with respect to municipal affairs does not necessarily protect a chartered city from state legislative control. For example, the state defines the tortious liability of a chartered city, and such city must operate within the general rules pertaining to property. A more detailed discussion follows.

59. State Controller's 1967 Annual Report of Financial Transactions Concerning Irrigation Districts of California 3.

60. Cal. Water Code § 22075.

61. Cal. Water Code §§ 22140-22146.

62. Cal. Water Code § 22160.

63. State Controller's 1966-1967 Annual Report of Financial Transactions Concerning Special Districts of California vii.

64. Cal. Water Code § 31020.

65. State Controller's Report, supra n. 63.

66. Cal. Water Code § 35401.

67. The enumeration is intended to be illustrative and not exhaustive.

68. Cal. Govt. Code § 61600.

69. State Controller's Report, supra n. 63.

70. Cal. Govt. Code § 71610.

71. State Controller's Report, supra n. 63.

72. Cal. Govt. Code § § 43000, 43001.

73. State Controller's Report, supra n. 63.

74. Cal. Govt. Code § 50910.

75. Cal. Water Code § 55330.

76. State Controller's Report, supra n. 63.

77. Cal. Pub. Util. Code § 16461.

78. State Controller's Report, supra n. 63.

79. Cal. Health and Safety Code § 13852(i).

80. Cal. Health and Safety Code § 14092(g).

81. State Water Resources Board, Bull. No. 16, Weather Modifications in California (1955); Dept. of Water Resources, Bull. Nos. 16-62 (1963), 16-63 (1964), 16-64 (1965), 16-65 (1966), 16-66 (1967), and 16-67 (1968). The Bulletins are entitled "Weather Modification Operations in California."

82. The federal funding for research involving intentional atmospheric modification was 13.8 million dollars, a figure which does not include funds for related research. Federal Council for Science and Technology, ICAS Rep. No. 11, National Atmospheric Sciences Program 7 (1967). ICAS Select Panel on Weather Modification has recommended an increase in federal funding to approximately 147 million dollars by fiscal year 1970. Ibid. at 111-3.
The response to this writer's inquiry from five public agencies active in operational precipitation-augmentation program indicates that none of them is engaged in laboratory research on weather modifica-

tion. The expenditure for field operations during the year 1966-1967 varied from a low of approximately $22,000 to $48,000 among the five responding public agencies.

83. State Controller's Report, supra n. 63, at 173.

84. State Controller's Report, supra n. 63, at 262.

85. See Break, Intergovernmental Fiscal Relations in the United States 63-76 (1967).

86. Two agencies responded to the inquiry concerning estimated benefit-cost ratio of their precipitation-augmentation program. One agency estimated a ratio of 34:1, and the other estimated a minimum of 6:1.

87. Where physical damage to the person or property of another is caused by weather-modification activity, there is no doubt that one has a legally protected interest in his person or property. The problem is at the level of determining the extent to which such interests should be protected against the activity of another. On the other hand, when a person is deprived of natural precipitation because of weather modification, the problem is at a rudimentary level of determining whether there is a legally protected interest in atmospheric resources. The basic issue is, of course, identical in both cases—*viz.* loss reallocation.

88. For a historical review of this doctrine, see Muskopf v. Corning Hosp. Dist., 55 Cal. 2d 211, 11 Cal. Rptr. 89, 359 P.2d 457 (1961); Van Alstyne, California Government Tort Liability § § 1.5–1.15 (1964); for example, Cal. Const. art. I, § 14.

The courts made a distinction between governmental and proprietary activities of the government and withheld the immunity from activities falling into the latter category. For example, People v. Superior Court, 29 Cal. 2d 754, 178 P.2d 1 (1947).

See Van Alstyne, Governmental Tort Liability § § 2.3-2.18 (1964).

89. Muskopf, v. Corning Hosp. Dist., 55 Cal. 2d 211, 11 Cal. Rptr. 89, 359 P.2d 457 (1961).

90. 1963 Cal. Stat. 3266.

91. Douglass v. City of Los Angeles, 5 Cal. 2d 123, 53 P.2d 353 (1936) (general law claims procedure for tort claim governs a chartered city since tort liability of a chartered city is determined by general law).

92. Cal. Govt. Code § 815.2 By the same token, the public entity generally enjoys the same immunity conferred upon the public employee.

93. Cal. Govt. Code § 820.

94. Cal. Govt. Code § 820.2.

95. 69 Cal. 2d 782, 73 Cal. Rptr. 240, 447 P.2d 352 (1968).

96. Cal. Govt. Code §§ 825, 825.2. There are minor exceptions to this rule.

97. 249 Cal. App. 2d 281, 57 Cal. Rptr. 312 (1967); ibid. at 290, 57 Cal. Rptr. at 317.

98. This may be an inquiry as to whether the judiciary is competent to prescribe a standard of care if negligence is the basis of liability.

99. Whether the nuisance doctrine as a basis of liability for public entities remains viable after the 1963 Act is in considerable doubt. Compare Cal. Govt. Code § 815 and the Legislative Committee Comment thereto, with Granone v. City of Los Angeles, 231 Cal. App. 2d 629, 42 Cal. Rptr. 34 (1965); Lombardy v. Peter Kiewit Sons' Co., 266 Cal. App. 2d 599, 72 Cal. Rptr. 240 (1968).

100. 62 Cal. 2d 250, 42 Cal. Rptr. 89, 398 P.2d 129 (1965).

101. Injuries resulting from inadvertent acts would not be compensable.

102. Youngblood v. Los Angeles County Flood Control Dist., 56 Cal. 2d 603, 15 Cal. Rptr. 904, 364 P.2d 840 (1961).

103. A local public entity is authorized to procure insurance for tort liability. Cal. Govt. Code § 990.

104. Cal. Govt. § 970.6. A local public entity is required to pay a tort judgment during the fiscal year in which it becomes final if funds are available, and, if not, in the following year; Cal. Govt. Code § 970.4, but installment payments may be made if payment in the succeeding fiscal year will cause an undue hardship. A local public entity is authorized to exceed any limitation on the amount of tax, assessment, rate or charge and also any debt limitation in order to pay tort judgments. Cal. Govt. Code § 971.

105. Cal. Govt. Code §§ 975-978.8.

106. See Long and Gregg, Property and Liability Insurance Handbook 103-105 (1965).

107. Federal Crop Insurance Act, 7 U.S.C.A. § 1501 et seq. (1964).

263

The regulations should be consulted to determine (1) the counties in which insurance is offered, (2) the crops covered, and (3) the hazards insured against. See 7 Code Fed. Reg. § 401.101 *et seq.* (1969); 112a National Flood Insurance Act of 1968, 82 Stat. 572 (1968); 42 U.S.C.A. §§ 4001 et seq. (1969 Supp.).

108. Under the former federal flood insurance, the administrator was authorized to establish insurance and reinsurance,guarantee loans made by public or private financing institutions, and make direct loans. Ibid.
    See, for example, Cal. Rev. and Tax. Code §§ 155.6, 155.11 (reassessment of property after lien date to reflect reduced value due to damage by flood or storm).

109. Although the occurrence of a rain shadow is debatable, it is assumed for the purpose of this discussion, that such result might occur and can be proved.

110. See, for example, Davis, The Legal Implications of Atmospheric Water Resources Development and Management, Rept. for Bur. of Reclamation, 16-30 (1968) and see footnote II-101 for citation of other materials. In a very recent case, Pennsylvania Natural Weather Assn. v. Blue Ridge Weather Modification Ass'n, 44 Pa. Dist. & Co. Rep. 2d 749 (1968), the court recognized private rights in the clouds and the water in them but also made the cryptic statement that "weather-modification activities undertaken in the public interest (as opposed to private interest) and under the direction and control of governmental authority should and must be permitted." It is far from clear whether the court meant that weather-modification activities undertaken under the control of governmental authority would merely be immune from an injunction or also immune from liability for an interference with private rights in clouds.

111. See, for example, City of Pasadena v. City of Alhambra, 33 Cal. 2d 908, 207 P.2d 17 (1949).

112. See Bain, Caves and Margolis, Northern California's Water Industry 332-338 (1966).

113. Statutory authority is found in Cal. Water Code App. § 40-27; see Orange County Water Dist. v. Farnsworth, 138 Cal. App. 2d 518, 292 P.2d 927 (1956) (sustaining validity of the assessment).

114. Cal. Water Code App. § 40-31.5.

115. Cal. Water Code §§ 400-415.

116. This observation is based on the assumption that, at least in the reasonably foreseeable future, weather-modification activity in Cali-

fornia will be conducted principally for precipitation augmentation.

117. Cal. Water Code §§ 174-175.

118. Cal. Water Code §§ 1255-1258. See Davis, The Legal Implications of Atmospheric Water Resources Development and Management, Rep. for Bur. of Reclamation, 122 (1968).

119. The local governmental units do not have constitutionally conferred authority over water resources allocative functions.

120. If the clouds are to be seeded in one county to increase precipitation in another county, must the modifier comply with regulations of both counties?

121. Professional Fire Fighters, Inc. v. City of Los Angeles, 60 Cal. 2d 276, 32 Cal. Rptr. 830, 384 P.2d 158 (1963), with Bishop v. City of San Jose, 1 Cal. 3d 56, 81 Cal. Rptr. 465, 460 P.2d 137 (1969).

122. Gilgert v. Stockton Port Dist., 7 Cal. 2d 384, 60 P.2d 847 (1936).

123. Moore v. Municipal Court, 170 Cal. App. 2d 548, 339 P.2d 196 (1959).

124. In some districts, a vote of an elector is weighted according to the value of property owned by him. See, for example, Cal. Water Code § 35003 (a voter in California water district has one vote for each dollar's worth of land which he owns). Property qualification for a franchise has been placed in great doubt. Kramer v. Union Free School Dist., 395 U.S. 621 (1969); Cipriano v. City of Houma, 395 U.S. 701 (1969), but compare Schindler v. Palo Verde Irrigation Dist., 1 Cal. App. 3d 831, 82 Cal. Rptr. 61 (1969), which sustained the validity of a weighted voting scheme in a special district.

125. Pipoly v. Benson, 20 Cal. 2d 366, 125 P.2d 482 (1942).

126. 70 Cal. 2d 851, 76 Cal. Rptr. 642, 452 P.2d 930 (1969).

127. Ibid. at 856, 76 Cal. Rptr. at 645-46, 452 P.2d at 933-34.

128. In re Hubbard, 62 Cal. 2d 119, 41 Cal. Rptr. 383, 396 P.2d 809 (1964).

129. Compare Galvan v. Superior Court, supra note 132 (sustaining local gun registration law); In re Hubbard, supra note 128 (sustaining local gambling prohibition), with In re Lane, 58 Cal. 2d 99, 22 Cal. Rptr. 857, 372 P.2d 897 (1962) (invalidating the local "resorting" ordinance).

130. It is not clear whether the state provisions cover operations for these purposes if the operations will have an indirect or unintended effect upon precipitation.

131. Cal. Pub. Util. Code §§ 701, 761, 768.

132. See Mitchell, The History and Scope of Public Utilities Regulation in California, 30 So. Cal. L. Rev. 118, 126 (1957).

133. See, for example, Hall v. City of Tuft, 47 Cal. 2d 177, 302 P.2d 574 (1956).

134. See, for example, Baldwin Park County Water Dist. v. County of Los Angeles, 208 Cal. App. 2d 87, 25 Cal. Rptr. 167 (1962).

135. For example, Hadacheck v. Sebastian, 239 U.S. 394 (1915).

136. For example, Jones v. City of Los Angeles, 211 Cal. 304, 295 Pac. 14 (1930) (preexisting sanitariums for mental patients in a residential zone cannot be eliminated). See City of Los Angeles v. Gage, 127 Cal. App. 2d 442, 274 P.2d 34 (1954) (sustaining an amortization scheme).

137. For example, Morris County Land Imp. Co. v. Township of Parsippany-Troy Hills, 40 N.J. 539, 193 A.2d 232 (1963) (regulation in effect compelled retention of marsh land in its natural state to provide a drainage basin and wild life sanctuary for the benefit of the community); Indiana Toll Road Comm. v. Jankovich, 244 Ind. 574, 193 N.E.2d 237 (1963), *cert. dismissed*, 379 U.S. 487 (1965) (building height regulation in the landing approach to airport). But cf. Consolidated Rock Products Co. v. City of Los Angeles, 57 Cal. 2d 515, 20 Cal. Rptr. 638, 370 P.2d 342, *appeal dismissed*, 371 U.S. 36 (1962).

138. In Southwest Engineering Co. v. Ernst, 79 Ariz. 403, 291 P.2d 764 (1955), the court sustained a statute which generally restricted the withdrawal of percolating groundwater in critical groundwater areas to those who had previously been pumping. A critical groundwater area was defined as an area where the groundwater supply was insufficient to provide a reasonably safe supply for irrigation at the current rate of withdrawal. The restriction imposed by the statute was clearly in derogation of an overlying landowner's right to a reasonable beneficial use of groundwater on the overlying land irrespective of injury to his neighbors.

Against the argument that the statute denies a person of the due process of law, the court answered that, where a choice must be made because of limited water supply between preserving presently cultivated lands as against potentially reclaimable land, there is no denial of due process to prefer the existing cultivated lands based on social policy considerations which are not unreasonable. Insofar as the equal protection clause was concerned, the court held that there was a rational basis for the classification. It reasoned that every new acreage reclaimed would result in destruction of an acre presently cultivated; there would be a destruction of capital investment similar to that caused by a catastrophe; and a classification which prevents this loss is not irrational.

See also Knight v. Grimes, 80 S.D. 517, 127 N.W.2d 708 (1964) (the legislature may, without compensation, abolish the rule of absolute ownership of unappropriated percolating water and substitute the doctrine of appropriation).

139. Neb. Rev. Stat. §§ 2-2428 to 2-2449 (1943).

140. Neb. Rev. Stat. § 2-2433 (1943).

141. The absence of a hearing and judicial review invalidated an earlier statute. Summerville v. North Platte Valley Weather, 170 Neb. 46, 101 N.W.2d 748 (1960).

142. Neb. Rev. Stat. § 2-2437 (1943).

143. Neb. Rev. Stat. § 2-2443 (1943).

144. Neb. Rev. Stat. § 2-2444 (1943).

145. Neb. Rev. Stat. § 2-2446 (1943).

146. N.D. Code Ann. § 2-07-06 (1969 Supp.).

147. N.D. Code Ann. § 2-07-06.3 (1969 Supp.).

148. N.D. Code Ann. § 2-07-02 (1969 Supp.).

149. N.D. Code Ann. § 58-03-07 (1969 Supp.).

8   The Atomic Energy Agency As a Model

Arthur W. Murphy

The legal framework for the control and development of atomic energy was established by the Atomic Energy Act of 1946 (the McMahon Act) and confirmed, with important changes, by the Atomic Energy Act of 1954. One major characteristic of the scheme adopted was that atomic energy was a government monopoly. The role of private companies was significant, but they functioned as contractors with the government rather than as independent operators. In the beginning, private owner-ship of significant amounts of fissionable material was prohibited, as was private ownership of facilities to make or use fissionable material. Although the 1954 Act relaxed the system to permit licensing of privately owned facilities and possession (though not ownership) of fissionable materials, elaborate regulations were promulgated to assure government control. Since 1954, there has been further relaxation, but the basic pattern remains. It is, for example, now possible for private industry to "own" nuclear fuel, although the ownership is subject to so many safeguards that it bears little resemblance to ownership as the term is usually understood. However, the AEC continues to hold the view (and the Act seems clearly to support its position) that even where new technology for production or utilization is developed privately—as, for example, the centrifuge—the AEC can impose regulatory controls to assure protection of the public health and safety and the national security.

The second major feature of the scheme was that, within the government, control was centralized in a specific agency, the AEC, which was created in 1946 to take over the monopoly from the Army. The AEC is responsible not only for the development of civilian uses but also for government applications, including military. AEC must review the safety aspects of its own operations and concur in the radiological safety standards for Department of Defense reactors and weapons, although these activities are exempt from licensing. Other federal agencies must obtain licenses from the AEC for use of the materials and facilities which are defined in the Atomic Energy Act.

AEC licensing and regulatory jurisdiction extends to those facilities (for example, reactors) and materials (for example, radioisotopes and special nuclear material) which are defined in the Atomic Energy Act. These definitions do not include all sources of radiation. For example, neither X-ray machines nor radium are within these definitions, and AEC has no jurisdiction regarding radiation from those sources.

Over the years the AEC has, through a number of bilateral agreements, yielded some of its jurisdiction to the states upon being satisfied that an adequate system of state regulation was in effect. The agreements with the state differ in many respects, but in all cases the AEC has retained control over major nuclear installations such as power plants, fuel reprocessing plants, etc.[1]

Although the Commission's responsibilities cover both peaceful and warlike uses of radioactive materials, we need only consider the former. Perhaps the most noteworthy aspect of the AEC role is that the 1954 Act charges it both to develop peaceful uses and to regulate them. This dual mission has been the occasion of much criticism over the years, and many proposals have been made for divorcing the two functions, including the spinning off of the regulatory function into a separate agency. So far the creation of a separate agency has been resisted (although there is still strong sentiment to do so); instead, the regulatory division of the Commission has been set up as a separated staff with elaborate safeguards to preserve its independence. The extent of Commission review varies with the type of license sought. For power-reactor licensing, the process is quite extensive. The staff conducts, through its own personnel and consultants, a detailed review of those aspects of the reactor and its location bearing on safety. Before construction is authorized, separate reviews are made by the Advisory Committee on Reactor Safeguards, (ACRS) and by a three man Safety and Licensing Board. The grant of a construction permit is only the first stage; thereafter an operating license must be applied for, and here again review by the AEC staff, the ACRS, and possibly by a Safety and

Licensing Board may be required. Close scrutiny continues throughout the lifetime of the reactor. Although AEC jurisdiction is exclusive, it has made it a practice to invite other agencies of the federal government to express their views as to the areas of their expertise. For example, the Weather Bureau may be asked to report on the meteorology of a proposed location, and the Coast and Geodetic Survey on its seismicity. State and local governments are entitled to notice of hearing on application for licenses, and to intervene as of right in the proceedings.

To what extent is the pattern of regulation of atomic energy a useful model for weather modification? The answer will depend largely on the extent to which the circumstances are the same and, of course, on one's assessment of the success of the AEC experience.

There are marked similarities between the fields. Both are largely dependent on technology: just as the shape of the regulatory program depended, in the case of the atom, on the character, size, and rate of advancement of the art, so too the shape of a program for weather will depend, at any given moment, on the feasibility of particular applications of technology. Many of the conclusions of the Special Commission on Weather Modification were based, for example, on its conclusions about the effectiveness of existing techniques, and it was explicitly recognized that different approaches would be required if and when the capability increased.

Again, as in the case of the atom, the implications of the subject are pervasive. Nuclear energy provides at the same time a whole new energy source, an invaluable research tool, and an important new medical technique; effective weather control would have consequences in substantially all phases of human activity. And both atomic energy and weather modification will affect almost all levels of government—local, state, federal, and international.

Notwithstanding all the similarities, however, there are important differences between the two fields which suggest different treatment. To begin with, in the case of weather modification, there is not the compelling urgency for tight control posed by the military potential of atomic energy.[2] Although the elaborate security program adopted for information control probably never made much sense, control over nuclear materials is still an important consideration in the effort to prevent proliferation of weapons. Second, it does not appear that weather-modification activities pose the specific health hazards of radioactive materials; thus, there is no need for a licensing system necessitated in the case of the atom by the fact that all radioactive materials are dangerous.[3] There may, of course, be other grounds for requiring a system of licenses—for example, a need to check on the qualifications of operators, or to prevent conflicting activities, might militate in favor of licenses—but certainly a comprehensive system of controls would not seem warranted at the present time.

On the promotional front, AEC activity has been far ranging, covering all phases of research and development. It has, for example, not only produced radioisotopes but pioneered in the development of new uses for isotopes in research, as power sources, in food sterilization, etc. Perhaps the best picture of the scope of operations can be given in connection with the development of atomic power, certainly the most dramatic of the peacetime programs. From the beginning, the production of economic electric power from nuclear energy was a major goal of the AEC. In the early stages most of the development work was done by the AEC, usually operating through private contractors. Many reactor types—pressurized and boiling water reactors, gas-cooled, and liquid metal with many variations—were investigated. Research on components such as fuel and metal was carried on even before 1954 when the door was opened to private industry under the license program. The AEC's activity was not by any means limited to basic research; it actually built, and operated under contract, some small and one large-scale power reactors to test their feasibility. Even after substantial private investment began, the AEC made significant R & D contributions to many early reactors. Although today there is little if any R & D contribution to water reactors, the AEC is still a major source of funds for other types—for example, the gas-cooled reactor recently authorized for construction at Greeley, Colorado. In the case of advanced reactor concepts such as the breeder reactor, the government is still the major factor. And, in such futuristic fields as fusion reactors or in a controversial field such as the peaceful use of nuclear explosives, both research and operations are almost entirely carried on by, or for, the AEC. On the whole the promotional program has become a success, economic electric power having become a reality in some areas of the country.

Is there a comparable need for promotion in weather modification? If so, should it be by a single agency? Should such an agency be the same agency charged with regulation? At the present time there would seem to be less need for promotion than was true with atomic energy, although it may be that certain types of needed basic research need increased support. So far as development programs are concerned, the

272

various operating agencies would seem to have gone ahead on programs within their sphere of interest. In view of these conclusions, it is less necessary to discuss the question of whether a single agency should have both promotional and regulatory functions.

So too, in terms of intragovernmental structure, there are major differences between weather modification now and the atom in 1946, or even 1954. In the case of the atom, substantially all knowledge in the field was concentrated in a few men; the program had been operated on a unified basis from the beginning—in the Manhattan Project. Unified management of the peacetime program was both a natural development and a practical necessity. Indeed, the original justification for a Commission rather than a single administrator was as a counterweight to what was viewed as necessary centralization of control.

By contrast, in the case of weather modification, almost everybody is already in the act. Although until recently the NSF has had major responsibility for basic research, interest in and responsibility for weather modification is already diffused throughout the government. It seems perfectly clear that even if it were thought desirable, it would not be feasible to concentrate responsibility for weather-modification activities in a manner even remotely approximating that of atomic energy. Moreover, there is at least some reason to believe that in important respects the AEC may have outlived the reason for its creation. Some years back, for example, there was considerable discussion of a proposal to replace the five-man Commission with a single administrator. One of the arguments in favor of the abolition of the Commission was that knowledge about the atom was now widely dispersed through the government, and there was no longer any need for a group of "wise men" to police the development of this unique new power. Many of the same arguments could be used to support dispersal of some of the Commission's functions throughout the government. All in all, it seems to me that it is probably unwise and almost certainly not politically feasible to try to establish anything like the AEC in the weather-modification field. The major need would seem to be for coordination of various government activities, and here it would seem that the example of the AEC's licensing other government agencies might be useful. So far, at least, it would not appear that a full-blown AEC licensing procedure, complete with public hearing would be necessary, but some procedure for advising a central agency of plans, in detail, and holding off implementation until the possible consequences of the proposed operations could be assessed would seem to be desirable.

It also seems appropriate to note that the AEC licensing system, although pervasive (some might say oppressive) is also very narrow in focus. The Commission has stoutly resisted any expansion of its jurisdiction beyond radioactivity. For example, intervenors in licensing and others have urged that the AEC consider the effects of heated water discharges from nuclear power plants into adjacent bodies of water and impose license conditions concerning such effects. The AEC's position has been that it lacks authority under the Atomic Energy Act to consider thermal effects, as opposed to radiological effects, in its licensing proceedings, even though, from the point of view of the public, that question may be the major one of substance. On January 13, 1969, the U.S. Court of Appeals for the First Circuit upheld the Commission's position in this regard (*The State of New Hampshire v. Atomic Energy Commission,* 406 F.2d 170 (1st Cir. 1969), *Cert.* denied, 395 U.S. 962 (1969)), although a more liberal reading of the statute by the Commission might well also have been sustained. The AEC supported legislation introduced in the 91st Congress which would require applicants for federal licenses to obtain advance certification from state water-pollution control agencies with respect to compliance with applicable state water-quality standards. The National Environmental Policy Act of 1969, Public Law 91-190, enacted January 1, 1970, may also have a bearing on the scope of AEC licensing jurisdiction over nonradiological environmental matters in future proceedings. In any event, it is very important that we avoid, in the case of weather modification, the narrow focus of the AEC, and that whatever structure is adopted should have as a primary objective that all questions of environmental effects be considered before any major project is undertaken.

Notes

1. Recently the State of Minnesota issued a waste disposal permit to a privately-owned utility which sets limits for the discharge of radioactive effluents from that utility's proposed nuclear power plant at a level less than those permitted by AEC regulations (10 CFR Part 20). The utility, Northern States Power Company, filed suits against the state in both the federal and state courts contesting these limitations. Among other things, the company contends that the Atomic Energy Act preempts to the federal government exclusive authority to regulate radioactive discharges from nuclear power plants. These cases are still pending.

2. This is not to say that there are not potential military applications, of course.

3. See Murphy, "Atomic Safety and Licensing Boards: An Experiment in Administrative Decision Making on Safety Questions," 33 *Law & Contemp. Prob.* 566 (1968).